GW00645051

LONDON

2 0 0 4

■ *Selection of hotels and restaurants*

Sélection d'hôtels et de restaurants ■

■ *Selezione di alberghi e ristoranti*

LONDON

Dear Reader

The Michelin Guide offers a selection of the best hotels and restaurants in many categories of comfort and price. It is compiled by a team of professionally trained inspectors who travel the country visiting new establishments as well as those already listed in the guide. Their mission is to check the quality and consistency of the amenities and service provided by the hotels and restaurants throughout the year. The inspectors are full-time Michelin employees and their assessments, made anonymously, are therefore completely impartial and independant.

The amenities found in each establishment are indicated by symbols, an international language which enables you to see at a glance whether a hotel has, for example, a car park or swimming pool. To take full advantage of the wealth of information contained in the guide, consult the introduction. A short descriptive text complements the symbols.

Entry in the Michelin Guide is completely free of charge and every year the proprietors of those establishments listed complete a questionnaire giving the opening times and prices for the coming year. Nearly 100,000 pieces of information are updated for each annual edition.

Our readers also contribute through the 45,000 letters and e-mails received annually commenting on hotels and restaurants throughout Europe.

Thank you for your support and please continue to send us your comments. We hope you enjoy travelling with the Michelin Guide 2004.

Consult the Michelin Guide at
www.Viamichelin.co.uk
and write to us at:
themichelinguide-gbirl@uk.michelin.com

Contents

Hotel facilities

In general the hotels we recommend have full bathroom and toilet facilities in each room.
This may not be the case, however for certain rooms in ↑.

30 rm	*Number of rooms*
|♦|	*Lift (elevator)*
▤	*Air conditioning*
TV	*Television in room*
⇥⇤	*Establishment either partly or wholly reserved for non-smokers*
☎	*Modem point in the bedrooms*
⅙	*Bedrooms accessible to people of restricted mobility*
🍽	*Meals served in garden or on terrace*
⛵ ⛴	*Outdoor or indoor swimming pool*
⌙ ⛉	*Exercise room – Sauna*
🌿	*Garden*
🌳	*Park*
✂ ⛳	*Hotel tennis court – Golf course and number of holes*
⚐ 150	*Equipped conference hall: maximum capacity*
🚗	*Hotel garage (additional charge in most cases)*
P	*Car park for customers only*
🐕	*Dogs are excluded from all or part of the hotel*
closed Saturday and August	*Dates when closed as indicated by the restaurateur*
season	*Probably open for the season – precise dates not available.* *Where no date or season is shown, establishments are open all year round.*
LL35 0SB	*Postal code*

Cuisine

Stars

*Certain establishments deserve to be brought
to your attention for the particularly fine quality
of their cooking. **Michelin stars** are awarded
for the standard of meals served. For such
restaurants we list three culinary specialities
typical of their style of cooking to assist
you in your choice.*

✿✿✿ Exceptional cuisine, worth a special journey

*One always eats here extremely well, sometimes
superbly. Fine wines, faultless service, elegant
surroundings. One will pay accordingly!*

✿✿ Excellent cooking, worth a detour

*Specialities and wines of first class quality.
This will be reflected in the price.*

✿ A very good restaurant in its category

*The star indicates a good place to stop on your journey.
But beware of comparing the star given
to an expensive «de luxe» establishment
to that of a simple restaurant where you can appreciate
fine cuisine at a reasonable price.*

🕮 The "Bib Gourmand"

Good food at moderate prices

*You may also like to know of other restaurants
with less elaborate, moderately priced menus
that offer good value for money
and serve carefully prepared meals.*
We bring them to your attention by marking them
with the **"Bib Gourmand"** 🕮 and Meals *in the text
of the Guide, e.g.* Meals 19.00/25.00.

Prices

Prices quoted are valid for autumn 2003. Changes may arise if goods and service costs are revised.

*Hotels and restaurants
have supplied details of all their rates
and have assumed responsibility for maintaining
them for all travellers in possession of this guide.*

*Prices are given in £ sterling.
All accommodation prices include both service and
V.A.T. All restaurant prices include V.A.T. Service is
also included when an s. appears after the prices.
Where no s. is shown, prices may be subject to the
addition of a variable service charge that is usually
between 10% - 15%.*

*Your recommendation is self-evident
if you always walk into a hotel guide in hand.*

Meals

Meals 13.00/28.00	**Set meals**
	Lowest 13.00, and highest 28.00 – prices for set meals including cover charge, where applicable
Meals 19.00/25.00	*See page 8*
s.	*Service included*
🍴	*Restaurants offering lower priced pre and/or post theatre menus*
🍷	*Wine served by the glass*

Meals a la carte	**A la carte meals**
20.00/35.00	*The prices represent the range of charges from a simple to an elaborate 3 course meal.*

*↑: Dinner in this category of establishment will generally be
offered from a fixed price menu of
limited choice, served at a set time to residents only.
Lunch is rarely offered. Many will not be licensed
to sell alcohol.*

Rooms

rm 120.00/250.00 *Lowest price 120.00, per room for a comfortable single*
and highest price 250.00 per room
for the best double or twin

suites *Check with the hotelier for prices*

rm ☕ 125.00/255.00 *Full cooked breakfast (whether taken or not)*
is included in the price of the room

☕ 9.50 *Price of breakfast*

Short breaks

Many hotels offer a special rate for a stay
of two or more nights which comprises dinner,
room and breakfast usually for a minimum
of two people. Please enquire at hotel for rates.

Alcoholic beverages-conditions of sale

The sale of alcoholic drinks is governed in Great Britain
and Ireland by licensing laws
which vary greatly from country to country.

Allowing for local variations, restaurants may stay
open and serve alcohol with a bona fide meal
during the afternoon. Hotel bars and public houses
are generally open between 11am and 11pm
at the discretion of the licensee. Hotel residents,
however, may buy drinks outside the permitted
hours at the discretion of the hotelier.

Children under the age of 14 are not allowed
in bars.

Deposits

Some hotels will require a deposit, which confirms
the commitment of customer and hotelier alike.
Make sure the terms of the agreement are clear.

Credit cards

⊕ ⒶⒺ ⓪ 𝘝𝘐𝘚𝘈 ᴶᶜᴮ *Credits cards accepted by the establishment:*
MasterCard (Eurocard) – American Express –
Diners Club – Visa – Japan Credit Bureau

London

✉ *SW7*	*Postal address*
London G.	*See the Michelin Green Guide*
BX A	*Letters giving the location of a place on the town plan*
🏌18	*Golf course and number of holes (handicap sometimes required, telephone reservation strongly advised)*
☀, ≤	*Panoramic view, viewpoint*
✈	*Airport*
🛈	*Tourist Information Centre*

Standard Time

In winter standard time throughout the British Isles is Greenwich Mean Time (G.M.T.). In summer British clocks are advanced by one hour to give British Summer Time (B.S.T.). The actual dates are announced annually but always occur over weekends in March and October.

Sights

Star-rating

★★★	*Highly recommended*
★★	*Recommended*
★	*Interesting*

Car, tyres

*The wearing of seat belts in Great Britain
is obligatory for drivers, front seat passengers
and rear seat passengers where seat belts are fitted.
It is illegal for front seat passengers
to carry children on their lap.*

Michelin tyre suppliers
ATS Euromaster tyre dealers

*The address of the nearest ATS Euromaster tyre dealer
can be obtained by contacting the address below
between 9am and 5pm.*

> *ATS Euromaster
> Jill Lane
> Sambourne
> Redditch
> Worcs. B96 6ES
> ☎ 0800 750 850*

Motoring organisations

*The major motoring organisations in Great Britain
are the Automobile Association and the Royal
Automobile Club. Each provides services in varying
degrees for non-resident members
of affiliated clubs.*

*AUTOMOBILE ASSOCIATION
Fanum House
Basingstoke, Hants
RG21 4EA
☎ (08705) 448866*

*ROYAL AUTOMOBILE CLUB
RAC House, Boston Drive
Bourne End Bucks SL8 5YS
☎ (01628) 843888*

Town plans

⊕ ● a   *Hotels – Restaurants*

Sights

Place of interest

Interesting place of worship

Roads

M 1   *Motorway*

❹ ❹   *Junctions: complete, limited*

Dual carriageway with motorway characteristics

Main traffic artery

A 2   *Primary route (GB) and National route (IRL)*

◀ ⁝⁝⁝⁝⁝   *One-way street – Unsuitable for traffic, street subject to restrictions*

Pedestrian street – Tramway

Piccadilly P P   *Shopping street – Car park – Park and Ride*

Gateway – Street passing under arch – Tunnel

Low headroom (16'6" max.) on major through routes

Station and railway

Funicular – Cable-car

△ B   *Lever bridge – Car ferry*

Various signs

🄸   *Tourist Information Centre*

Church/Place of worship – Mosque – Synagogue

Communications tower or mast – Ruins

Garden, park, wood – Cemetery

Stadium – Racecourse – Golf course

Golf course (with restrictions for visitors) – Skating rink

Outdoor or indoor swimming pool

View – Panorama

Monument – Fountain – Hospital – Covered market

Pleasure boat harbour – Lighthouse

✈ ⊖ ● 🚐   *Airport – Underground station – Coach station*

Ferry services:
- passengers and cars

✉   *Main post office*

Public buildings located by letter:

C H J   *County Council Offices – Town Hall – Law Courts*

M T U   *Museum – Theatre – University, College*

POL   *Police (in large towns police headquarters)*

London

BRENT WEMBLEY   *Borough – Area*

Borough boundary

Congestion Zone-Charge applies Monday-Friday 07.00-18.30

13

A. Leprince / Michelin

- [ ] a. 🏠 *Charming guesthouse ?*
- [ ] b. 💶 *Room for €40 or less per night ?*
- [ ] c. 😋 *That little extra, not to be missed ?*

Can't decide ?

Then simply open a copy of Michelin Charming Places to Stay !

From a remote country farmhouse to a mansion surrounded by vineyards, from a tiny rustic B&B to a château amid acres of parkland, this guide offers a selection of hotels and guesthouses for each region in France, chosen for their character, peace and quiet and hospitality to suit all budgets.

Discover the pleasure of travel with the Michelin Charming Places to Stay.

☐ a. *Island of Bréhat ?*
☐ b. *Pontusval Point ?*
☐ c. *Penhir Point ?*

Can't decide ?

Then immerse yourself in the Michelin
Green Guide !

- Everything to do and see
- The best driving tours
- Practical information
- Where to stay and eat
The Michelin Green Guide:
the spirit of discovery.

Cher lecteur,

Le Guide Michelin vous propose,
dans chaque catégorie de confort et de prix,
une sélection des meilleurs hôtels et restaurants.
Cette sélection est effectuée par une équipe
d'inspecteurs, professionnels de formation
hôtelière, qui sillonnent le pays toute l'année
pour visiter de nouveaux établissements
et ceux déjà cités afin d'en vérifier la qualité
et la régularité des prestations.
Salariés Michelin, les inspecteurs travaillent
en tout anonymat et en toute indépendance.

Les équipements et services sont signalés
par des symboles, langage international
qui vous permet de voir en un coup d'œil
si un hôtel dispose, par exemple, d'un parking
ou d'une piscine. Pour bien profiter
de cette très riche source d'information,
plongez-vous dans l'introduction.
Un texte décrivant l'atmosphère
de l'hôtel ou du restaurant complète
ces renseignements.

L'inscription dans le guide est totalement
gratuite. Chaque année, les hôteliers
et restaurateurs cités remplissent
le questionnaire qui leur est envoyé,
nous fournissant les dates d'ouverture
et les prix pour l'année à venir.
Près de 100 000 informations
sont mises à jour pour chaque édition
(nouveaux établissements, changements
de tarif, dates d'ouverture).

Une grande aide vient aussi des commentaires
des lecteurs avec près de 45 000 lettres
et Email par an, pour toute l'Europe.

Merci d'avance pour votre participation
et bon voyage avec le Guide Michelin 2004.

Consultez le Guide Michelin sur
www.Viamichelin.co.uk
et écrivez-nous à :
themichelinguide-gbirl@uk.michelin.com

Sommaire

Comprendre

Le choix d'un hôtel, d'un restaurant

Ce guide vous propose une sélection d'hôtels et restaurants établie à l'usage de l'automobiliste de passage. Les établissements, classés selon leur confort, sont cités par ordre de préférence dans chaque catégorie.

Catégories

🏨🏨🏨	XXXXX	*Grand luxe et tradition*
🏨🏨	XXXX	*Grand confort*
🏨🏨	XXX	*Très confortable*
🏨	XX	*De bon confort*
🏨	X	*Assez confortable*
	🍺	*Traditionnel pub anglais servant des repas*
🏠		*Autres formes hébergement conseillé (maison d'hôtes et cottages)*
without rest.		*L'hôtel n'a pas de restaurant*
	with rm	*Le restaurant possède des chambres*

Agrément et tranquillité

Certains établissements se distinguent dans le guide par les symboles rouges indiqués ci-après.
Le séjour dans ces hôtels se révèle particulièrement agréable ou reposant.
Cela peut tenir d'une part au caractère de l'édifice, au décor original, au site, à l'accueil et aux services qui sont proposés, d'autre part à la tranquillité des lieux.

🏨🏨🏨 à 🏨, 🏠	*Hôtels agréables*
XXXXX à X	*Restaurants agréables*
🤚	*Hôtel très tranquille ou isolé et tranquille*
🤚	*Hôtel tranquille*
⩽ London	*Vue exceptionnelle*
⩽	*Vue intéressante ou étendue*

L'installation

Les chambres des hôtels que nous recommandons possèdent, en général, des installations sanitaires complètes. Il est toutefois possible que dans les 🏠, certaines chambres en soient dépourvues.

30 ch	Nombre de chambres
🛗	Ascenseur
▤	Air conditionné
TV	Télévision dans la chambre
⚡	Établissement entièrement ou en partie réservé aux non-fumeurs
📞	Prise modem dans la chambre
♿	Chambres accessibles aux personnes à mobilité réduite
🌳	Repas servis au jardin ou en terrasse
🏊 🏊	Piscine : de plein air ou couverte
🏋 ⮝s	Salle de remise en forme – Sauna
🌿	Jardin de repos
🏞	Parc
🎾 ⛳	Tennis à l'hôtel – Golf et nombre de trous
🅰 150	Salles de conférences : capacité maximum
🚗	Garage dans l'hôtel (généralement payant)
P	Parking réservé à la clientèle
🚫	Accès interdit aux chiens (dans tout ou partie de l'établissement)
closed Saturday and August	Fermeture communiquée par le restaurateur
LL35 0SB	Code postal de l'établissement

La table

Les étoiles

Certains établissements méritent d'être signalés à votre attention pour la qualité de leur cuisine. Nous les distinguons par les étoiles de bonne table. Nous indiquons, pour ces établissements, trois spécialités culinaires qui pourront orienter votre choix.

ஜஜஜ **Une des meilleures tables, vaut le voyage**

On y mange toujours très bien, parfois merveilleusement, grands vins, service impeccable, cadre élégant... Prix en conséquence.

ஜஜ **Table excellente, mérite un détour**

Spécialités et vins de choix... Attendez-vous à une dépense en rapport.

ஜ **Une très bonne table dans sa catégorie**

L'étoile marque une bonne étape sur votre itinéraire. Mais ne comparez pas l'étoile d'un établissement de luxe à prix élevés avec celle d'une petite maison où à prix raisonnables, on sert également une cuisine de qualité.

Le "Bib Gourmand"

Repas soignés à prix modérés

Vous souhaitez parfois trouver des tables plus simples, à prix modérés; c'est pourquoi nous avons sélectionné des restaurants proposant, pour un rapport qualité-prix particulièrement favorable, un repas soigné.
Ces restaurants sont signalés par le **"Bib Gourmand"** ☺ et Meals.
Ex. ☺ Meals 19.00/25.00.

Les prix

Les prix que nous indiquons dans ce guide
ont été établis en automne 2003. Ils sont susceptibles
de modifications, notamment en cas de variations
des prix des biens et services.

Les hôtels et restaurants nous ont donné tous leurs prix
et se sont engagés, sous leur propre responsabilité,
à les appliquer aux touristes de passage
porteurs de notre guide.

Les prix sont indiqués en livres sterling
(1 L = 100 pence). Les tarifs de l'hébergement
comprennent le service et la T.V.A.
La T.V.A. est également incluse dans les prix des repas.
Toutefois, le service est uniquement compris dans les
repas si la mention « s » apparaît après le prix.
Dans le cas contraire, une charge supplémentaire
variant de 10 à 15 % du montant de l'addition
est demandée.

*Entrez à l'hôtel le guide à la main, vous montrerez
ainsi qu'il vous conduit là en confiance.*

Repas

Meals 13.00/28.00	**Repas à prix fixe**
	Minimum 13.00, *Maximum* 28.00. *Ces prix s'entendent couvert compris*
Meals 19.00/25.00	*Voir page 24*
s.	*Service compris*
🎭	*Restaurants proposant des menus à prix attractifs servis avant ou après le théâtre*
🍷	*Vin servi au verre*

Meals à la carte	**Repas à la carte**
20.00/35.00	*Le 1ᵉʳ prix correspond à un repas simple mais soigné, comprenant : petite entrée, plat du jour garni, dessert.*

Le 1er prix correspond à un repas simple mais soigné,
comprenant : petite entrée, plat du jour garni, dessert.
Le 2e prix concerne un repas plus complet, comprenant :
hors-d'œuvre, plat principal, fromage ou dessert.

↑: *Dans les établissements de cette catégorie, le dîner
est servi à heure fixe exclusivement aux personnes ayant
une chambre. Le menu, à prix unique, offre un choix
limité de plats. Le déjeuner est rarement proposé.
Beaucoup de ces établissements ne sont pas autorisés
à vendre des boissons alcoolisées.*

Chambres

rm 120.00/250.00

Prix minimum 120.00 *d'une chambre pour une personne
et prix maximum* 250.00 *de la plus belle chambre
occupée par deux personnes*

suites

Se renseigner auprès de l'hôtelier

rm ☕ 125.00/255.00

*Le prix du petit déjeuner à l'anglaise est inclus
dans le prix de la chambre,
même s'il n'est pas consommé*

☕ 9.50

Prix du petit déjeuner

Short breaks

*Certains hôtels proposent des conditions
avantageuses ou «Short Break» pour un séjour
minimum de 2 nuits. Ce forfait, calculé
par personne pour 2 personnes au minimum,
comprend la chambre, le dîner et le petit déjeuner.
Se renseigner auprès de l'hôtelier.*

La vente de boissons alcoolisées

*En Grande-Bretagne, la vente de boissons alcoolisées est
soumise à des lois pouvant varier d'une région à l'autre.*

*D'une façon générale, les restaurants peuvent demeurer
ouverts l'après-midi et servir des boissons alcoolisées
dans la mesure où elles accompagnent un repas
suffisamment consistant. Les bars d'hôtel et les pubs
sont habituellement ouverts de 11 heures à 23 heures.
Néanmoins, l'hôtelier a toujours la possibilité
de servir, à sa clientèle, des boissons alcoolisées
en dehors des heures légales.*

Les enfants au-dessous de 14 ans n'ont pas accès aux bars.

Les arrhes

*Certains hôteliers demandent le versement d'arrhes.
Il s'agit d'un dépôt-garantie qui engage l'hôtelier
comme le client. Bien faire préciser les dispositions
de cette garantie.*

Cartes de crédit

Ⓜ️Ⓞ ᴀᴇ Ⓓ *VISA* ᴊᴄʙ

*Cartes de crédit acceptées par l'établissement :
MasterCard (Eurocard) – American Express –
Diners Club – Visa – Japan Credit Bureau*

Londres

✉ SW7	Bureau de poste desservant la localité
London G.	Voir le guide vert Michelin
BX A	Lettres repérant un emplacement sur le plan
⛳18	Golf et nombre de trous (Handicap parfois demandé, réservation par téléphone vivement recommandée)
❋, ≤	Panorama, point de vue
✈	Aéroport
🛈	Information touristique

Heure légale

Les visiteurs devront tenir compte de l'heure officielle
en Grande-Bretagne : une heure de retard
sur l'heure française.

Les curiosités

Intérêts

★★★	Vaut le voyage
★★	Mérite un détour
★	Intéressant

La voiture, les pneus

En Grande-Bretagne, le port de la ceinture
de sécurité est obligatoire pour le conducteur
et le passager avant ainsi qu'à l'arrière, si le
véhicule en est équipé. La loi interdit au passager
avant de prendre un enfant sur ses genoux.

Fournisseurs de pneus michelin
ATS Euromaster Spécialistes du pneu

Des renseignements sur le plus proche point
de vente de pneus ATS Euromaster pourront être
obtenus en s'informant entre 9 h et 17 h
à l'adresse indiquée ci-dessous.

ATS Euromaster
Jill Lane
Sambourne
Redditch
Worcs. B96 6ES
☏ 0800 750 850

Automobile clubs

Les principales organisations de secours automobile
dans le pays sont l'Automobile Association
et le Royal Automobile Club,
toutes deux offrant certains de leurs services
aux membres de clubs affiliés.

AUTOMOBILE ASSOCIATION
Fanum House
Basingstoke, Hants
RG21 4EA
☏ (08705) 448866

ROYAL AUTOMOBILE CLUB
RAC House, Boston Drive
Bourne End Bucks SL8 5YS
☏ (01628) 843888

Les plans

@ ● a   *Hôtels – Restaurants*

Curiosités

Bâtiment intéressant
Édifice religieux intéressant

Voirie

Autoroute
- échangeurs : complet, partiel
Route à chaussées séparées de type autoroutier
Grand axe de circulation
Itinéraire principal (Primary route : GB)
(National route : IRL)
Sens unique – Rue impraticable, réglementée
Rue piétonne – Tramway
Piccadilly *Rue commerçante – Parking – Parking Relais*
Porte – Passage sous voûte – Tunnel
Passage bas (inférieur à 16'6") sur les grandes voies
de circulation
Gare et voie ferrée
Funiculaire – Téléphérique, télécabine
Pont mobile – Bac pour autos

Signes divers

Information touristique
Église/édifice religieux – Mosquée – Synagogue
Tour ou pylône de télécommunication – Ruines
Jardin, parc, bois – Cimetière
Stade – Hippodrome – Golf
Golf (réservé) – Patinoire
Piscine de plein air, couverte
Vue – Panorama
Monument – Fontaine – Hôpital – Marché couvert
Port de plaisance – Phare
Aéroport – Station de métro – Gare routière
Transport par bateau :
- passagers et voitures
Bureau principal
Bâtiment public repéré par une lettre :
C H   *- Bureau de l'Administration du Comté – Hôtel de ville*
M T U   *- Musée – Théâtre – Université, grande école*
POL J   *- Police (commissariat central) – Palais de Justice*

Londres

BRENT WEMBLEY   *Nom d'arrondissement (borough) – de quartier (area)*
Limite de « borough »
Zone à péage du centre-ville Lundi-Vendredi 07.00-18.30

29

Caro lettore,

*La Guida Michelin le propone,
per ogni categoria di confort e di prezzo,
una selezione dei migliori alberghi e ristoranti
effettuata da un'équipe di professionisti
del settore. Gli ispettori, dipendenti Michelin,
attraversano il paese tutto l'anno
per visitare nuovi esercizi e verificare la qualità
e la regolarità delle prestazioni di quelli
già citati, lavorando nel più stretto anonimato
e in tutta autonomia.*

*Le attrezzature ed i servizi sono indicati
da simboli, un immediato linguaggio
internazionale che ti permetterà di capire
in un attimo se, per esempio, un albergo
dispone di parcheggio o di piscina.
Per trarre il meglio da questa ricca fonte
d'informazioni, le consigliamo di consultare
l'introduzione. Le indicazioni sono poi completate
da un testo che descrive l'atmosfera dell'albergo o
del ristorante.*

*L'iscrizione nella guida è completamente
gratuita. Ogni anno gli albergatori
e i ristoratori citati compilano
un questionario inviato loro per fornirci i periodi
di aperturae i prezzi per l'anno a venire.
Circa 100 000 dati sono aggiornati
ad ogni edizione (nuovi esercizi, variazioni
di tariffe, periodi di apertura).*

*Di grande aiuto sono anche i commenti
dei lettori che ci inviano circa 45 000 lettere
ed e-mail all'anno da tutta l'Europa.*

*Grazie sin d'ora per la sua partecipazione
e buon viaggio con la Guida Michelin 2004.*

Consultate la Guida Michelin at
www.Viamichelin.co.uk
e scriveteci presso :
themichelinguide-gbirl@uk.michelin.com

Sommario

Come servisi della guida

La scelta di un albergo, di un ristorante

*Questa guida propone una selezione
di alberghi e ristoranti stabilita ad uso
dell'automobilista di passaggio. Gli esercizi,
classificati in base al confort che offrono,
vengono citati in ordine di preferenza
per ogni categoria.*

Categorie

🏨	XXXXX	*Gran lusso e tradizione*
🏨	XXXX	*Gran confort*
🏨	XXX	*Molto confortevole*
🏨	XX	*Di buon confort*
🏛	X	*Abbastanza confortevole*
	🍴	*Pub tradizionali con cucina*
↑		*Altra forme di alloggio consigliate (Pensioni e Case private)*
without rest.		*L'albergo non ha ristorante*
	with rm	*Il ristorante dispone di camere*

Amenità e tranquillità

*Alcuni esercizi sono evidenziati nella guida dai
simboli rossi indicati qui di seguito. Il soggiorno
in questi alberghi dovrebbe rivelarsi particolarmente
ameno o riposante.*

*Ciò può dipendere sia dalle caratteristiche
dell'edifico, dalle decorazioni non comuni,
dalla sua posizione e dal servizio offerto,
sia dalla tranquillità dei luoghi.*

🏨 a 🏛, ↑	*Alberghi ameni*
XXXXX a X	*Ristoranti ameni*
🖐	*Albergo molto tranquillo o isolato e tranquillo*
🖐	*Albergo tranquillo*
⇐ London	*Vista eccezionale*
⇐	*Vista interessante o estesa*

Installazioni

*Le camere degli alberghi che raccomandiamo
possiedono, generalmente, delle installazioni sanitarie
complete. È possibile tuttavia che
↱ alcune camere ne siano sprovviste.*

30 rm	*Numero di camere*
🛗	*Ascensore*
▤	*Aria condizionata*
TV	*Televisione in camera*
⇥	*Esercizio riservato completamente o in parte ai non fumatori*
📞	*Presa modem in camera*
♿	*Camere accessibili a persone con difficoltà motoria*
☂	*Pasti serviti in giardino o in terrazza*
⌁ ⌁	*Piscina: all'aperto, coperta*
⌁ ⇌	*Palestra – Sauna*
⌁	*Giardino*
⌁	*Parco*
✂ 18	*Tennis appatenente all'albergo – Golf e numero di buche*
⌁ 150	*Sale per conferenze: capienza massima*
⌁	*Garage nell'albergo (generalmente a pagamento)*
P	*Parcheggio riservato alla clientela*
⌁	*Accesso vietato ai cani (in tutto o in parte dell'esercizio)*
closed Saturday and August	*Periodo di apertura, comunicato dall'albergatore*
LL35 OSB	*Codice postale dell'esercizio*

La tavola

Le stelle

Alcuni esercizi meritano di essere segnalati alla Vostra attenzione per la qualità tutta particolare della loro cucina. Noi li evidenziamo con le «stelle di ottima tavola».
Per questi ristoranti indichiamo tre specialità culinarie e alcuni vini locali che potranno aiutarVi nella scelta.

✿✿✿ **Una delle migliori tavole, vale il viaggio**

Vi si mangia sempre molto bene, a volte meravigliosamente, grandi vini, servizio impeccabile, ambientazione accurata... Prezzi conformi.

✿✿ **Tavola eccellente, merita una deviazione**

Specialità e vini scelti...
AspettateVi una spesa in proporzione.

✿ **Un'ottima tavola nella sua categoria**

La stella indica una tappa gastronomica sul Vostro itinerario.
Non mettete però a confronto la stella di un esercizio di lusso, dai prezzi elevati, con quella di un piccolo esercizio dove, a prezzi ragionevoli, viene offerta una cucina di qualità.

🍴 Il "Bib Gourmand"

Pasti accurati a prezzi contenuti

Per quando desiderate trovare delle tavole più semplici a prezzi contenuti abbiamo selezionato dei ristoranti che, per un rapporto qualità-prezzo particolarmente favorevole, offrono un pasto accurato.
Questi ristoranti sono evidenziati nel testo con il **"Bib Gourmand"** 🍴 *e* Meals *evidenziata in rosso, davanti ai prezzi.*
Ex. 🍴 Meals 19.00/25.00.

I prezzi

I prezzi che indichiamo in questa guida sono stati stabiliti nel l'autunno 2003. Potranno pertanto subire delle variazioni in relazione ai cambiamenti dei prezzi di beni e servizi.

Gli alberghi e i ristoranti vengono menzionati quando gli albergatori ci hanno comunicato tutti i loro prezzi e si sono impegnati, sotto la propria responsabilità, ad applicarli ai turisti di passaggio, in possesso della nostra guida.

I prezzi sono indicati in lire sterline (1 £ = 100 pence).

Tutte le tariffe per il soggiorno includono sia servizio che I.V.A. Tutti i prezzi dei ristoranti includono l'I.V.A., il servizio è incluso quando dopo il prezzo appare s. Quando non compare s., il prezzo può essere soggetto ad un aumento per il servizio solitamente compreso tra il 10% e il 15%.

Entrate nell'albergo o nel ristorante con la guida in mano, dimostrando in tal modo la fiducia in chi vi ha indirizzato.

Pasti

Meals 13.00/28.00 — **Prezzo fisso**
Prezzo minimo 13.00, *massimo* 28.00.

Meals 19.00/25.00 — *Vedere p. 36*

s. — *Servizio compreso*

🍽 — *Ristoranti che offrono menù a prezzi ridotti prima e/o dopo gli spettacoli teatrali*

🍷 — *Vino servito a bicchiere*

Meals a la carte — **Alla carta**
20.00/35.00 — *Il 1° prezzo corrisponde ad un pasto semplice comprendente : primo piatto, piatto del giorno con contorno, dessert. Il 2° prezzo corrisponde ad un pasto più completo comprendente : antipasto, piatto principale, formaggio e dessert*

↟ *: Negli alberghi di questa categoria, la cena viene servita, ad un'ora stabilita, esclusivamente a chi vi alloggia. Il menu, a prezzo fisso, offre una scelta limitata di piatti. Raramente viene servito anche il pranzo. Molti di questi esercizi non hanno l'autorizzazione a vendere alcolici.*

37

Camere

rm 120.00/250.00

Prezzo minimo 120.00, per una camera singola
e prezzo massimo 250.00 per la camera più bella
per due persone

suites
Informarsi presso l'albergatore

rm ⊑ 125.00/255.00

Il prezzo della prima colazione inglese è compreso
nel prezzo della camera anche se non viene consumata

⊑ 9.50

Prezzo della prima colazione

«Short Breaks»

Alcuni alberghi propongono delle condizioni
particolarmente vantaggiose o short break
per un soggiorno minimo di due notti.
Questo prezzo, calcolato per persona e per un minimo
di due persone, comprende; camera, cena
e prima colazione. Informarsi presso l'albergatore.

La vendita di bevande alcoliche

La vendita di bevande alcoliche in Gran Bretagna
è regolata da leggi che variano considerevolmente
da regione a regione.

Eccezion fatta per varianti locali, i ristoranti possono
rimanere aperti o servire bevande alcoliche con i pasti
il pomeriggio. I bar degli hotel e i pub sono generalmente
aperti dalle 11 alle 23, a discrezione del gestore.
I clienti dell'hotel, comunque, possono acquistare bevande
al di fuori delle ore stabilite se il direttore lo permette.
Il bambini al di sotto del 14 anni non possono entrare
nei bar.

La caparra

Alcuni albergatori chiedono il versamento
di una caparra. Si tratta di un deposito-garanzia
che impegna tanto l'albergatore che il cliente.
Vi raccomandiamo di farVi precisare le norme
riguardanti la reciproca garanzia.

Carte di credito

Carte di credito accettate dall'esercizio :
MasterCard (Eurocard) – American Express –
Diners Club – Visa – Japan Credit Bureau

Londra

⊠ SW7	*Sede dell'ufficio postale*
London G.	*Vedere la Guida Verde Michelin*
BX A	*Lettere indicanti l'ubicazione sulla pianta*
🏌18	*Golf e numero di buche (handicap generalmente richiesto, prenotazione telefonica vivamente consigliata)*
☀, ≼	*Panorama, punto di vista*
✈	*Aeroporto*
🛈	*Ufficio informazioni turistiche*

Ora legale

I visitatori dovranno tenere in considerazione l'ora ufficiale in Gran Bretagna: un'ora di ritardo sull'ora italiana.

Luoghi d'interesse

Grado di interesse

★★★	*Vale il viaggio*
★★	*Merita una deviazione*
★	*Interessante*

L'automobile, I pneumatici

In Gran Bretagna, l'uso delle cinture di sicurezza
è obbligatorio per il conducente e il passeggero
del sedile anteriore, nonchè per i sedili posteriori,
se ne sono equipaggiati. La legge non consente
al passaggero seduto davanti di tenere un bambino
sulle ginocchia.

Pneumatici Michelin

Potrete avere delle informazioni sul più vicino
punto vendita di pneumatici ATS Euromaster,
rivolgendovi, tra le 9 e le 17, all'indirizzo indicato
qui di seguito :

> ATS Euromaster
> Jill Lane
> Sambourne
> Redditch
> Worcs. B96 6ES
> ☎ 0800 750 850

Le nostre Succursali sono in grado di dare ai
nostri clienti tutti i consigli relativi alla migliore
utilizzazione dei pneumatici.

Automobile clubs

Le principali organizzazioni di soccorso
automobilistico sono l'Automobile Association
ed il Royal Automobile Club :
entrambe offrono alcuni loro servizi
ai membri dei club affiliati.

AUTOMOBILE ASSOCIATION
Fanum House
Basingstoke, Hants
RG21 4EA
☎ (08705) 448866

ROYAL AUTOMOBILE CLUB
RAC House, Boston Drive
Bourne End Bucks SL8 5YS
☎ (01628) 843888

Le piante

⊖ ● a *Alberghi – Ristoranti*

Curiosità

Edificio interessante
Costruzione religiosa interessante

Viabilità

M 1 *Autostrada*
➍ ➍ *- svincoli: completo, parziale*
Strada a carreggiate separate di tipo autostradale
Asse principale di circolazione
A 2 *Itinerario principale (Primary route : GB)*
(National Route : IRL)
◀ ⅼ=====ⅼ *Senso unico – Via impraticabile, a circolazione regolamentata*
Via pedonale – Tranvia
.Piccadilly 🅿 🄿 *Via commerciale – Parcheggio – Parcheggio Ristoro*
✛ ⅃⊢ ⅃⊢ *Porta – Sottopassaggio – Galleria*
15.3 *Sottopassaggio (altezza inferiore a 16'6") sulle grandi*
vie di circolazione
Stazione e ferrovia
o⁺⁺⁺⁺⁺⁺o o⁻●⁻●⁻●o *Funicolare – Funivia, Cabinovia*
⚠ 🅱 *Ponte mobile – Traghetto per auto*

Simboli vari

🅸 *Ufficio informazioni turistiche*
Ծ ŏ ⊠ *Chiesa/edificio religioso – Moschea – Sinagoga*
⌄ ⸫ *Torre o pilone per telecomunicazioni – Ruderi*
🄸ₗ *Giardino, parco, bosco – Cimitero*
◯ 🐎 ⌐9 *Stadio – Ippodromo – Golf*
⌐ ⌐ *Golf riservato – Pattinaggio*
≋ ≋ *Piscina all'aperto, coperta*
◂ ≋ *Vista – Panorama*
■ ⊙ ⊞ ⊟ *Monumento – Fontana – Ospedale – Mercato coperto*
⚓ ⚑ *Porto per imbarcazioni da diporto – Faro*
✈ ⊖ ● 🚌 *Aeroporto – Stazione della Metropolitana – Autostazione*
⤙ *Trasporto con traghetto:*
- passeggeri ed autovetture
⊗ *Ufficio centrale*
🄻 *Edificio pubblico indicato con lettera:*
C H *- Sede dell'Amministrazione di Contea – Municipio*
M T U *- Museo – Teatro – Università, grande scuola*
POL. J *- Polizia (Questura, nelle grandi città) – Palazzo di Giustizia*

Londra

BRENT WEMBLEY *Nome del distretto amministrativo (borough) –*
del quartiere (area)
Limite del «borough»
Area con circolazione a pagameto Lunedì-Venerdì 07.00-18.30

41

E. Baret / Michelin - (06 - Roubion)

☐ a. **D17 ?**
☐ b. **N202 ?**
☐ c. **D30 ?**

Which road will get you there?
To find out, simply open a Michelin map!

The Michelin Atlases and new NATIO-NAL, REGIONAL, LOCAL and ZOOM map series offer clear, accurate map-ping to help you plan your route and find your way.

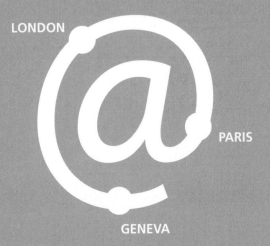

London

🄸 Victoria Station Forecourt – City of London Information Centre, St. Paul's Churchyard, EC4 ℘ (020) 7332 1456 – Selfridges, Basement Services Arcade, Oxford Street, WI – Britain Visitor Centre, I Regent Street, WI.

✈ Heathrow, ℘ 08700 000123, p. 10 AX – **Terminal** : Airbus (A1) from Victoria, Airbus (A2) from Paddington – Underground (Piccadilly line) frequent service daily.

✈ Gatwick, ℘ 08700 002468 p. 11 : by A 23 EZ and M 23 – **Terminal** : Coach service from Victoria Coach Station (Flightline 777, hourly service) – Railink (Gatwick Express) from Victoria (24 h service).

✈ London City Airport ℘ (020) 7646 0000, p. 9 HV.

✈ Stansted, at Bishop's Stortford, ℘ 08700 000303, NE : 34 m. p. 9 : by M 11 JT and A 120.

British Airways : Ticket sales and reservations 213 Piccadilly, London W1, ℘ 0845 6060747.

Major hotel groups
Central reservation telephone numbers

Principales chaînes hôtelières
Centraux téléphoniques de réservation

Principali catene alberghiere
Centrali telefoniche di prenotazione

ACCOR HOTELS (IBIS, MERCURE & NOVOTEL) — *0208 2834500*
CHOICE HOTELS — *0800 444444 (Freephone)*
CORUS & REGAL HOTELS — *08457 334400*
DE VERE HOTELS PLC — *0870 6063606*
HILTON HOTELS — *08705 515151*
HOLIDAY INN WORLDWIDE — *0800 897121 (Freephone)*
HYATT HOTELS WORLDWIDE — *0845 8881234*
INTERCONTINENTAL HOTELS LTD — *0800 0289387 (Freephone)*
JURYS/DOYLE HOTELS — *0870 9072222*
MACDONALD HOTELS PLC — *08457 585593*
MARRIOTT HOTELS — *0800 221222 (Freephone)*
MILLENNIUM & COPTHORNE HOTELS PLC — *0845 3020001*
PREMIER LODGES — *08702 010203*
QUEENS MOAT HOUSES PLC — *0500 213214 (Freephone)*
RADISSON EDWARDIAN HOTELS — *0800 374411 (Freephone)*
SHERATON HOTELS — *0800 353535 (Freephone)*
THISTLE HOTELS — *0800 181716 (Freephone)*
TRAVEL INNS — *0870 2428000*
TRAVELODGES — *08700 850950*

PRACTICAL INFORMATION

Banks

Open, generally 9.30 am to 4.30 pm weekdays (except public holidays). Most have cash dispensers. You need ID (passport) for cashing cheques. Banks levy smaller commissions than hotels.
Many 'Bureaux de Change' around Piccadilly open 7 days.

Congestion Charging

The congestion charge is £5 per day on all vehicles (except motor cycles and exempt vehicles) entering the central zone between 7.00 am and 6.30 pm - Monday to Friday except on Bank Holidays.
Payment can be made in advance, on the day, by post, on the Internet, by telephone (0845 900 1234) or at retail outlets.
A charge of up to £80 will be made for non-payment.
Further information is available on the Transport for London website - www.cclondon.com.

Getting around

As driving and parking in London are difficult, it is advisable to take the Underground, a bus or taxi and full details of these services can be obtained from London Transport Travel Enquiries ℘ (020) 7222 1234.

Underground – an extensive network covers the whole capital and a map can be found at the back of this guide. Single or return tickets may be purchased from tube stations only. To calculate an estimated journey time, count three minutes between stations and an average of fifteen minutes to change lines. Last trains run from Central London until 0.50am Mondays to Fridays and until 12 midnight on Sundays.

Buses – Bus-routes are displayed in bus shelters as well as inside the buses themselves. White signs with the red logo indicate bus stops at which all listed buses must stop – red signs with the white logo are request stops at which passengers must wave to the bus to stop and make a pick up.

Taxis – The traditional London cab is available at railway termini, Heathrow airport taxi ranks and cruising the streets. An orange roof light displays whether or not they are available for pick-up and when iluminated they can be hailed in the street.

Travelcards – Multi-journey zoned passes are more economical for a stay in the capital and these Travelcards are available for one day, a weekend, a week or longer.

Medical Emergencies

To contact a doctor for first aid, emergency medical advice and chemists night service: 07000 372255.
Accident & Emergency: dial 999 for Ambulance, Police or Fire Services.

Post Offices

Open Monday to Friday 9 am to 5.30 pm. Late collections made from Leicester Square.

Shopping

Most stores are found in Oxford Street (Selfridges, M & S), Regent Street (Hamleys, Libertys) and Knightsbridge (Harrods, Harvey Nichols). Open usually Monday to Saturday 9 am to 6 pm. Some open later (8 pm) once a week; Knightsbridge Wednesday, Oxford Street and Regent Street Thursday. Other areas worth visiting include Jermyn Street and Savile Row (mens outfitters), Bond Street (jewellers and haute couture).

Theatres

The "West End" has many major theatre performances and can generally be found around Shaftesbury Avenue. Most daily newspapers give details of performances. A half-price ticket booth is located in Leicester Square and is open Monday-Saturday 1 - 6.30 pm, Sunday and matinée days 12 noon - 6.30 pm. Restrictions apply.

Tipping

When a service charge is included in a bill it is not necessary to tip extra. If service is not included a discretionary 10% is normal.

Sights

Curiosités

Le curiosità

HISTORIC BUILDINGS AND MONUMENTS

Palace of Westminster★★★ : House of Lords★★, Westminster Hall★★ (hammerbeam roof★★★), Robing Room★, Central Lobby★, House of Commons★, Big Ben★, Victoria Tower★, 39 ALX — Tower of London★★★ (Crown Jewels★★★, White Tower or Keep★★★, St. John's Chapel★★, Beauchamp Tower★, Tower Hill Pageant★) 34 ASU — British Airways London Eye (views★★★) 32 AMV.

Banqueting House★★ 31 ALV — Buckingham Palace★★ (Changing of the Guard★★, Royal Mews★★) 38 AIX — Kensington Palace★★ 27 ABV — Lincoln's Inn★★ 32 AMT — London Bridge★ 34 ARV — Royal Hospital Chelsea★★ 37 AGZ — St. James's Palace★★ 30 AJV — Somerset House★★ 32 AMU — South Bank Arts Centre★★ (Royal Festival Hall★, National Theatre★, County Hall★) 32 AMV — The Temple★★ (Middle Temple Hall★) 32 ANU — Tower Bridge★★ 34 ASV.

Albert Memorial★ 36 ADX — Apsley House★ 30 AHV — Burlington House★ 30 AIV — Charterhouse★ 19 UZD — George Inn★, Southwark 33 AQV — Gray's Inn★ 32 AMV — Guildhall★ (Lord Mayor's Show★★) 33 AQT — International Shakespeare Globe Centre★ 33 APV — Dr Johnson's House★ 32 ANT — Lancaster House★ 30 AIV — Leighton House★ 35 AAX — Linley Sambourne House★ 35 AAX — Lloyds Building★★ 34 ARU — Mansion House★ (plate and insignia★★) 33 AQV — The Monument★ (⚹★) 34 ARU — Old Admiralty★ 31 AKV — Royal Albert Hall★ 36 ADX — Royal Exchange★ 34 ARU — Royal Opera Arcade★ (New Zealand House) 31 AKV — Royal Opera House★ (Covent Garden) 31 ALU — Spencer House★★ 30 AIV — Staple Inn★ 32 ANT — Theatre Royal★ (Haymarket), 31 AKV — Westminster Bridge★ 39 ALX.

CHURCHES

The City Churches

St. Paul's Cathedral★★★ (Dome ⩽★★★) 33 APU.

St. Bartholomew the Great★★ (choir★) 33 APT — St. Dunstan-in-the-East★★ 34 ARU — St. Mary-at-Hill★★ (woodwork★★, plan★) 34 ARU — Temple Church★★ 32 ANU.

All Hallows-by-the-Tower (font cover★★, brasses★) 34 ARU — Christ Church★ 33 APT — St. Andrew Undershaft (monuments★) 34 ARU — St. Bride★ (steeple★) 32 ANU — St. Clement Eastcheap (panelled interior★★) 34 ARU — St. Edmund the King and Martyr (tower and spire★) 34 AQV — St-Giles Cripplegate★ 33 AQT — St. Helen Bishopsgate★ (monuments★★) 34 ART — St. James Garlickhythe (tower and spire★, sword rests★) 33 AQU — St. Magnus the Martyr (tower★, sword rest★) 34 ARU — St. Margaret Lothbury★ (tower and spire★, woodwork★, screen★, font★) 33 AQV — St. Margaret Pattens (spire★, woodwork★) 34 ARU — St. Martin-within-Ludgate (tower and spire★, door cases★) 33 APU — St. Mary Abchurch★ (reredos★★, tower and spire★, dome★) 33 AQU — St. Mary-le-Bow (tower and steeple★★) 33 AQU — St. Michael Paternoster Royal (tower and spire★) 35 AQU — St. Nicholas Cole Abbey (tower and spire★) 33 APU — St. Olave★ 34 ARU — St. Peter upon Cornhill (screen★) 34 ARU — St. Stephen Walbrook★ (tower and steeple★, dome★) 33 AQU — St. Vedast (tower and spire★ ceiling★), 33 APT.

Other Churches

Westminster Abbey★★★ (Henry VII Chapel★★★, Chapel of Edward the Confessor★★, Chapter House★★, Poets' Corner★) 39 ALX.

Southwark Cathedral★★ 33 AQV.

Queen's Chapel★ 30 AJV — St. Clement Danes★ 32 AMU — St. James's★ 30 AJV — St. Margaret's★ 39 ALX — St. Martin-in-the-Fields★ 31 ALV — St. Paul's★ (Covent Garden) 31 ALU — Westminster Roman Catholic Cathedral★ 39 ALX.

PARKS

Regent's Park★★★ 11 QZC (terraces★★, Zoo★★).

Hyde Park 29 AFV — Kensington Gardens★★ 28 ACV (Orangery★) 27 ABV — St. James's Park★★ 31 AKV.

STREETS AND SQUARES

The City★★★ 33 AQT.

Bedford Square★★ 31 AKT – *Belgrave Square*★★ 37 AGX – *Burlington Arcade*★★ 30 AIV – *Covent Garden*★★ *(The Piazza*★★ *)* 31 ALU – *The Mall*★★ 31 AKV – *Piccadilly*★ 30 AIV – *The Thames*★★ 32 ANU – *Trafalgar Square*★★ 31 AKV – *Whitehall*★★ *(Horse Guards*★ *)* 31 ALV.

Barbican★ 33 AQT – *Bond Street*★ 30 AIU – *Canonbury Square*★ 13 UZB – *Carlton House Terrace*★ 31 AKV – *Cheyne Walk*★ 23 PZG – *Fitzroy Square*★ 18 RZD – *Jermyn Street*★ 30 AJV – *Leicester Square*★ 31 AKU – *Merrick Square*★ 19 VZE – *Montpelier Square*★ 37 AFX – *Neal's Yard*★ 31 ALU – *Piccadilly Arcade*★ 30 AIV – *Portman Square*★ 29 AGT – *Queen Anne's Gate*★ 39 AKX – *Regent Street*★ 30 AIU – *Piccadilly Circus*★ 31 AKU – *St. James's Square*★ 31 AJV – *St. James's Street*★ 30 AIV – *Shepherd Market*★ 30 AHV – *Soho*★ 31 AKU – *Trinity Church Square*★ 19 VZE – *Victoria Embankment gardens*★ 31 ALV – *Waterloo Place*★ 31 AKV.

MUSEUMS

British Museum★★★ 31 AKL – *National Gallery*★★★ 31 AKV – *Science Museum*★★★ 36 ADX – *Tate Britain*★★★ 39 ALY – *Victoria and Albert Museum*★★★ 36 ADY – *Wallace Collection*★★★ 29 AGT.

Courtauld Institute Galleries★★ *(Somerset House)* 32 AMU – *Gilbert Collection*★★ *(Somerset House)* 32 AMU – *Museum of London*★★ 33 APT – *National Portrait Gallery*★★ 31 AKU – *Natural History Museum*★★ 36 ADY – *Sir John Soane's Museum*★★ 32 AMT – *Tate Modern*★★ *(views*★★★ *from top floors)* 33 APV.

Clock Museum★ *(Guildhall)* 33 AQT – *Imperial War Museum*★ 40 ANY – *London's Transport Museum*★ 31 ALU – *Madame Tussaud's*★ 17 QZD – *Museum of Mankind*★ 33 DM – *National Army Museum*★ 37 AGZ – *Percival David Foundation of Chinese Art*★ 18 SZD – *Planetarium*★ 15 HVL – *Wellington Museum*★ *(Apsley House)* 30 AHV.

OUTER LONDON

Blackheath 8 HX *terraces and houses*★, *Eltham Palace*★ **A**
Brentford 5 BX *Syon Park*★★, *gardens*★
Bromley 7 GXY *The Crystal Palace Park*★
Chiswick 6 CV *Chiswick Mall*★★, *Chiswick House*★ **D**, *Hogarth's House*★ **E**
Dulwich 11 *Picture Gallery*★ FX **X**
Greenwich 7 and 8 GHV *Cutty Sark*★★ GV **F**, *Footway Tunnel* (≼ ★★ *)*, *Fan Museum*★ 10 GV **A**, *National Maritime Museum*★★ *(Queen's House*★★ *)* GV **M²** *Royal Naval College*★★ *(Painted Hall*★, *the Chapel*★ *)* GV **G**, *The Park and Old Royal Observatory*★ *(Meridian Building : collection*★★ *)* HV **K**, *Ranger's House*★ GX **N**
Hampstead *Kenwood House*★★ *(Adam Library*★★, *paintings*★★ *)* 2 EU **P**, *Fenton House*★★ 11 PZA
Hampton Court 5 BY *(The Palace*★★★, *gardens*★★★, *Fountain Court*★, *The Great Vine*★ *)*
Kew 6 CX *Royal Botanic Gardens*★★★ : *Palm House*★★, *Temperate House*★, *Kew Palace or Dutch House*★★, *Orangery*★, *Pagoda*★, *Japanese Gateway*★
Hendon★ 2 *Royal Air Force Museum*★★ CT **M³**
Hounslow 5 BV *Osterley Park*★★
Lewisham 7 GX *Horniman Museum*★ **M⁴**
Richmond 5 and 6 CX *Richmond Park*★★, ✳★★★ CX, *Richmond Hill*✳★★ CX, *Richmond Bridge*★★ BX **R**, *Richmond Green*★★ BX **S**, *(Maids of Honour Row*★★, *Trumpeter's House*★ *)*, *Asgill House*★ BX **B**, *Ham House*★★ BX **V**
Shoreditch 14 XZ *Beffrye Museum*★ **M**
Tower Hamlets 7 GV *Canary Wharf*★★ B, *Isle of Dogs*★ *St. Katharine Dock*★ 34 ASV
Twickenham 5 BX *Marble Hill House*★ **Z**, *Strawberry Hill*★ **A**.

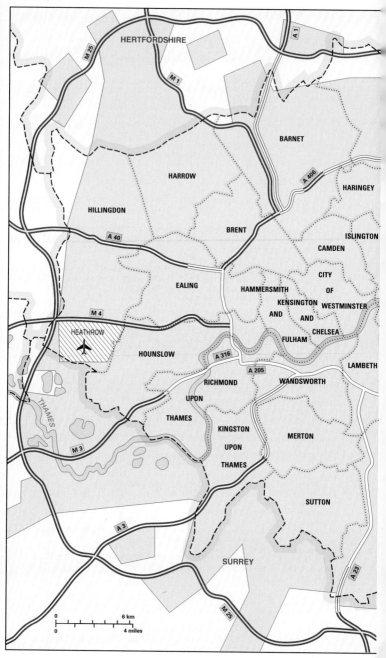

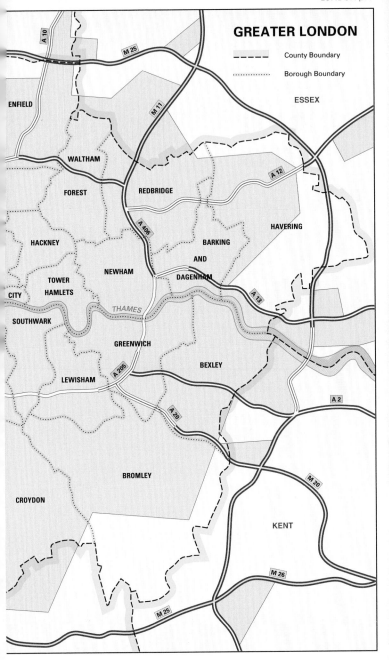

GREATER LONDON

- - - - County Boundary

·············· Borough Boundary

ESSEX

ENFIELD

WALTHAM

FOREST

REDBRIDGE

HAVERING

HACKNEY

NEWHAM

BARKING

AND

DAGENHAM

TOWER

HAMLETS

CITY

SOUTHWARK

THAMES

GREENWICH

BEXLEY

LEWISHAM

A 2

BROMLEY

CROYDON

KENT

A 10

M 25

M 11

A 12

A 406

A 13

A 205

A 20

M 20

M 26

M 25

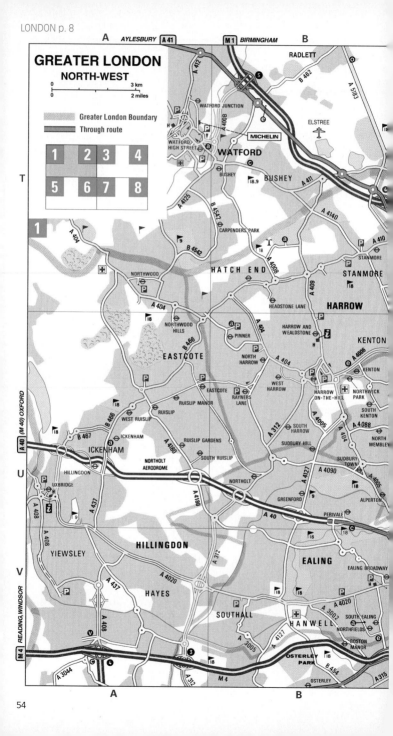

GREATER LONDON
NORTH-WEST

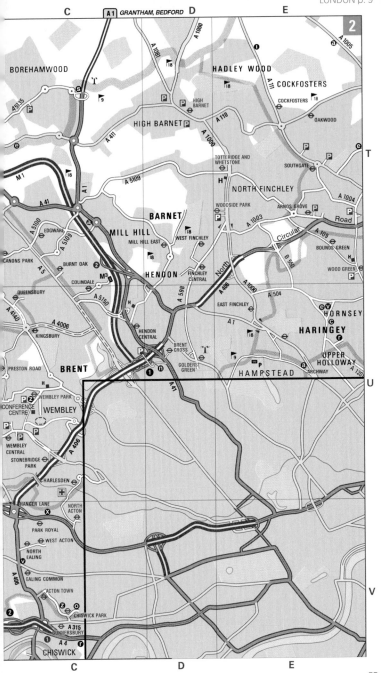

2

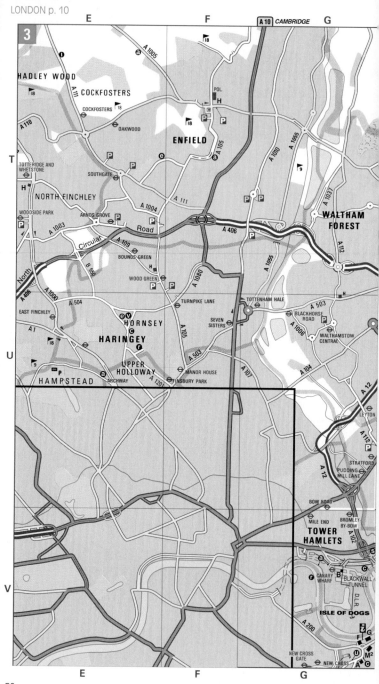

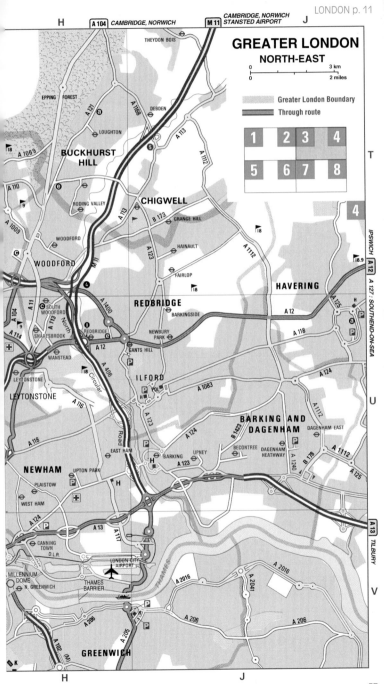

GREATER LONDON
NORTH-EAST

Greater London Boundary
Through route

| 1 | 2 | 3 | 4 |
| 5 | 6 | 7 | 8 |

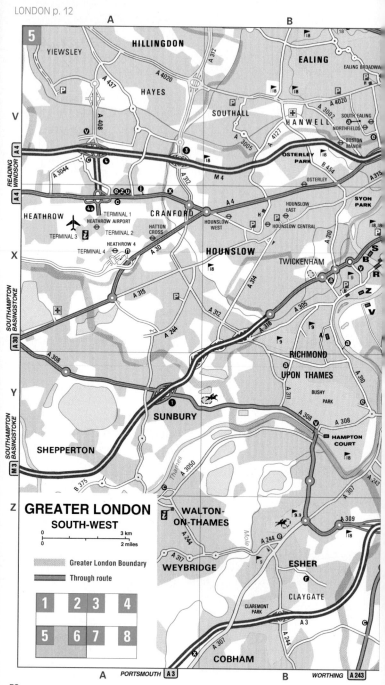

GREATER LONDON
SOUTH-WEST

0 ——— 3 km
0 ——— 2 miles

Greater London Boundary
Through route

| 1 | 2 | 3 | 4 |
| 5 | 6 | 7 | 8 |

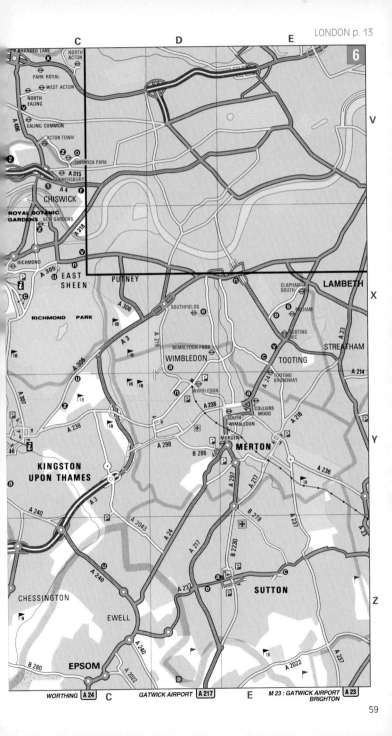

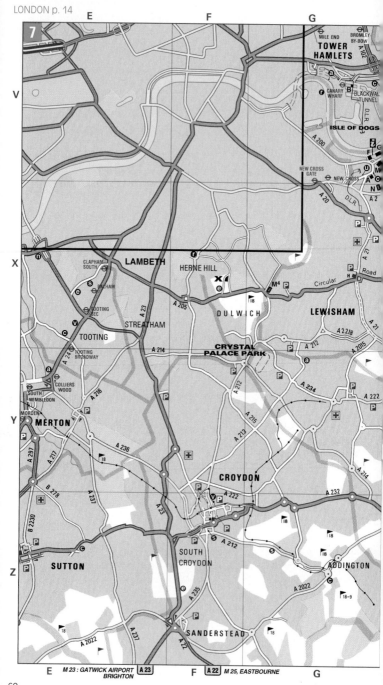

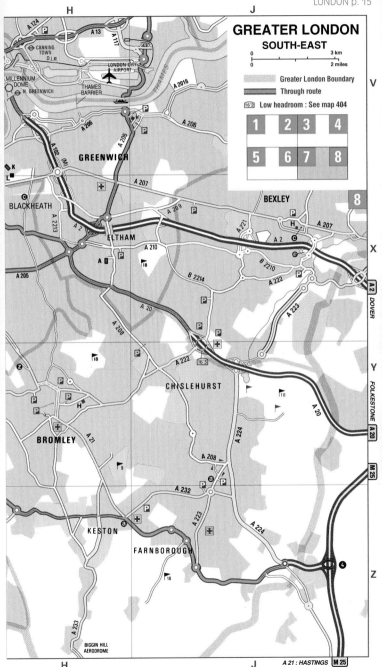

GREATER LONDON
SOUTH-EAST

0   3 km
0   2 miles

Greater London Boundary
Through route
16.2 Low headroom : See map 404

| 1 | 2 | 3 | 4 |
| 5 | 6 | 7 | 8 |

8

A 124
A 13
A 111
CANNING TOWN D.L.R.
LONDON CITY AIRPORT
MILLENNIUM DOME
N. GREENWICH
THAMES BARRIER
THAMES
A 2016
A 206
A 206
A 205
A 102 (M)
GREENWICH
A 207
BLACKHEATH
A 2213
A 2
ELTHAM
A 209
BEXLEY
A 221
A 207
A 2
A 210
A 205
B 2214
B 2210
A 222
A 20
A 208
A 223
CHISLEHURST
16.3
A 222
A 224
A 20
BROMLEY
A 21
A 208
A 232
A 224
A 223
KESTON
FARNBOROUGH
A 233
BIGGIN HILL AERODROME

DOVER A2
FOLKESTONE A 20
M 25
4

LONDON CENTRE

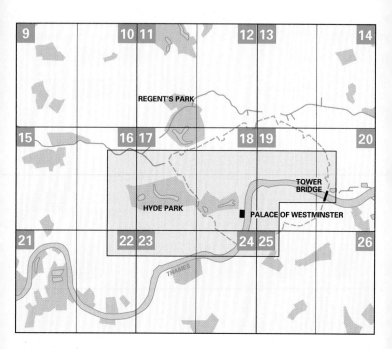

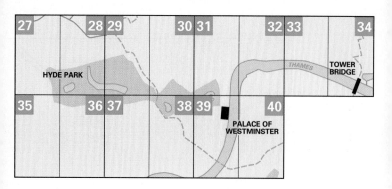

INDEX OF STREET NAMES IN LONDON CENTRE

9

Brent Reservoir

K

L

North Circular Road

A 406

Crest Road

Coles Green Rd

Edgware Rd

A 5

Avenue

Brook Rd

Lane

Cricklewood

NEASDEN JUNCTION

Tanfield

Dollis

Hill

ZA

Neasden

A 4088

Dudden

GLADSTONE PARK

BRENT

Mora Rd

Sneyd Rd

Heber Rd

Neasden

Lane

Hill

Kendal Rd

Anson Road

North Pk Ave

Burnley Road

Sherrick Green Rd

15'3

Dollis Hill

Denzil Road

Chapter Road

Willesden Green

Lane

High Road

Lane

WILLESDEN GREEN

High Road

a

Walm

e

A 407

357

Brondesbury

Rd

482

Roundwood Road

Pound Lane

WILLESDEN CEMETERY

Peter Ave

KILBURN

Sidmouth

Mount Pleasant Rd

Church Road

351

196

ROUNDWOOD PARK

Harlesden Road

Donnington Road

Chamberlayne

Road

ZB

A 404

352

Manor Park Rd

Doyle

Avenue

Hardinge Rd

College

480

Rd

Acton Lane

High Street

Wrottesley Road

Road

All Souls Gdns

Clifford Gdns

KENSAL RISE

Harley La.

Furness Road

Bathurst Gdns

Rd

Willesden Junction

Harrow Road

Mortimer

ZC

Oak Lane

A 404

Kensal Green

Harrow

K

15

L

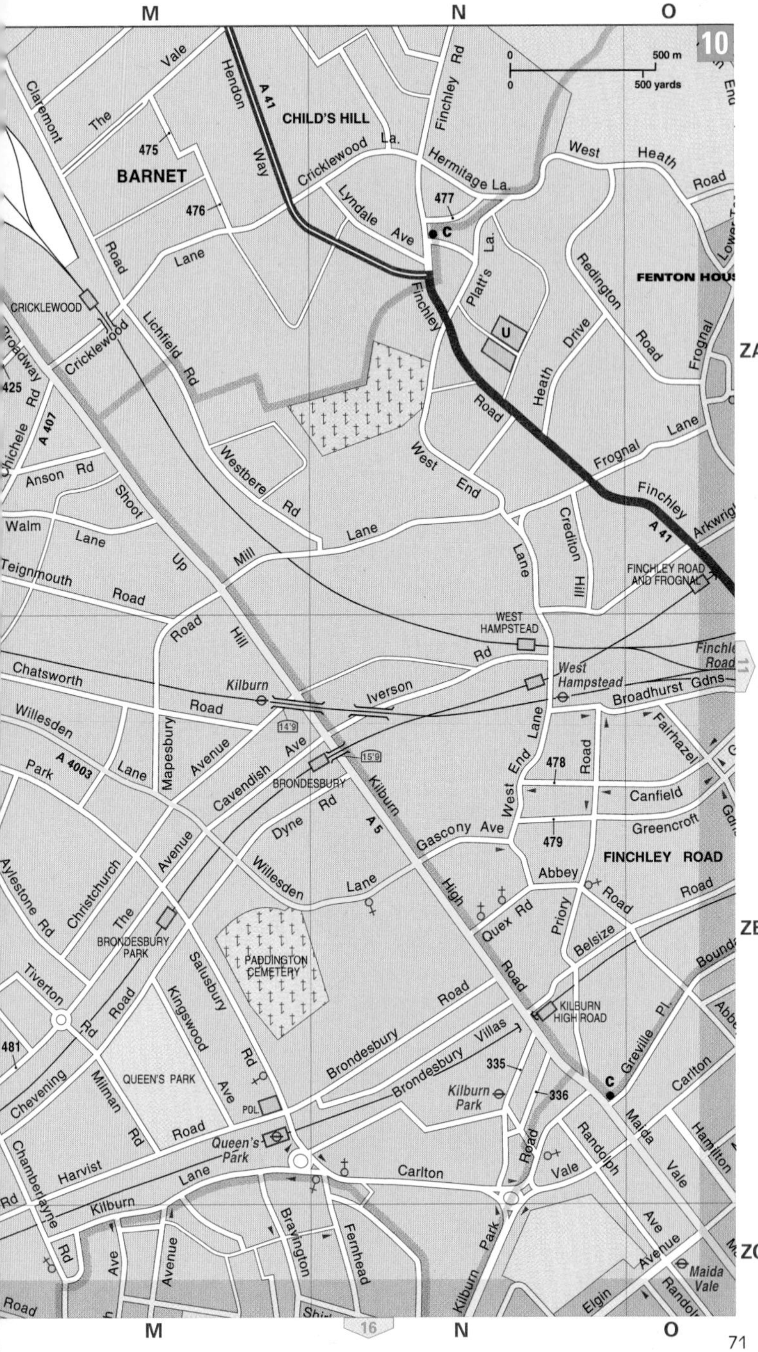
M
N
O
10
0
500 m
0
500 yards
CHILD'S HILL
BARNET
FENTON HOUSE
CRICKLEWOOD
WEST HAMPSTEAD
West Hampstead
FINCHLEY ROAD AND FROGNAL
Kilburn
BRONDESBURY
BRONDESBURY PARK
PADDINGTON CEMETERY
QUEEN'S PARK
Queen's Park
Kilburn Park
KILBURN HIGH ROAD
FINCHLEY ROAD
Maida Vale
A 41
A 407
A 4003
A 5
Hendon Way
Finchley Rd
Cricklewood La.
Hermitage La.
West Heath Road
Lyndale Ave
Platt's La.
Redington Road
Heath Drive
Frognal
Frognal Lane
West End Lane
Crediton Hill
Cricklewood Broadway
Lichfield Rd
Westbere Rd
Mill Lane
Shoot Up Hill
Anson Rd
Walm Lane
Teignmouth Road
Chichele Rd
Chatsworth Road
Willesden Lane
Mapesbury Road
Iverson Rd
Broadhurst Gdns
Fairhazel
Canfield
Greencroft
Abbey Road
Belsize Road
Priory Road
Quex Rd
Gascony Ave
Dyne Rd
Cavendish Ave
Kilburn High Road
Christchurch Avenue
Aylestone Rd
Tiverton Rd
Salusbury Rd
Kingswood Ave
Brondesbury Road
Brondesbury Villas
Chevening Rd
Milman Rd
Harvist Road
Chamberlayne Rd
Kilburn Lane
Carlton Vale
Randolph Ave
Maida Vale
Hamilton
Greville Pl.
Boundary
Bravington
Fernhead
Elgin Avenue
Kilburn Park Road
Cleve Road
475
476
477
425
478
479
481
335
336
14'9
15'9
POL.
U
C
11
16
ZA
ZB
ZC

O   P   Q

11

HAMPSTEAD HEATH

Kenwood
Ladies Pond

0 500 m
0 500 yards

North End Way A 502 Spaniards Road

Vale of
Health Pond

Mixed Bathing
Pond PARLIAMENT HILL

Heath Road

Whitestone
Pond East Heath Road

Heath South End Rd Parliament Hill

ZA

208 305 **v**

FENTON HOUSE

171 Well Walk **HAMPSTEAD**

227 Hampstead Willow

209 324 479 236 **s** Nassington Rd GOSPEL OAK

a 139 **M** 390 Savernake

x 106 HAMPSTEAD
HEATH 362 Mansfield Rd 13

Lane Rosslyn **e** Pond St Fleet Rd

Frognal Arkwright Road A 502 Lawn Southampton Rd Malden

A 41 Finchley **c** Lyndhurst Rd Hill **r** Belsize Park Parkhill Road

FINCHLEY ROAD
AND FROGNAL Gdns Fitzjohns 22 Lane Oman Rd Belsize Av. Haverstock

Netherhall Nutley Ter. Belsize 19 Belsize Park Gardens

10 Finchley
Road **CAMDEN**

Roadhurst Gdns Avenue Lancaster Grove 323 Hill Prince

Fairhazel Gdns Fairfax Road Eton Ave Chalk Farm Chalk

Canfield Gdns **n** **SWISS COTTAGE** Primrose

Greencroft **v** Swiss Cottage Adelaide Road

FINCHLEY ROAD **s** **e** **a** Adelaide Road **a** **b** Gloucester Ave **z**

Road SOUTH
HAMPSTEAD 297 Road Road Regents

ZB

Boundary Road 379 Elsworthy Rd Park

Loudoun Finchley Grove Avenue Rd PRIMROSE HILL Prince

Abbey Hill Road Ordnance Rd Circle **ZOO**

Carlton Place Queen's St John's Wood

Greville Pl. **b** **r** Marlborough Acacia Rd Wellington Allitsen Rd 79

Hamilton Road Circus 29 Prince Albert **REGENT'S** **PARK**

Maida Vale 277 Outer

ZC

Ave Maida Hall Terrace REGENT'S PARK
AND MARYLEBONE Canal Boating
Lake

Randolf Grove Road LORD'S CRICKET
GROUND **v** Road QUEEN MARY'S

12

Swains Lane

Dartmouth Park

Archway Road

Holloway Road

Hornsey Park

Tollington

DARTMOUTH PARK

UPPER HOLLOWAY

A 1

Tollington Way

Tollington Road

Chetwynd Road

Junction Hill

Highgate Rd

Tufnell Park

Tufnell Park Road

Holloway Road

Seven Sisters

Hornsey Road

ZA

A 503

Highgate Road

Fortess Road

Lady Margaret Rd

Carleton Rd

Dalmeny Rd

Dalmeny Ave

Parkhurst Road

Road

Caledonian

Hol R

n

x

Leighton Rd

Camden Road

Hillmarton Road

ISLING

Spring Place

Willes Road

A 400

Kentish Town

Islip Street

Torriano Ave

Busby Place

Hungerford Road

North

Caledonian Road

KENTISH TOWN

16'6

Gaisford Street

Patshull Road

Road

Wales Road

Town St

16

A 503

Camden Road

York Road

Market Road

Brewery Road

Mackenzie Roman W

A 5203

CALEDONIAN AND BARNSBI

13

Farm

Pancras

Agar

Grove

A 5200

Way

Caledonian

15'6

Offord a

CAMDEN ROAD

15'0

15

Road

Richmor

ZB

366

Camden Town

Parkway

Camden Rd

Royal

College St

Pancras Way

York Way

Copenhagen St

Road

Rd

Albert Rd

Camden St

Camden High St

Pratt Street

Delancey

Crowndale Rd

Pancras Rd

455

M

P

Caledonian

Calshot St

Outer

Park Village East

Mornington Crescent

Hampstead Road

Eversholt

KING'S CROSS

P

Pentonville

Albany

Ossulston St

Midland Rd

ST PANCRAS

King's

TERRACES

Circle

REGENT'S PARK

Robert Street

EUSTON

BRITISH LIBRARY

Euston Road

Judd

417

ZC

Chester Rd

St

P

P

18

r s

Gra Cross

R

S

T

73

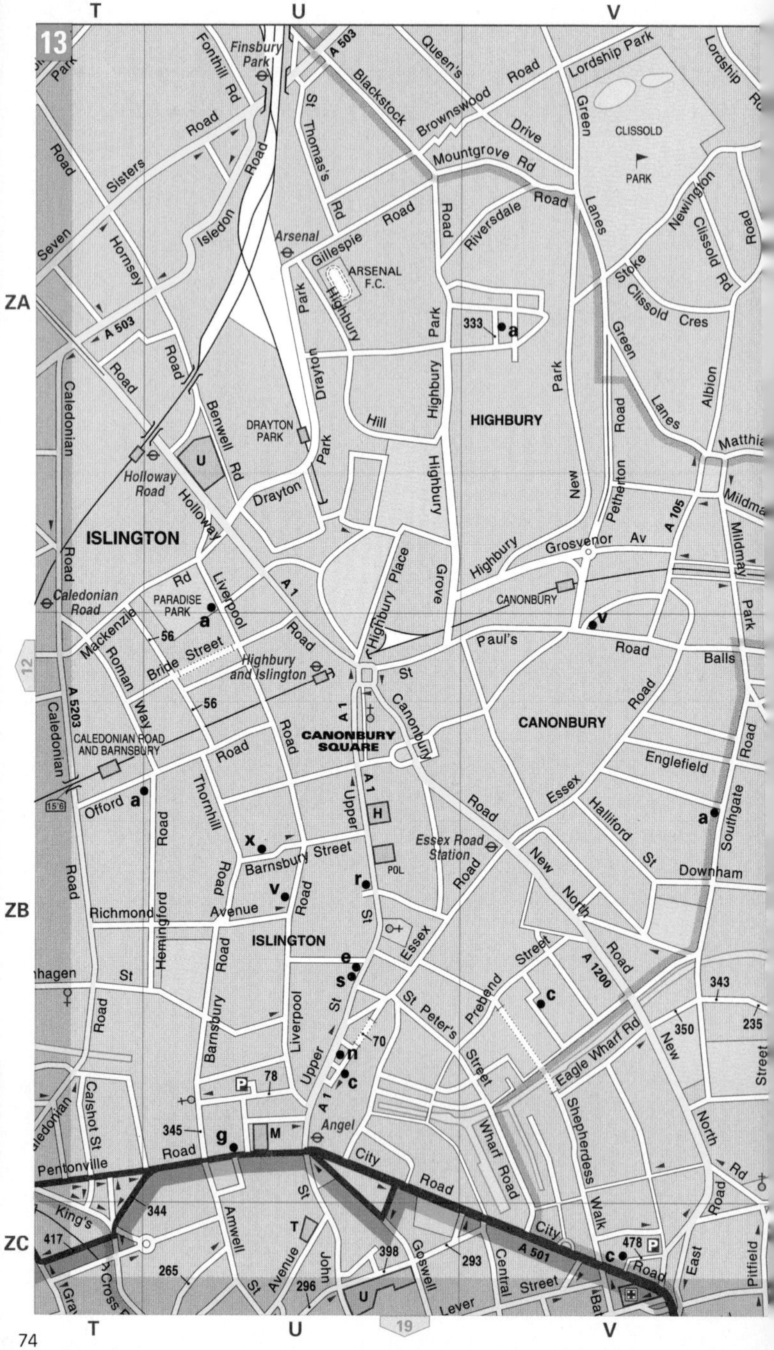

T
U
V
13
Finsbury Park
Fonthill Rd
A 503
Queen's
Blackstock
Road
Lordship Park
Lordship
Seven Sisters Road
St Thomas's Rd
Brownswood
Drive
Mountgrove Rd
Green Lanes
CLISSOLD PARK
Hornsey Road
Isledon
Arsenal
Gillespie Road
ARSENAL F.C.
Riversdale Road
Stoke Newington
Clissold Rd
Clissold Cres
ZA
A 503
Road
Road
Highbury Park
333
a
Drayton Park
Highbury Hill
Green Lanes
Albion Road
Caledonian Road
Benwell Rd
DRAYTON PARK
HIGHBURY
Highbury
Park
New
Petherton Road
Matthias
U
Holloway Road
Holloway
Drayton
Mildmay
A 105
ISLINGTON
Highbury Grove
Highbury
Grosvenor Av
Mildmay Park
Rd
Liverpool
A 1
Highbury Place
Grove
CANONBURY
Caledonian Road
PARADISE PARK
a
Mackenzie
56
Road
St Paul's Road
v
Roman Way
Bride Street
Highbury and Islington
St
Balls
12
Canonbury
A 1
56
A 5203
Caledonian
CALEDONIAN ROAD AND BARNSBURY
Road
Road
CANONBURY SQUARE
CANONBURY
Road
Road
Englefield
15'6
Offord a
Thornhill
Upper St
A 1
H
Essex Road Station
Essex
Halliford St
Southgate
a
Road
Road
x
Barnsbury Street
POL
Road
New North
Downham
Road
v
r
ZB
Richmond Avenue
Road
Hemingford
Essex
ISLINGTON
Street
A 1200
Road
Barnsbury Road
e
s
Prebend
c
343
hagen St
Road
St Peter's
Street
235
Liverpool
Upper St
70
n
c
350
New
Eagle Wharf Rd
Street
Road
Calshot St
P
78
Caledonian
A 1
Angel
Shepherdess Walk
North
345
g
M
Wharf Road
Rd
Pentonville Road
City Road
St
Road
King's
344
Amwell
T
City
417
ZC
398
Goswell
293
478
P
c
Road
East
Pitfield
265
Cross
St
Avenue
John
296
U
Central
A 501
Street
Lever
Bat
19
T
U
V

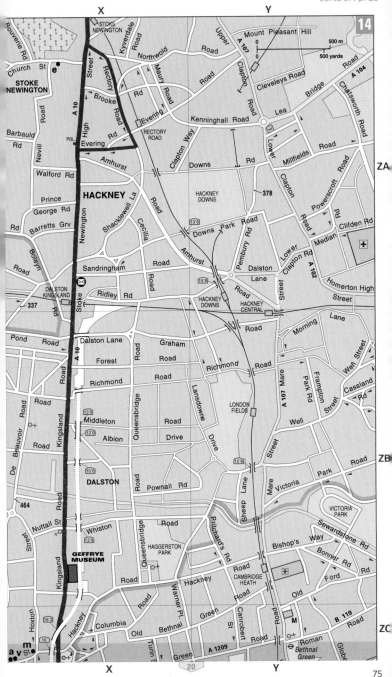

15

ZC

ZD

ZE

ZF

K   9   L   21

Willesden Junction

Oak Lane

Victoria Rd

Old

Grand Union Canal

Harrow Road

A 404   Kensal Green

Harrow

KENSAL GREEN CEMETERY

Mortimer

A 219

Scrubs Lane

Barlby

St Quintin

Highlever Road

Wood Lane

WORMWOOD SCRUBS

Oak Common Lane

Wulfstan Street

East Acton

The Fairway

Brassie Ave

Western Ave

Du

Westway

Westway   A 40

Cane   Road

East Acton Lane

Bromyard

Ashfield Rd

Avenue

EALING

The Vale

Larden Road

Cobbold Road

Emlyn Road

The Avenue

Blenheim Rd

Abinger Rd

Old Oak Road

Yew Tree Rd

Steventon Rd

Wormholt Road

Bryony Road

Sawley Road

Uxbridge Road   A 4020

Askew Road

Goldhawk Road

387

462

463   c

Prebend Gdns

Bath Road

Stamford Brook

Goldhaw Road

RAVENSCOURT PARK

Paddenswick Rd

Goldhawk Road   A 402

13

Ravenscourt Park

Turnham Green

Bloemfontein

South Africa Road

SHEPHERD'S BUSH

LOFTUS ROAD STADIUM

White City

BBC

Wood Lane

Shepherd's Bush

Uxbridge Road

Lime Grove

454

Goldhawk Road

Coningham Road

Hammersmith

Brackenbury Rd

Banim St

Glenthorne Road

HAMMERSMITH

Shepherd's Bush

Brook

x

a

500 m / 500 yards

16

ZC

ZD

ZE

ZF

M   N   O

BAYSWATER
AND MAIDA VALE

Maida
Vale

Lauderdale Rd

Delaware Rd

Warwick

Sutherland Rd

Canal

Harrow

Road

A 404

Royal
Oak

Westway

Westbourne
Park

Ladbroke
Grove

Westbourne

Park

Chepstow

Road

Grove

Westbourne

Pembridge Villas

Dawson

Place

Porchester

Gdns

Bayswater

Queensway

Queensway

Bayswat

NORTH
KENSINGTON

Clarendon

Road

Notting

Hill Gate

Notting
Hill Gate

Kensington

Kensington Church

Campden

Broad

ORANGERY

Ro
Pa

KENSINGTON
PALACE

Kensington

Gardens

Walk

Street

KENSINGTON

Holland

Park

HOLLAND   PARK

Abbotsbury

Holland

Holland

Holland St

U

LINLEY
SAMBOURNE
HOUSE

St

H

High Street
Kensington

KENSINGTON
AND CHELSEA

LEIGHTON
HOUSE

Kensington

Edwardes
Square

POL

Earls

Marloes

NAT

Olympia

OLYMPIA

Warw

Pembroke Rd.

Cromwell

Road

A 315

Green

North

M   N   O

77

17

O   P   Q

ZC

REGENT'S PARK AND MARYLEBONE

LORD'S CRICKET GROUND

Boating Lake

500 m
500 yards

QUEEN MARY'S GARDENS

Avenue
Maida
Hall
Terrace

Randolph
Maida   Vale

v

Wood   Road

Park   Road

TERRACES

U

Regent's

St John's

Lisson

Rossmore   Rd

Outer

TERRACES

dale Rd

Ave

348

Clifton Gdns

Frampton   St

Church   St

MARYLEBONE

Baker   Street

s

MADAME TUSSAUD'S

n   e

Warwick

Avenue

ZD

p   c   a

Blomfield

Warwick Av.

Edgware   Road

Maida   Vale   Av.

Road

Broadley

Marylebone

St

A 501

Road

Paddington S

WATER
AIDA VALE
Road

Edgware   Road

Westway

Crawford

WALLACE COLLECTION

Royal
Oak

PADDINGTON

Praed   Street

Gardens

Edgware

PORTMAN SQUARE

Gloucester

Sussex

Kendal St

Seymour   St

Marble Arch

Oxford   St

ter Gdns

Queensway

Terrace

Bayswater   Road

Road

Lancaster
Gate

North   Carriage   Drive

Marble Arch

16

ay   Bayswater

HYDE   PARK

Park

Lane

The   Long   Water

CITY OF WESTMINSTER

ORANGERY

KENSINGTON   GARDENS

Serpentine

Road

Broad

Round
Pond

ZE

The   Serpentine

KENSINGTON PALACE

Walk

HYDE PARK AND KNIGHTSBRIDGE

ALBERT MEMORIAL

Road

Knightsbridge

Hyde Park
Corner

Kensington

Knightsbridge

ROYAL ALBERT HALL

U

Exhibition   Rd

MONTPELIER SQUARE

Road

BELGRAVE SQUARE

Queen's

Sloane

ENSINGTON
D CHELSEA

SCIENCE MUSEUM

VICTORIA AND ALBERT MUSEUM

Brompton

Pont   Street

Street

Lyall

NATURAL HISTORY MUSEUM

Cadogan
Square

ZF

Cromwell
Gloucester   Road

Road

South
Kensington

Walton   Street

Sloane

Gloc

Gate

Pelham   St

MICHELIN HOUSE

23

O   P   23   Q

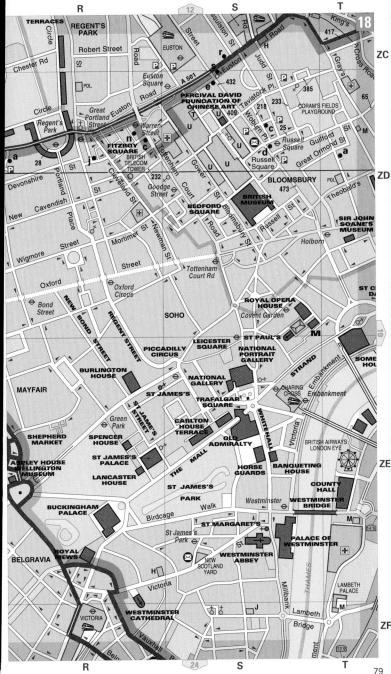

19

T U V

ZC

ng's

344

Amwell

T

398

Goswell

City

478 P

c

East

Pitfield

Walk

Cross Road

265

296

John

St

Avenue

U

293

Lever

Central

Street

A 501

Bath

Old Street

ZC

Gray's

a

65

b

n

Percival St

e

FINSBURY

Road

Old

Street

Whitecross

City

Road

Worship

FIELDS
OUND

M

Inn

Farringdon

110

43

Aldersgate

Burhill

141

P

St

Road A 105

lford St

mond St

Rosebery

474

A 5201

r

U

166

St

Row

ZD

a

Rd

M

CHATERHOUSE

Barbican

Chiswell

St

Sun

Theobald's

Farringdon

Beech

St

Wilson

POL

113

MUSEUM OF
LONDON

Moorgate

GRAY'S
INN

Chancery

Road

ST BARTHOLOMEW
THE GREAT

A 1211

London

Wall

SIR JOHN
SOANE'S
MUSEUM

Lane

STAPLE
INN

Holborn Viaduct

GUILDHALL

LINCOLN'S
INN

Fleet

Street

ST PAUL'S
CATHEDRAL

ROYAL
EXCHANGE

ST CLEMENT
DANES

ST BRIDE

CITY OF
LONDON

Cannon

ST MARY-
LE-BOW

Bank

Gracechurch

St

TEMPLE

Blackfriars

Blackfriars

Mansion House

Cannon

MANSION
HOUSE

Temple

Victoria

Embankment

Upper

Street

MONUMENT

Thames

ankment

nkment

Bridge

SOMERSET
HOUSE

THAMES

St

GLOBE
CENTRE

LONDON
BRIDGE

SOUTH BANK
ARTS CENTRE

M

TATE
MODERN

SOUTHWARK
CATHEDRAL

LONDON
BRIDGE

A AIRWAYS
ON EYE

IMAX

Blackfriars

Southwark

BRAMAH MUSEUM
OF TEA AND COFFEE

St

Thomas

GEORGE
INN

386

T

ZE

UNTY
ALL
NSTER
GE

WATERLOO

T

Union

Street

Bridge

High

Newcomen
Street

P

Iveston

M

Webber

Suffolk

St

Borough

408

Long

OF
TER

Westminster

Lamberth North

Road

Street

Borough

SOUTHWARK

Road

349

TRINITY CHURCH
SQUARE

St

Great

Dover

Street

LAMBETH
PALACE

M

Bridge

Rd

POL

Lambeth

Road

St

London

George's

U

Southwark

Rd

A 3

J

Trinity

Harper

St

MERRICK
SQUARE

A 2

ZF

D

500 m

500 yards

IMPERIAL WAR
MUSEUM

Kennington

ELEPHANT AND CASTLE
SHOPPING CENTRE

New

163

306

Kent

Heygate

St

Rodh

Road

Falmouth

Rd

A 201

WALWORTH

13 9

T U V

25

80

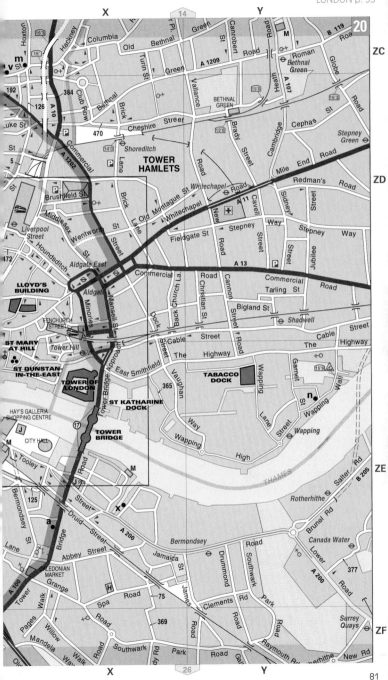

21

K   15   L

ZF

RAVENSCOURT PARK

HAMMERSMITH   x

14'6   Bath   Road   Prebend Gdns   Stamford Brook   Goldhawk   Rd

Turnham Green   12'0

13

Ravenscourt Park   Glenthorne   Road   Grove

389   Hammersmith

r   x   Chiswick   High   n   Road

u   King   H   Street

A 315

CHISWICK

Road   Great   West   Road   Talgarth

y   Devonshire

Chiswick

Hammersmith   431

21   Fulham

HOUNSLOW   a   West   402   Rd

A 4   CHISWICK   MALL

Bridge

Castelnau

A 219

Rainmoch Rd

ZG

HOGARTH'S HOUSE

A 316

Great

Lane

Burlington

Road

Lonsdale

Rainville Road

CHISWICK HOUSE

r

Verdun

Road

A 306

Castelnau

THAMES

WILDFOWL AND WETLANDS TRUST

Suffolk   Road

Ferry

NATURE RESERVE

Lonsdale

Road

Road

Stevenage

a

Church   Road   x   Rocks

404

The Terrace

BARNES

Lane

16'6

Mill   Hill   Road

ZH

BARNES BRIDGE

e

RICHMOND UPON THAMES

Station

BARNES

Rocks

Lane

Mill   Hill   Road

PUTNEY

s   Richmond

White   Hart

Road

Road

COMMON

B 306   Ride   Lower

COMMON

Vine

BARNES

Rocks

Queen's

Erpingham Rd

Hotham Road

Upper   Richmond   Road   West   Upper

A 205

Hertford   Ave

Priory   Lane

Roehampton   Lane

Richmond

A 306

House   Road

Dover

Road

A 205

PUTNEY

Lane

Howards

Gwendolen Ave

0   500 m
0   500 yards

K   L

M   16   N   O

22

ZF

ZG

ZH

OLYMPIA

Green   A 315   North   Road   Warwick   Pembroke Rd.   Cromwell   Court   Road

Hammersmith   Edith   Gunterstone Rd   Road   West   End   West Kensington   EARL'S COURT   Road   Earl's Court

182   Talgarth   Road   101   99   SOU KENSIN

Barons Court   Baron's Court Rd   Star Road   North   Road   Brompton

St. Dunstan's Rd.   HAMMERSMITH AND FULHAM   EARL'S COURT EXHIBITION BLDG   West Brompton   BROMPTON   Redcliffe   Gardens

Greyhound   Road   Palace   Lillie   Musard Road   Lillie   Road   Halford Rd   Seagrave Rd   CEMETERY   202

164   Lillie   Road   Road   Ryston Road   End   Road   CHELSEA F.C.   King's   Road

203   Dawes   Road   Dawes   Road   207   Fulham Broadway   Fulham   Lots   V

450   Munster   Road   Filmer   Bishops   Road   Road   A 304   Harwood Road   King's   Imperial Road

Woodlawn   Fulham   Palace   Road   Bishops   Road   Parsons   A 146   EEL BROOK COMMON   New King's Road   Wandsworth   A 217   Bagley's

Finlay   Street   A 219   FULHAM   Munster   Road   Fulham   Road   Parsons Green   Green   La.   Road   A 308   Studdridge Street   Clancarty Road   Bridge   Lane   Road

Bishop's Park Rd   FULHAM PALACE GARDENS   King's   15'0   New   Road   Peterborough   Broomhouse   SOUTH PARK   Hugon Rd   Stephendale

172   Hurlingham Road   HURLINGHAM PARK   Road   Lane   Carnwath   Road   Road   Townmead

Putney   Putney Bridge   Road   THAMES   437

Charlwood Rd   Road   Putney   Bridge   WANDSWORTH PARK   A 3209   Bridge   Swandon   Way   WANDSWORTH TOWN

POL.   Putney   High St   Putney   A 219   Disraeli   Oxford Road   WANDSWORTH PARK   Fawe Park Road   Road   a

358   Upper   Richmond   Rd   PUTNEY   East Putney   15   Oakhill   Road   7   165

M   N   O   83

O   P   17   Q

23

NATURAL HISTORY MUSEUM

ZF

South Kensington

Cadogan Square

Cromwell Road
Gloucester Road
Road

Pelham St

MICHELIN HOUSE

Sloane Street

23

101

SOUTH KENSINGTON

Gloucester Rd

Onslow Gdns

Fulham

Sidney Street

Cale St

Sloane

Ave

King's Road

Sloane Square

Pimlic

99

Drayton Gds

Cranley Gdns

Road

Old

Church

King's

Oakley Street

Flood Street

Royal

Smith St

CHELSEA

Hospital Road

Chelse

Brompton

Gliston Rd

Beaufort

Street

Street

NATIONAL ARMY MUSEUM

THE ROYA
HOSPITAL

Redcliffe
Gardens

Fulham

Park

Walk

n

Street

CHEYNE   WALK

Chelsea

Embankmen

ZG

Road

Edith Grove

e

d

WALK

CHEYNE

Battersea

Albert

THAMES

202

P

Road

Bridge

Battersea
Bridge

Albert
Bridge

The Parade

Carriage

Drive

Carriage

v

r

King's

Lots Rd

Lots Road

Battersea Church Rd

c

Parkgate Rd

Bridge

Carriage

BATTERSEA   PARK

22

b

Road

Bridge

Drive

j

Imperial Road

B 305

Westbridge

Surrey Lane

Road

Prince   of   Wales   Park

Bagley's

Lane

Road

433

10'9

BATTERSEA

449

x

Carriage   Drive

Battersea

A 3205

12'6

Stephendale

Townmead

B 305

266

15'9

Latchmere

15'6

ZH

Road

Road

York

Falcon

Road

WANDSWORTH

Road

A 3220

H

Gowrie

437

Road

CLAPHAM JUNCTION

14'9

A 3036

Lavender

Elspeth Rd

Hill

Marney Rd

Clapham

a

Swandon   Way

WANDSWORTH TOWN

441

Plough

York

John's

St

A 3

St. John's Rd

Rise

Northcote Rd

The   Avenue

155

Road

Hill

Battersea

92

165

316

O   P   Q

ZF

ZG

ZH

R   S   T

WESTMINSTER CATHEDRAL

VICTORIA

Belgrave

Vauxhall   Bridge   Road

Road   Pimlico

TATE BRITAIN

Lambeth Bridge

Millbank

Albert   Embankment

13.9

14.6

13.3

49

Vauxhall Bridge

Kennin

Ke

150

Harleyford   Rd

Rd

341

290

Vauxhall

Rd   14.9

Grosvenor   Road

Chelsea Bridge

North   Queenstown

Rd

Elms

Lane

Nine

Fentiman

Road

Dorset   Rd

420

NEW COVENT GARDEN MARKET

SOUTH LAMBETH

Lambeth

South

Way

Stockwell

Drive East

361

BATTERSEA PARK

14.9

QUEENSTOWN ROAD

15.6

South   Drive

Road

Wandsworth

Road

Landsdowne

Lane

Larkhall

Binfield Rd

Stockwel

Clapham

Stockwell

Sidney

A 3036

Silverthorne   Road

Union

Jeffrey's   Road

Lingham

Road

St

Road

Road

WANDSWORTH ROAD

Road

Queenstown   Road

Wandsworth   Road

B 224

North   Street

Rectory

Grove

Clapham

Grove

CLAPHAM HIGH ST.

Landor

A 3

Clapham North

ZH

c

436

a

CLAPHAM

Cedars

Road

Rd

426

428

Manor   St

Clapham Common

Clapham High St

Triangle Pl.

V

Clapham

Park

B 221

Bedford   Road

Common   North   Side   Long   Road

King's   Ave.

Acre   Lane

Acre

Clapham Common South Side

Crescent   Lane

Park   Hill

CLAPHAM   COMMON

A 24

e

Brixto

0   500 m
0   500 yards

R   S   T

24

25

25 M

IMPERIAL WAR
MUSEUM

ELEPHANT AND CASTLE
SHOPPING CENTRE

A 201

New

ZF

13.9

Kennington

Kent

Road

WALWORTH

Heygate St

163

Rodney

306

Flint St

St

Kennington

Lane

Penton Place

M

East

Street

East

Portland

Thurl

Kennington

Road

A 3204

Braganza St

Manor

POL

Walworth

Pl.

Street

Kennington

Park

Road

Kennington

Road

Kennington Lane

150

KENNINGTON

A 23

A 3

Chapter Rd

Road

ZG

Harleyford Rd

Kennington

THE OVAL

Oval 211

Oval

KENNINGTON
PARK

Kennington

Camberwell

John

Ruskin

Street

14.6

Albany

Wells

BURGESS
PARK

Church Rd

Way

Camberwell

New

Edmund St

Southampt

Dorset Rd

man

Road

420

Caldwell St

Road

Road

Vassall

Foxley Rd

Road

New

Wyndham

Lothian Rd

A 202

Rd.

Comber Gro.

Lomond Gro.

Road

Elmington

Benhill

LAMBETH

Brixton

Calais St

Flodden Rd

Road

Road

Church Street
Camberwell

Camberwe

Way

Stockwell

Groveway

Mostyn Road

Road

Akerman

Knatchbull

Carew St

13.6

Warner

Denmark

Road

Hill

Grove

Clapham

Park

Rd

Road

Road

Lilford

Road

Denmark Rd

Lane

Stockwell

Sidney Rd

Loughborough Rd

Loughborough

Minet Rd

Rd

Coldharbour

DENMARK
HILL

Champion
Park

Grove

Camberwe

ZH

Road

Angell Dr.

Barrington Rd

14.3

LOUGHBOROUGH
JUNCTION

Herne

Road

Road

RUSKIN PARK

Denmark

Hill

A 23

Wiltshire

Road

Brixton

Road

14.3

Brixton

A 2217

Coldharbour

Lane

Road

Shakespeare

Road

Milkwood

Fawnbrake Avenue

Road

Ferndene

Rd

Hill

A 215

Sunray

Denmark

Hill

Acre

Hill

Lane

Kellett Rd

Railton

Road

Herne

Hill

Red Post Hill

Avenue

Brixton

Effra Rd

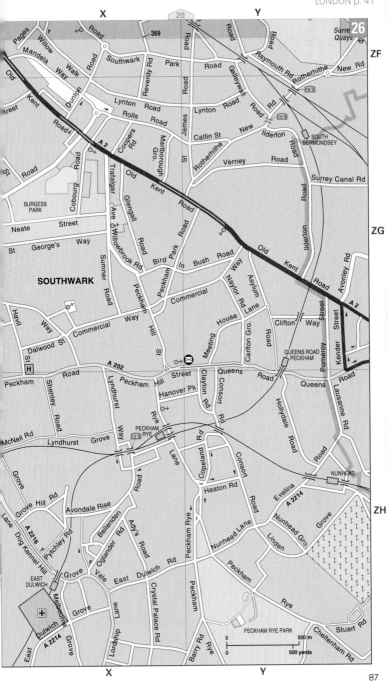

27

Grand Union Canal

200 m
200 yards

Westbourne Park

Great

Western

A 40

Westway

Harrow Road

Bourne Terrace

BAYSWATER
AND MAIDA VALE

Harrow

T

Tavistock Rd

St Luke's Rd

Westbourne

Ledbury

Talbot

Road

Road

Park

Road

Chepstow Rd

Westbourne Park Villas

Talbot

Hereford

Westbourne Park Road

Porchester

Royal Oak

Gloucester

Westbourne Gdns

197

P

NORTH KENSINGTON

Colville

Ter.

Artesian

Road

Newton

Rd

Bishop's Bridge

P

Colville Rd

Ledbury

Grove

Villas

Chepstow

Hereford

a

V

Westbourne Grove

Garway

b

Kensington Gdns Sq.

Queensway

Inverness

Gdns

U

Westbourne

Road

Villas

Pembridge

Chepstow

c

Leinster Sq.

Road

Porchester

Queensborough

a

Portobello

84

Dawson

Pembridge Cres.

Pl.

Moscow

Road

Road

Bayswater

Kensington

Park

Road

Pembridge

Square

Pembridge

Palace

St Petersburgh

Bark

Place

Queensway

Terrace

P

Ladbroke Square

Road

n

Linden

Gdns

Ossington St.

Court

Pl.

Queensway

c

328

Ladbroke

Road

u

Pembridge Gdns

Hill

Gate

Bayswater

Road

Broad

Holland Park Ave

Notting

e

Uxbridge St

Notting Hill Gate

Campden Hill Square

Kensington

Place

r

z

Kensington

Palace

Gardens

Walk

Aubrey

Walk

Bedford

Gardens

c

ORANGERY

Holland

u

Campden

Hill

Sheffield

Terrace

KENSINGTON AND CHELSEA

Campden Hill

Rd

Church

St

KENSINGTON PALACE

Palace

35

28

AC AD AE

T

U

29

V

452

Road

Grand

Union

Harrow Road

Road

Church St

Edgware

Bell Street

POL P Edgware Road

c Chapel

Road

Harrow Road

Sale Place

Street

North Wharf Road

Bishop's

Bridge

Canal

South Wharf Road

Praed

PADDINGTON

ST MARY'S

Nonfolk

Gardens

Terrace

Orsett Ter.

Road

Cleveland

Gloucester

Westbourne

Terrace

Eastbourne Terrace

St

Terrace Rd

London Street

Praed Street

Street

Street

v

Radnor Place

156

156

67

Sussex

94

Cleveland Square

Chilworth Terrace

Gardens

Gloucester Square

Hyde Park Square

Sussex

Sussex

Pl

Leinster

Queen's Gardens

136

Craven

Terrace

Spring St

Sussex Square

93

a

257

448

Westbourne St

158

Hyde Park Gardens

Porchester

Craven Hill

Craven Ter.

P e

Hyde

z

M

s

Lancaster Gate

Bayswater

e r Gate P

Terrace

Leinster Ter.

Lancaster

v

Bayswater Road

FOUNTAIN GARDEN

The Long Water

The Ring

KENSINGTON GARDENS

Round Pound

Broad

The Ring

The

Rotten

36

AC AD AE

89

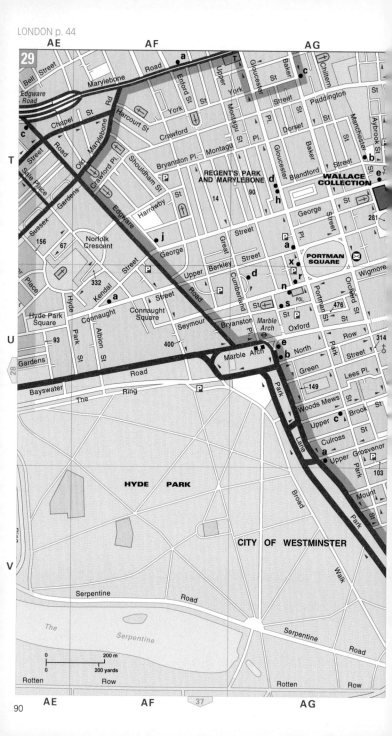

AH AI AJ

30

BRITISH TELECOM TOWER 232

Charlotte
Cleveland
Goodge St

Wimpole
Harley
Street
Cavendish
Great
Foley
St
MIDDLESEX
Goodge
Berner's
Newman
Weymouth
Portland
New
Langham
Titchfield
Wells
Marylebone High St
Cavendish
Harley
Street
Street
Place
Portland
Mortimer
Wells
New St
Queen
Anne
Street
z
228
Street
Eastcastle
Welbeck
Wimpole
Street
St
Margaret
286
Poland
Noel
413
287
Cavendish Sq.
Holles St
Oxford
Oxford
189
26
Wigmore
Henrietta Pl.
Princes St
Oxford
Circus
Argyll
D'Arblay St
Duke St
Vere St
South Molton
NEW BOND ST
Hannover Sq.
Hanover St
REGENT ST
Great Marlborough St
Marshall
Broadwick

Bond St
Gilbert
Davies St
Brook St
Maddox
Kingly St
Carnaby
Beak
James
Golden Sq
Brew

184
12
Brook's Mews
NEW BOND ST
George St
Savile
Row
444
179
MAYFAIR
Grosvenor Square
Brook
Conduit
PDL
Vigo St
REGENT ST
Grosvenor
Mount Row
Bruton Street
NEW BOND ST
322
38
BURLINGTON HOUSE
Adam's Row
Berkeley Square
62
225
BURLINGTON ARCADE
PICCADILLY
Mount
Farm
Dover
Berkeley
OLD BOND ST
Sackville St
ST JAM
Hay's Mews
168
PICCADILLY ARCADE
JERMYN
Charles
Curzon St
Bolton Street
Street
Duke
143
Hill
Bury
ST JAMES SQUARE
132
178
Curzon
Bolton
c
6
JAMES ST
King
421
d
Shepherd Market
Green Park
Queen's
Pall Mall
SHEPHERD MARKET
153
116
QUEEN'S CHAPEL
Hertford
St
SPENCER HOUSE
Brick
PICCADILLY
ST JAMES PALACE
205
GREEN PARK
Walk
WELLINGTON MUSEUM
APSLEY HOUSE
LANCASTER HOUSE

AH AI AJ

38

91

31

AJ AK AL

Charlotte St
Goodge St
Tottenham
Court
St
256
Gower
St
U
U
Old Gloucester St
Boswell St
473
s
BLOOMSBURY
292
a

Goodge St
State
St
BRITISH
MUSEUM

Store St
BEDFORD
SQUARE
260

Bloomsbury
Russell
Bloomsbury
Sq.
9
473

T
Berner's
St
Newman
e
a
e
v
u
r
Percy
St
f
Bloomsbury
Museum
St
Bury
St
Street

y
Great
a
k
St
Oxford
e
r
Newton St
Kingsway
Great Queen

c
n
r
St
Wells St
Wardour
St
c
210
Street
St Giles
Circus
n
New
Holborn
Macklin St
Parker
b
b

26
Oxford
Dean
St
Tottenham
Court Rd
St Giles
High
St
High
St
Drury
Lane
T
Great Queen
Wild

Noel
St
b
Greek
St
Soho
Sq.
d
134
Shaftesbury Ave
x
NEAL'S
YARD
x
g
Shorts Gdns
Neal
s
Endell St
Long Acre
b
ROYAL
OPERA
HOUSE

D'Arblay
St
w
x
Frith
St
v
u
88
d
Earlham
e
St
Shelton St
88
Bow
St
Russell St
M

Broadwick
St
Lexington
St
e
26
SOHO
m
18
t
b
Old
Compton
368
Cambridge
Circus
q
p
430
Floral
Long
Covent Gdn
COVENT
GARDEN
b
187
f

Golden
Sq.
444
Brewer
261
Wardour
St
y
f
174
Lisle
j
191
Garrick St
King St
z
ST
PAUL'S
COVENT
GARDEN
M
Tavistock
217
n
Exeter
388
83
STRAND
T
a

179
133
Rupert
St
Shaftesbury
Coventry St
115
Leicester Sq.
Cross Rd
New
Row
v
e
243
Chandos Pl.
c
245
Savoy
PICCADILLY
CIRCUS
T
LEICESTER
SQUARE
St Martin's
T
T
238
T

ST
REGENT
C
Haymarket
Panton
St
Orange
191
St
NATIONAL PORTRAIT
GALLERY
s
Lane
POL
St Martin
VICTORIA
EMBANKMENT
GARDENS

e
a
e
ST JAMES'S
ST
JERMYN
ST
r
143
THEATRE
ROYAL
n
k
191
a
Charles II
St
NATIONAL
GALLERY
ROYAL OPERA
ARCADE
WATERLOO
PLACE
39
TRAFALGAR
SQUARE
ST MARTIN-
IN-THE-FIELDS
147
a
STRAND
CHARING
CROSS
Craven St
Charing
Cross
Northumberland
Embankment
Hungerford

ST JAMES'S
SQUARE
ST JAMES'S
Pall Mall
CARLTON HOUSE
TERRACE
74
Carlton H
OLD ADMIRALTY
WHITEHALL
Whitehall
a
460
Horse Guards Ave

QUEEN'S
CHAPEL
THE
MALL
Horse
Guards
HORSE
GUARDS
BANQUETING
HOUSE

ST JAMES'S
PALACE
ST JAMES' PARK
234

0 200 m
0 200 yards

AJ AK 39 AL

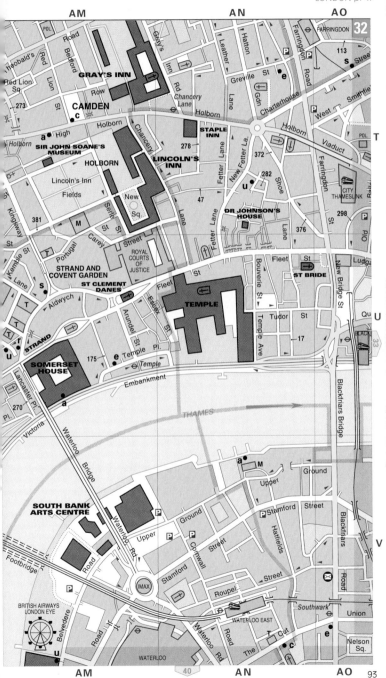

AM AN AO

32

FARRINGDON

POL

Theobald's Red Red Lion Bedford Road Gray's Inn Leather Hatton Farringdon 113

GRAY'S INN

Row Greville St e

Red Lion Lane Charterhouse West Smithfie

Sq.

– 273

CAMDEN Holborn Chancery Lane Gdn Viaduct

c Holborn

High Holborn Chancery **STAPLE INN** Holborn POL

a 278 New Fetter La. 372 Farringdon CITY THAMESLINK

SIR JOHN SOANE'S MUSEUM

HOLBORN **LINCOLN'S INN** 282 298

u

Lincoln's Inn Fetter 47 **DR. JOHNSON'S HOUSE** 376

Fields New Shoe

381 Sq. M Lane

Kingsway Serle St Fleet St Ludga

St Carey Street Bouverie **ST BRIDE** New Bridge St

Portugal **ROYAL COURTS OF JUSTICE** St

STRAND AND COVENT GARDEN Fleet St

Kemble St s **ST CLEMENT DANES** Essex **TEMPLE** Tudor St Qu

Aldwych St 17 BLACK

T Arundel St Temple Ave

T **STRAND** 175 e Temple Pl.

u **SOMERSET HOUSE** Temple

a Embankment

270 Lancaster Pl.

Victoria *THAMES*

Waterloo Bridge

a M Ground

Upper Ground Blackfriars

SOUTH BANK ARTS CENTRE P Stamford Street Blackfriars

P Upper Ground Hatfields V

Footbridge P Stamford Street

IMAX Roupel St Southwark

P Waterloo Road Street

BRITISH AIRWAYS LONDON EYE WATERLOO EAST The Cut e Nelson Sq.

BELVEDERE Road c

u WATERLOO 40

AM AN AO

93

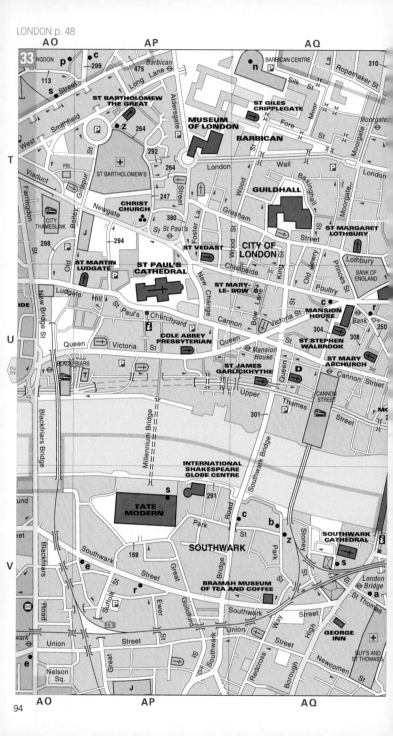

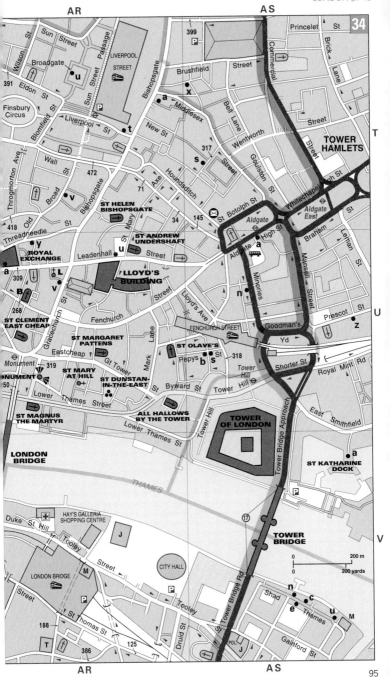

35

27

0 200 m
0 200 yards

U

KENSINGTON

Campden Walk

Hornton St

Holland

Kensington Church St

Kensington Green

c P Kensingto

r

u

241

HOLLAND PARK

Argyll Rd

Phillimore Gdns

Holland Walk

H P

Street

High

Kensington

Young Street

LINLEY SAMBOURNE HOUSE

Street

n

High Street Kensington

Kensington Square

241

242

X

Melbury Road

High Street

LEIGHTON HOUSE

Kensington

Kensington

Abingdon

Villas

Marloes

Kensington

St Alban's Grov

c

Cornwall

Edwardes Square

PDL

Scarsdale Rd

Road

Earls Court

Cornwall

c
V

Warwick Gardens

342

Road

Earls

Lexham

Road

Gardens

Lexham Gdns

Cromwell

Y

Warwick

Gardens

P

P

Pembroke

Road

Logan Place

Cromwell

119

Road

Earls Court

Road

Road

n

Knaresborough Pl

Courtfield Gdns

101

Courtfield Gdns

99

Longridge

Nevern Pl.

Kenway Rd

Earls Court Gdns

Barkston Gdns

e

Bramham Gdns

Nevern Square

s

410

a c

n

Earl's Court

Road

Earls

Court Rd

Bolton Gardens

u

Trebovir

EARL'S COURT

Penywern

Road

Warwick

Philbeach Gardens

Road

Earl's Court Sq.

e

Road

Redcliffe

Old

The

151

EARL'S COURT EXHIBITION BLDG

Brompton

Finborough

Square

Z

North End

WEST KENSINGTON

Road

Seagrave Rd

West Brompton

BROMPTON CEMETERY

a

Redcliffe Gardens

Road

Lillie

Road

P

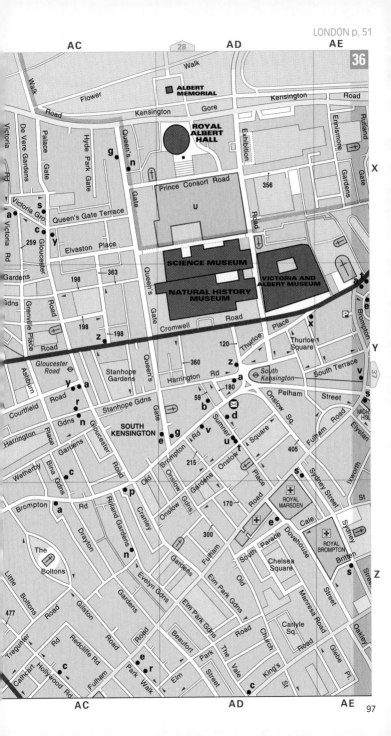

37

HYDE PARK AND KNIGHTSBRIDGE

AE   AF   AG

29

a

Road
Knightsbridge   Knightsbridge   x   e
Road   The   Carriage   h   468   t
Knightsbridge   m z e   s
z e   d   Lowndes
P   a   214   BELGRAVIA
MONTPELIER   b   Square   BELGRA
SQUARE   r   f
Trevor Sq.   Crescent   h
West Halkin St
r   n   P
Cheval Pl.   v   Hans   Cadogan Pl.   Lowndes St
x   Place   Pont   Street   Chesham
n   d   c u   Place
Beauchamp Pl.   Street   c u
Brompton   c   Pont   Street   Lyall   Eat
a f h   e   a   b   Chesham St   Eaton
e   162   Cadogan   u
161   Lennox   Place   Eaton
160   Gardens   Cadogan   220   Road
CHELSEA   263   Square   Street
South Terrace   Hasker St   Milner   Cadogan Gdns
v   Moore St   u
j   v   Rawlings St   r 23   King's
s u   f   Mossop St   c   Chester
Draycott   407   Sloane Sq.   Holbein
Elystan   Sloane   Cadogan   Sloane Sq.
z   Whiteheads Grove   Avenue   c   Lower   Pl.
n d   POL.   Draycott   y   Sloane
Elystan   Place   45
ROYAL   Jubilee   Markham St   Cheltenham   a 223   Pimlico
BROMPTON   Place   Terrace   u
Sydney   Britten   King's   Smith   Franklin's Row   Chelsea
s   x   e   St. Leonard's Ter.   Road
Chelsea   BURTON'S COURT   THE ROYAL
s   Radnor   HOSPITAL
Z   Shawfield   Walk   329   Hospital   Ct
Manor   367   Tedworth   Square
Oakley   Flood   Christchurch St   Tite   NATIONAL ARMY   0   200 m
Glebe   Royal   c   MUSEUM   0   200 yards
Pl.   Chelsea

AE   AF   AG

98

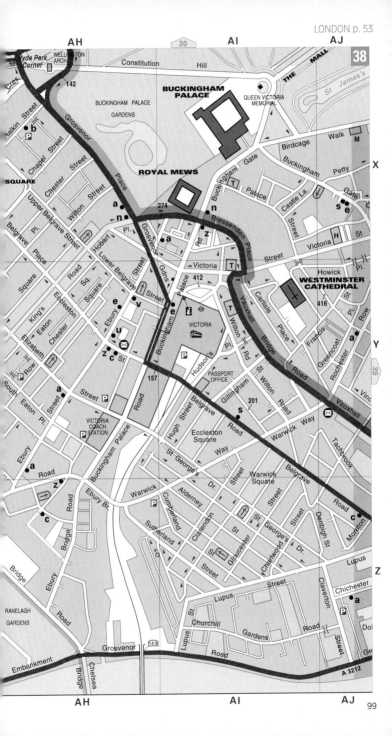

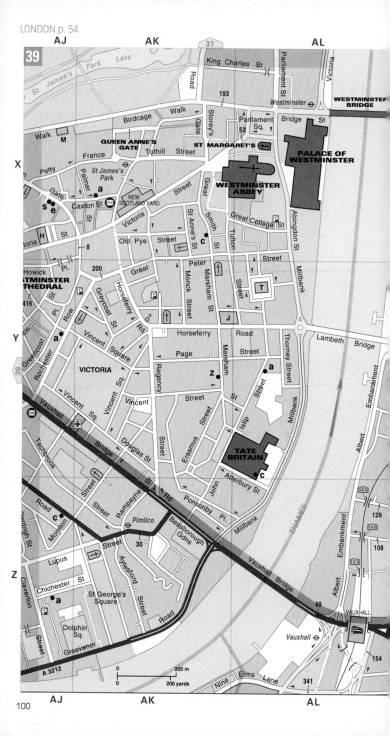

39

AM 32 AN AO

40

COUNTY HALL

a

Westminster

M

York

Bridge

Road

Lower

Marsh

Rd

Baylis

St

Pearman

Webber

Waterloo

Street

Blackfriars

Road

Road

St THOMAS'S

14'9

Palace

Road

Hercules

Road

Kennington

Road

Lambeth

North

Westminster Bridge

St

POL.

Road

Road

St George's

Lambeth

London Rd

173

X

LAMBETH PALACE GARDENS

LAMBETH PALACE

M

Lambeth

Road

IMPERIAL WAR MUSEUM

GERALDINE MARY HARMSWORTH PARK

Road

West Sq.

Hayles

St

Road

Lambeth

Walk

LAMBETH

Brook

West Sq.

Drive

a

Juxon

St

14'6

15'0

Walnut

Tree

Walk

x

Walcot

Square

Fitzalan

Street

Kennington

Road

Wincott

Street

Renfrew

Rd

Dante Rd

Y

Lambeth High

St

12'9

13'9

Black

13'6

Prince

Rd

Walk

Street

Vauxhall

Black

Prince

Rd

Chester

Way

Kennington

Lane

e

Johnathan

St

Sancroft

St

Newburn

Courtenay

St

Street

Kennington

Road

Road

Kennington

SPRING GARDENS

Tyers

Street

Tyers

St

Cleaver

J

Street

219

Stannary

St

Park

De

Laune

St

Braganza

St

Kennington

Z

s

Kennington

Lane

Kennington

Lane

150

Vauxhall

St

Clayton

St

Kennington

Oval

Road

Kennington

Cooks Rd

Harleyford

Road

THE OVAL

KENNINGTON PARK

AM AN AO

101

Alphabetical list of hotels and restaurants
Liste alphabétique des hôtels et restaurants
Elenco alfabetico degli alberghi e ristoranti

A

B

C

D

E

U - V - W

X - Y - Z

Starred establishments in London
Les établissements à étoiles de Londres
Gli esercizi con stelle a Londra

🌼🌼🌼

🌼🌼

Good food at moderate prices
Repas soignés à prix modérés
Pasti accurati a prezzi contenuti

"Bib Gourmand"

Particularly pleasant hotels and restaurants
Hôtels et restaurants agréables
Alberghi e ristoranti ameni

Restaurants classified according to type
Restaurants classés suivant leur genre
Ristoranti classificati secondo il loro genere

Bangladeshi

page
184 *Bayswater & Maida Vale* X Ginger

Chinese

192 *Mayfair*	XXXX The Oriental		135 *Fulham*	XX	Mao Tai
195 *Mayfair*	XXX Kai		131 *Ealing*	XX	Maxim
115 *Mill Hill*	XX Good Earth		158 *Kensington*	XX	Memories of China
153 *Chelsea*	XX Good Earth		187 *Hyde Park & Knightsbridge*	XX	Mr Chow
120 *Bloomsbury*	XX ✿ Hakkasan				
168 *South Woodford*	XX Ho-Ho		117 *Orpington*	XX	Xian
129 *City of London*	XX Imperial City		123 *Hampstead*	XX	ZeNW3
151 *Chelsea*	XX Mao Tai		211 *Soho*	X	Fung Shing

Danish

163 *South Kensington* XX Lundum's

English

192 *Mayfair*	XXXX Grill Room (at Dorchester H.)		217 *Victoria*	XXX	Shepherd's
194 *Mayfair*	XXX Brian Turner Mayfair		212 *Strand & Covent Garden*	XX	Rules
195 *Mayfair*	XXX Scotts				

French

191 *Mayfair*	XXXX ✿✿ (Le) Gavroche		121 *Bloomsbury*	XX	Mon Plaisir
127 *City of London*	XXX Coq d'Argent		170 *Hampton Hill*	XX	Monsieur Max
144 *Islington*	XX Almeida		151 *Chelsea*	XX	Poissonnerie de l'Avenue (Seafood)
137 *Crouch End*	XX (Les) Associés				
204 *Regent's Park & Marylebone*	XX L'Aventure		151 *Chelsea*	XX 🍷	Racine
207 *St. James's*	XX 🍷 Brasserie Roux		217 *Victoria*	XX ✿	Roussillon
			166 *Kennington*	X	Lobster Pot (Seafood)
151 *Chelsea*	XX Chez Max				
136 *Shepherd's Bush*	XX Chez Moi		171 *Twickenham*	X 🍷	Ma Cuisine
128 *City of London*	XX ✿ Club Gascon		218 *Victoria*	X	(La) Poule au Pot
153 *Chelsea*	XX (Le) Colombier				
165 *Surbiton*	XX (The) French Table		153 *Chelsea*	X	Thierry's
			210 *Soho*	X	(La) Trouvaille

111

Greek

133 *Hoxton*	※※ Real Greek	134 *Hoxton*	※ Mezedopolio

Indian

193 *Mayfair*	※※※※ Benares
163 *South Kensington*	※※※ Bombay Brasserie
150 *Chelsea*	※※※ Chutney Mary
216 *Victoria*	※※※ (The) Cinnamon Club
209 *Soho*	※※※ Red Fort
194 *Mayfair*	※※※ ✿ Tamarind
216 *Victoria*	※※※ Quilon
172 *Bermondsey*	※※ Bengal Clipper
178 *Spitalfields*	※※ Bengal Trader
209 *Soho*	※※ Café Lazeez
178 *Whitechapel*	※※ ⊛ Café Spice Namaste
197 *Mayfair*	※※ Chor Bizarre
153 *Chelsea*	※※ Haandi
129 *City of London*	※※ Kasturi
163 *South Kensington*	※※ Khan's of Kensington
121 *Bloomsbury*	※※ Malabar Junction
164 *South Kensington*	※※ Memories of India
207 *St James's*	※※ Mint Leaf
151 *Chelsea*	※※ (The) Painted Heron
130 *Addington*	※※ Planet Spice
202 *Regent's Park & Marylebone*	※※ (La) Porte des Indes
203 *Regent's Park & Marylebone*	※※ Rasa Samudra (Seafood) (Vegetarian)
179 *Southfields*	※※ ⊛ Sarkhel's
156 *Earl's Court*	※※ Sticklebackpink
165 *Herne Hill*	※※ 3 Monkeys
152 *Chelsea*	※※ Vama
197 *Mayfair*	※※ Yatra
157 *Kensington*	※※ ✿ Zaika
180 *Wandsworth*	※ Bombay Bicycle Club
164 *South Kensington*	※ Café Lazeez
143 *Finsbury*	※ Café Lazeez City
180 *Tooting*	※ Kastoori (Vegetarian)
159 *Kensington*	※ ⊛ Malabar
122 *Bloomsbury*	※ Mela
141 *Archway*	※ ⊛ (The) Parsee
134 *Stoke Newington*	※ Rasa (Vegetarian)
116 *Willesden Green*	※ ⊛ Sabras (Vegetarian)
210 *Soho*	※ ⊛ Soho Spice
198 *Mayfair*	※ Veeraswamy

Italian

194 *Mayfair*	※※※ Cecconi's
150 *Chelsea*	※※※ Floriana
217 *Victoria*	※※※ (L') Incontro
187 *Hyde Park & Knightsbridge*	※※※ Isola
202 *Regent's Park & Marylebone*	※※※ ✿ Locanda Locatelli
217 *Victoria*	※※※ Santini
208 *Soho*	※※※ Quo Vadis
194 *Mayfair*	※※※ Sartoria
150 *Chelsea*	※※※ Toto's
196 *Mayfair*	※※ Alloro
183 *Bayswater & Maida Vale*	※※ Al San Vincenzo
158 *Kensington*	※※ (The) Ark
203 *Regent's Park & Marylebone*	※※ Bertorelli
203 *Regent's Park & Marylebone*	※※ Caldesi
152 *Chelsea*	※※ Caraffini
217 *Victoria*	※※ (Il) Convivio
160 *North Kensington*	※※ Edera
179 *Putney*	※※ Enoteca Turi
203 *Regent's Park & Marylebone*	※※ Latium
144 *Islington*	※※ ⊛ Metrogusto
120 *Bloomsbury*	※※ Neal Street
152 *Chelsea*	※※ Pellicano
177 *Canary Wharf*	※※ Quadrato
135 *Hammersmith*	※※ ✿ River Café
203 *Regent's Park & Marylebone*	※※ Rosmarino
120 *Bloomsbury*	※※ Sardo
195 *Mayfair*	※※ Teca

112

Japanese

Kosher

Lebanese

Moroccan

North African

Polish

Pubs

Scottish

Seafood

South East Asian

Spanish

Thai

Turkish

Vegetarian

Vietnamese

Boroughs and areas

Greater London *is divided, for administrative purposes, into 32 boroughs plus the City : these sub-divide naturally into minor areas, usually grouped around former villages or quarters, which often maintain a distinctive character.*

BARNET *Gtr London.*

Brent Cross *Gtr London* – ✉ *NW2.*

🏨 **Holiday Inn London Brent Cross**   2 DU **n**
Tilling Rd, NW2 1LP, ✆ *(020) 8201 8686, Fax (020) 8455 4660*
|≑|, ⇄ rm, 🗐 📺 📞 & 🅿 – 🏛 50. 🆗 🆎 ⑩ *VISA* 🇯🇨🇧. ✦
Meals 15.00 and a la carte – ☄ 13.95 – **153 rm** 165.00.
 ♦ A ten storey purpose-built group hotel, usefully located at the foot of the M1. Well-equipped bedrooms are triple-glazed and business rooms are available. Informal restaurant and all-day open bar.

Child's Hill *Gtr London* – ✉ *NW2.*

🍴🍴 **Philpott's Mezzaluna**   2 NZA **C**
424 Finchley Rd, NW2 2HY, ✆ *(020) 7794 0455, Fax (020) 7794 0452*
🏮 – 🗐. 🆗 🆎 *VISA*
closed 25-26 December, 1 January, Saturday lunch and Monday – **Meals** - *Italian influences* - 19.00/23.00.
 ♦ Homely Italian restaurant, affably run by patrons. Huge lunar artefacts complement the plain walls. Weekly changing menus offer tasty, modern cuisine at moderate prices.

Mill Hill *Gtr London* – ✉ *NW7.*

🏌 *100 Barnet Way, Mill Hill* ✆ *(020) 8959 2282* CT.

🍴🍴 **Good Earth**   2 CT **a**
143 The Broadway, NW7 4RN, ✆ *(020) 8959 7011, Fax (020) 8959 1464*
🗐. 🆗 🆎 *VISA* 🇯🇨🇧
closed 23-30 December – **Meals** - *Chinese* - 25.00/35.00 (dinner) and a la carte 9.95/25.10.
 ♦ Smart, well-kept Chinese restaurant set slightly back from the busy A1 outside. Spacious and comfortable with efficient staff. Authentic menu; extensive vegetarian choice.

BEXLEY *Gtr London.*

Bexley *Kent* – ✉ *Kent.*

🏨 **Holiday Inn**   8 JX **e**
Black Prince Interchange, Southwold Rd, DA5 1ND, *on A 2,* ✆ *(0870) 4009006,*
bexley@6c.com, Fax (01322) 526113
|≑|, ⇄ rm, 🗐 rest, 📺 📞 & 🅿 – 🏛 130. 🆗 🆎 ⑩ *VISA*
Meals *(closed Saturday lunch)* (carving lunch Sunday) 13.50/15.00 and dinner a la carte 16.15/26.15 **s.** – ☄ 13.95 – **108 rm** 129.00.
 ♦ A commercial hotel with mock Tudor exterior, convenient for Bexleyheath town centre. Modern, well-equipped bedrooms in a Scandinavian style. Rustic public bar. Busy, informal restaurant.

Bexleyheath *Kent* – ⊠ *Kent.*

🏨 **Bexleyheath Marriott**   8   JX **C**
1 Broadway, DA6 7JZ,   ℰ (0870) 4007245,   *bexleyheath@marriott.co.uk,*
Fax (0870) 4007345
ℱ₆, ▨ – ▮, ⊱ rm, ▤ 📺 📞 & 🄿 – 🛎 250. 🆖 🄰🄴 ⓪ *VISA* ᴊᴄʙ
Copper : Meals *(closed lunch Saturday and Sunday)* a la carte 22.25/33.60 ♀ –
⊐ 13.95 – **142 rm** 99.00.
  ♦ A group hotel offering extensive conference facilities as well as a leisure
club in a Graeco-Roman theme. Comfortable and spacious bedrooms with
marble bathrooms. Popular carvery restaurant.

BRENT *Gtr London.*

Wembley *Middx* – ⊠ *Middx.*

🏨 **Premier Lodge**   2   CU **Z**
151 Wembley Park Drive, HA9 8HQ,   ℰ (0870) 7001446, *wembleypremierlodge*
@snr.co.uk, Fax (0870) 7001447
▮ ⊱ ▤ 📺 📞 & 🄿 🆖 🄰🄴 ⓪ *VISA* ᴊᴄʙ. ⌘
Meals (grill rest.) (dinner only) a la carte approx. 14.50 – **153 rm** 56.00.
  ♦ Lodge offering good value accommodation. All of the spacious modern
bedrooms are carefully planned and feature king size beds. Bright, colourful
restaurant.

Willesden Green *Middx* – ⊠ *Middx.*

🍴 **Sabras**   9 KZB **e**
263 High Rd, NW10 2RX,   ℰ (020) 8459 0340, *Fax (020) 8459 0541*
🆖 *VISA* ᴊᴄʙ
closed 25-26 December and Monday – **Meals** - Indian Vegetarian - (dinner
only) a la carte 15.50/22.00.
  ♦ Inexpensive Indian vegetarian food served in modest, but friendly, surroundings. Framed awards and write-ups garnered since opening in 1973
bear testament to its popularity.

🍴 **Sushi-Say**   9 LZB **a**
33B Walm Lane, NW2 5SH,   ℰ (020) 8459 2971, *Fax (020) 8907 3229*
🆖 🄰🄴 *VISA* ᴊᴄʙ
closed 25-26 December, 1 January, Easter, 1 week August and Monday –
Meals - Japanese - (dinner only and lunch Saturday and Sunday)/dinner
18.20/28.60 and a la carte 13.75/36.50.
  ♦ Friendly service provided by the owner in traditional dress. From bare
wooden tables, watch her husband in the open-plan kitchen carefully prepare
authentic Japanese food.

Write to us...
If you have any comments on the contents of this Guide.
Your praise as well as your criticisms will receive careful
consideration and, with your assistance, we will be able to add
to our stock of information and, where necessary, amend
our judgments.
Thank you in advance!

BROMLEY *Gtr London.*

🏌18, 🏌9 *Cray Valley, Sandy Lane, St. Paul's Cray, Orpington* 🕿 *(01689) 837909* JY.

Bromley *Kent –* ✉ *Kent.*

🏌9 *Magpie Hall Lane* 🕿 *(020) 8462 7014* HY.

🏛 **Bromley Court**   8 HY **Z**
Bromley Hill, BR1 4JD, 🕿 *(020) 8464 5011, bromleyhotel@btinternet.com,*
Fax (020) 8460 0899
🍽, 🛬, 🚬, 🚶 – 🛗, ⇆ rm, 🖿 📺 📞 🅿 – 🔬 150. 🆖 🆎 ⑩ 𝘝𝘐𝘚𝘈
Meals *(closed Saturday lunch)* 15.15/18.95 and dinner a la carte 22.65/27.45 –
113 rm � 105.00/118.00, 2 suites.
◆ A grand neo-Gothic mansion in three acres of well-tended garden. Popular
with corporate guests for the large conference space, and the bedrooms
with modems and voicemail. Conservatory or terrace dining available.

Farnborough *Kent –* ✉ *Kent.*

❀❀❀ **Chapter One**   8 HZ **a**
Farnborough Common, Locksbottom, BR6 8NF, 🕿 *(01689) 854848, info@cha*
ptersrestaurants.com, Fax (01689) 858439
🖿 🅿. 🆖 🆎 ⑩ 𝘝𝘐𝘚𝘈 𝗝𝗖𝗕
closed 2-7 January – **Meals** 19.50/26.95 ☆.
◆ The mock Tudor exterior belies the stylish, light and contemporary interior.
Precise and well executed modern European menu. West End sophistication
without the prices.
Spec. Ballottine of chicken, foie gras parfait and roast hazelnuts. Roast hali-
but, Tarte Tatin of beetroot, onion purée and horseradish sauce. Lemon grass
panna cotta with raspberry compote.

Orpington *Kent –* ✉ *Kent.*

🏌18 *High Elms, High Elms Rd, Downe, Orpington* 🕿 *(01689) 858175.*

❀❀ **Xian**   8 JY **a**
324 High St, BR6 0NG, 🕿 *(01689) 871881*
🖿. 🆖 🆎 ⑩ 𝘝𝘐𝘚𝘈 𝗝𝗖𝗕
closed 25-26 December and Sunday lunch – **Meals** - Chinese (Peking, Szechuan) - 9.50/25.00 and a la carte 10.80/32.50.
◆ Modern, marbled interior with oriental artefacts make this personally run
Chinese restaurant a firm favourite with locals. Specialises in the hotter dishes
of Peking.

Penge *Gtr London –* ✉ *SE20.*

⌂ **Melrose House**   7 GY **a**
89 Lennard Rd, SE20 7LY, 🕿 *(020) 8776 8884, melrose.hotel@virgin.net,*
Fax (020) 8325 7636
without rest., 🚬 – ⇆ 📺 🔧 🅿. 🆖 𝘝𝘐𝘚𝘈. 🚭
closed Christmas-New Year – **6 rm** ⊆ 40.00/85.00.
◆ An imposing Victorian house with a conservatory sitting room. Breakfast is
taken "en famille" and the older bedrooms still have their original fireplaces.

In this guide
a symbol or a character,
printed in red *or* **black,** *in light or bold type*
does not have the same meaning.
Pay particular attention to the explanatory pages.

Bloomsbury *Gtr London –* ✉ *NW1/W1/WC1.*

🏛 **Le Meridien Russell**   18 SZD **d**
Russell Sq, WC1B 5BE, ☏ (020) 7837 6470, *sales.russell@lemeridien.com,*
Fax (020) 7837 2857
|⃞| 🛬 rm, ▤ 📺 📞 – 🔬 400. ⓜ⓪ 🄰🄴 ⓞ *VISA* 🄹🄲🄱. ℠
Meals 16.95/22.50 and dinner a la carte 20.90/32.00 ♈ – ☐ 19.50 – **369 rm**
182.10/211.50, 2 suites.
♦ An impressive Victorian building dominating Russell Square. Boasts many
original features including the imposing marbled lobby and staircase. Tradi-
tional or modern rooms. Restaurant has noticeable feel of grandeur.

🏛 **Holiday Inn Kings Cross**   19 UZD **a**
1 Kings Cross Rd, WC1X 9HX, ☏ (020) 7833 3900, *reservations@holidayinnlond*
on.com, Fax (020) 7917 6163
ƒ₆, 🚭, 🗔 – |⃞|, 🛬 rm, ▤ 📺 📞 ₺ – 🔬 220. ⓜ⓪ 🄰🄴 ⓞ *VISA*. ℠
Lahore : Meals - Indian - *(closed Saturday lunch)* a la carte 20.00/40.00
Carriages : Meals a la carte 32.50/42.00 – ☐ 12.50 – **403 rm** 190.00, 2 suites.
♦ In a fast developing part of town and close to Kings Cross station. Comfortable bedrooms with all mod cons. Clubby lobby bar with deep leather
armchairs and sofas. Lahore offers bold surroundings. Carriages is half
lounge, half restaurant.

🏛 **Marlborough**   31 AKT **k**
9-14 Bloomsbury St, WC1B 3QD, ☏ (020) 7636 5601, *resmarl@radisson.com,*
Fax (020) 7636 0532
|⃞|, 🛬 rm, ▤ rest, 📺 📞 ₺ – 🔬 200. ⓜ⓪ 🄰🄴 ⓞ *VISA* 🄹🄲🄱. ℠
Glass : Meals *(closed Sunday)* 27.50 and a la carte 30.00/36.00 – ☐ 15.00 –
171 rm 229.00/298.45, 2 suites.
♦ A Victorian building around the corner from the British Museum. The lobby
has been restored to its original marbled splendour and the bedrooms offer
good comforts. Bright, breezy restaurant with suitably modish cooking.

🏛 **Mountbatten**   31 ALU **d**
20 Monmouth St, WC2H 9HD, ☏ (020) 7836 4300, *Fax (020) 7240 3540*
ƒ₆ – |⃞|, 🛬 rm, ▤ 📺 📞 – 🔬 90. ⓜ⓪ 🄰🄴 ⓞ *VISA* 🄹🄲🄱. ℠
Dial : Meals 27.50 and a la carte 30.00/36.00 – ☐ 15.00 – **149 rm** 302.00/
371.30, 2 suites.
♦ Photographs and memorabilia of the eponymous Lord Louis adorn the
walls and corridors. Ideally located in the heart of Covent Garden. Compact
but comfortable bedrooms. Bright, stylish restaurant.

🏛 **Covent Garden**   31 ALU **x**
10 Monmouth St, WC2H 9HB, ☏ (020) 7806 1000, *covent@firmdale.com,*
Fax (020) 7806 1100
ƒ₆ – |⃞| ▤ 📺 📞 – 🔬 50. ⓜ⓪ 🄰🄴 *VISA*. ℠
Brasserie Max : Meals (booking essential) a la carte 26.50/40.00 ♈ – ☐ 18.00
– **56 rm** 229.00/346.60, 2 suites.
♦ Individually designed and stylish bedrooms, with CDs and VCRs discreetly
concealed. Boasts a very relaxing first floor oak-panelled drawing room with
its own honesty bar. Informal restaurant.

🏛 **Grafton**   18 RZD **n**
130 Tottenham Court Rd, W1P 9HP, ☏ (020) 7388 4131, *resgraf@radisson.co*
m, Fax (020) 7387 7394
ƒ₆ – |⃞|, 🛬 rm, ▤ 📺 📞 ₺ – 🔬 100. ⓜ⓪ 🄰🄴 ⓞ *VISA* 🄹🄲🄱. ℠
Aston's : Meals 27.50 and a la carte 30.00/36.00 – ☐ 12.00 – **326 rm** 229.10/
298.50, 4 suites.
♦ Just yards from Warren Street tube. Discreet Edwardian charm that belies
its location in one of London's busier streets. Bedrooms to becalm in soft
beige tones. Open-plan restaurant and bar.

🏨 **Kenilworth**   31 AKT **a**
97 Great Russell St, WC1B 3BL, ℘ (020) 7637 3477, *resmarl@radisson.com*, *Fax (020) 7631 3133*
₤ᵇ – |‡|, ⇌ rm, 🖵 TV ✆ ♿ – 🏋 100. ⚙️ AE ⓞ VISA JCB. ⚘
Meals - Asian - 27.50 and a la carte 30.00/36.00 – ⌷ 15.00 – **186 rm** 229.00/298.50.
    ◆ Usefully placed for the shops of Oxford Street. Stylish interiors and modern designer hi-tech bedrooms, equipped to meet the needs of the corporate traveller. Smart dining room with a modern style.

🏨 **Jurys Gt Russell St**   31 AKT **n**
16-22 Gt Russell St, WC1B 3NN, ℘ (020) 7347 1000, *gtrussellstreet@jurysdoyle .com, Fax (020) 7347 1001*
|‡|, ⇌ rm, 🖵 TV ✆ ♿ – 🏋 220. ⚙️ AE ⓞ VISA. ⚘
Lutyens : **Meals** a la carte approx. 29.00 – ⌷ 16.00 – **168 rm** 225.00, 1 suite.
    ◆ Neo-Georgian building by Edward Lutyens, built for YMCA in 1929. Smart comfortable interior decoration from the lounge to the bedrooms. Facilities include a business centre. Restaurant has understated traditional style.

🏨 **Montague on the Gardens**   31 ALT **a**
15 Montague St, WC1B 5BJ, ℘ (020) 7637 1001, *bookmt@rchmail.com*, *Fax (020) 7637 2516*
🏮, ₤ᵇ, ⇌s, ⇌ – |‡|, ⇌ rm, 🖵 TV ✆ ♿ – 🏋 120. ⚙️ AE ⓞ VISA
Blue Door Bistro : **Meals** 13.50/19.00 and a la carte 27.95/36.00 � – ⌷ 16.50 – **98 rm** 205.60/229.10, 6 suites.
    ◆ A period townhouse with pretty hanging baskets outside. The hushed conservatory overlooks a secluded garden. The clubby bar has a Scottish golfing theme. Rich bedroom décor. Restaurant divided into two small, pretty rooms.

🏨 **Holiday Inn Bloomsbury**   18 SZD **C**
Coram St, WC1N 1HT, ℘ (0870) 4009222, *bloomsbury@ichotelsgroup.com*, *Fax (020) 7837 5372*
|‡|, ⇌ rm, 🖵 TV ✆ ♿ – 🏋 300. ⚙️ AE ⓞ VISA JCB. ⚘
Meals *(closed Saturday and Sunday lunch)* 15.00 and a la carte 19.65/28.85 **s.** – ⌷ 14.95 – **313 rm** 179.00.
    ◆ Bright, modern bedrooms in warm, neutral tones. Have a drink in either the stylish bar with leather chairs or Callaghans Irish themed bar. Relaxed and contemporary dining.

🏨 **Thistle Bloomsbury**   31 ALT **r**
Bloomsbury Way, WC1A 2SD, ℘ (020) 7242 5881, *bloomsbury@thistle.co.uk*, *Fax (020) 7831 0225*
|‡|, ⇌ rm, 🖵 rest, TV ♿ – 🏋 80. ⚙️ AE ⓞ VISA JCB. ⚘
Meals *(closed lunch Saturday, Sunday and Bank Holidays)* 23.95 – ⌷ 14.95 – **138 rm** 215.00/246.75.
    ◆ Established over 100 years ago and retains much charm. Quiet and discreet lobby. An old fashioned lift leads up to the bedrooms that have a very English feel. Combined bar and dining room.

🏨 **Myhotel**   31 AKT **X**
11-13 Bayley St, Bedford Sq, WC1B 3HD, ℘ (020) 7667 6000, *bloomsbury@my hotels.co.uk, Fax (020) 7667 6001*
₤ᵇ – |‡| ⇌ 🖵 TV ✆ – 🏋 40. ⚙️ AE ⓞ VISA JCB
Yo! Sushi : **Meals** - Japanese - a la carte 16.00/22.00 – ⌷ 16.00 – **78 rm** 223.25/258.50.
    ◆ The minimalist interior is designed on the principles of feng shui; even the smaller bedrooms are stylish and uncluttered. Mybar is a fashionable meeting point. Diners can enjoy Japanese food from conveyor belt.

🏨 Bonnington in Bloomsbury
31 ALT **S**

92 Southampton Row, WC1B 4BH, ✆ (020) 7242 2828, *sales@bonnington.com, Fax (020) 7831 5758*

₤₃ – 🛗, ✳ rm, 🖥 📺 ☎ ♿ – 🏛 250. 🄼🄾 🄰🄴 🄾 *VISA*. 🚫

Meals *(closed Sunday)* (bar lunch)/dinner 20.95 **s.** ♀ – **239 rm** ⊑ 125.00/159.00, 8 suites.

♦ Built in 1911 and providing easy access to a number of tourist attractions. Functional, but well-kept, bedrooms offer traditional comforts with many modern extras. Classically decorated dining room.

✗✗✗ Pied à Terre
31 AJT **e**

❀❀ 34 Charlotte St, W1T 2NH, ✆ (020) 7636 1178, *p-a-t@dircon.co.uk, Fax (020) 7916 1171*

✳ 🖥. 🄼🄾 🄰🄴 *VISA*

closed last week December, first week January, Sunday and lunch Monday and Saturday – **Meals** 24.00/49.00 ♀.

♦ Frosted glass front hints at the understated, cool interior. The kitchen offers an elaborate and adventurous, yet refined take on modern French cuisine. Well-chosen wine list.

Spec. Seared and poached foie gras in a Sauternes consommé. Saddle of rabbit with Pommery mustard sauce. Chocolate tart with stout ice cream.

✗✗ Incognico
31 AKU **q**

117 Shaftesbury Ave, WC2H 8AD, ✆ (020) 7836 8866, *Fax (020) 7240 9525*

🖥. 🄼🄾 🄰🄴 🄾 *VISA*

closed 4 days Easter, 10 days Christmas, Sunday and Bank Holidays – **Meals** 12.50 (lunch) and a la carte 29.00/46.00 🍴 ♀.

♦ Opened in 2000 with its robust décor of wood panelling and brown leather chairs. Downstairs bar has a window into the kitchen, from where French and English classics derive.

✗✗ Neal Street
31 ALU **S**

26 Neal St, WC2H 9QT, ✆ (020) 7836 8368, *Fax (020) 7240 3964*

🄼🄾 🄰🄴 🄾 *VISA* 🄹🄲🄱

closed 25 December-2 January and Sunday – **Meals** - Italian - 25.00 (lunch) and a la carte 27.50/39.50 ♀.

♦ Light, bright and airy; tiled flooring and colourful pictures. Dishes range from the simple to the more complex. Mushrooms a speciality. Has its own shop next door.

✗✗ Sardo
18 RZD **C**

45 Grafton Way, W1T 5DQ, ✆ (020) 7387 2521, *info@sardo-restaurant.com, Fax (020) 7387 2559*

🄼🄾 🄰🄴 🄾 *VISA* 🄹🄲🄱

closed Saturday lunch, Sunday and Bank Holidays – **Meals** - Italian (Sardinian specialities) - a la carte 20.50/32.40.

♦ Simple, stylish interior run in a very warm and welcoming manner with very efficient service. Rustic Italian cooking with a Sardinian character and a modern tone.

✗✗ Hakkasan
31 AKT **C**

❀ 8 Hanway Pl, W1T 1HD, ✆ (020) 7907 1888, *mail@hakkasan.com, Fax (020) 7907 1889*

🖥. 🄼🄾 🄰🄴 🄾 *VISA*

Meals - Chinese (Canton) - a la carte 28.80/79.00 ♀.

♦ A distinctive, modern interpretation of Cantonese cooking in an appropriately contemporary and cavernous basement. The lively, bustling bar is an equally popular nightspot.

Spec. Stir-fry scallop and prawn cake. Pan-fried rib-eye of beef, sweet soya and almonds. Jasmine tea smoked chicken.

XX **Fino** 31 AJT **a**
33 Charlotte St (entrance on Rathbone St), W1T 1RR, ✆ (020) 7813 8010, *info @finorestaurant.com, Fax (020) 7813 8011*
MB AE O VISA
closed 25 December, Easter, Saturday lunch, Sunday and Bank Holidays –
Meals - Spanish - a la carte 16.00/29.50 ☒.
◆ Spanish-run basement Tapas bar with modern style décor and banquette seating. Wide-ranging menu of authentic dishes; 2 set-price selections offering an introduction to tapas.

XX **Mon Plaisir** 31 ALU **g**
21 Monmouth St, WC2H 9DD, ✆ (020) 7836 7243, *eatafrog@mail.com, Fax (020) 7240 4774*
MB AE O VISA JCB
closed 25-26 and 31 December, 1 January and lunch Saturday and Sunday –
Meals - French - 15.95 (lunch) and a la carte 25.50/32.20 ☒ ☒.
◆ London's oldest French restaurant and family-run for over fifty years. Divided into four rooms, all with a different feel but all proudly Gallic in their decoration.

XX **Archipelago** 18 RZD **c**
110 Whitfield St, W1T 5ED, ✆ (020) 7383 3346, *Fax (020) 7383 7181*
MB AE O VISA JCB
closed 25 December, Saturday lunch, Sunday and Bank Holiday Mondays –
Meals 20.50/38.50.
◆ Eccentric in both menu and décor and not for the faint hearted. Crammed with knick-knacks from cages to Buddhas. Menu an eclectic mix of influences from around the world.

XX **Malabar Junction** 31 AKT **y**
107 Great Russell St, WC1B 3NA, ✆ (020) 7580 5230, *Fax (020) 7436 9942*
▤. **MB AE VISA**
Meals - South Indian - a la carte 20.50/31.00 ☒.
◆ Specialising in dishes from southern India. Bright restaurant with a small fountain in the centre of the room below a large skylight. Helpful and attentive service.

X **Passione** 31 AKT **u**
10 Charlotte St, W1T 2LT, ✆ (020) 7636 2833, *Liz@passione.co.uk, Fax (020) 7636 2889*
MB AE O VISA JCB
closed 23 December-2 January, Saturday lunch, Sunday and Bank Holidays –
Meals - Italian - (booking essential) a la carte 31.00/42.00.
◆ Compact but light and airy. Modern Italian cooking served in informal surroundings, with friendly and affable service. Particularly busy at lunchtime.

X **Cigala** 19 TZD **a**
54 Lamb's Conduit St, WC1N 3LW, ✆ (020) 7405 1717, *tasty@cigala.co.uk, Fax (020) 7242 9949*
MB AE O VISA JCB
closed 25 December – **Meals** - Spanish - 18.00 (lunch) and a la carte approx. 26.50 ☒ ☒.
◆ Spanish restaurant on the corner of attractive street. Simply furnished with large windows and open-plan kitchen. Robust Iberian cooking. Informal tapas bar downstairs.

✗ **Paolo**   31 AKT   f
16 Percy St, W1T 1DT,   ℰ (020) 7637 9900,   *info@paolorestaurant.com*, *Fax (020) 7637 9696*
▤. ⓂⓈ AE � *VISA* JCB
closed 24-26 December and Sunday – **Meals** - Italian - 17.50 (lunch) and a la carte 24.00/35.00 🐾 ♀.
♦ Wood floored restaurant with intimate basement and brighter ground floor dining rooms. Authentic, rustic Italian dishes with a predominately Northern Italian style.

✗ **Mela**   31 AKU   e
152-156 Shaftesbury Ave, WC2H 6HL,   ℰ (020) 7836 8635, *info@melarestauran t.co.uk, Fax (020) 7379 0527*
ⓂⓈ AE � *VISA* JCB
closed 25 December – **Meals** - Indian - 10.95/35.95 (dinner) and a la carte 11.35/26.85 **s.**
♦ Vibrantly decorated dining room with a simple style in a useful location close to Theatreland. Enjoy thoroughly tasty Indian food in a bustling, buzzy environment.

✗ **Abeno**   31 ALT   e
47 Museum St, WC1A 1LY,   ℰ (020) 7405 3211, *okonomi@abeno.co.uk, Fax (020) 7405 3212*
▤. ⓂⓈ AE � *VISA* JCB
closed 25-26 and 31 December and 1 January – **Meals** - Japanese (Okonomi-Yaki) - 6.50/16.50 (lunch) and a la carte 12.25/30.80.
♦ Specialises in Okonomi-yaki: little Japanese "pancakes" cooked on a hot-plate on each table. Choose your own filling and the size of your pancake.

Euston *Gtr London* – ✉ *WC1.*

🏨 **Novotel London Euston**   18 SZC   r
100-110 Euston Rd, NW1 2AJ,   ℰ (020) 7666 9000, *h5309@accor-hotels.com, Fax (020) 7666 9100*
🛋, ⇌s – |≑|, ↪ rm, ▤ 📺 ℰ ♿ – 🔬 450. ⓂⓈ AE � *VISA* JCB. ⧚
Meals 16.00 (lunch) and a la carte 23.50/29.90 ♀ – ⌻ 14.50 – **311 rm** 160.00/180.00, 1 suite.
♦ Extensive conference facilities that include the redeveloped Shaw theatre. Large marbled lobby. Modern bedrooms that offer views of London's rooftops from the higher floors. Lobby-based restaurant and bar look onto busy street.

🏨 **Euston Plaza**   18 SZD   e
17-18 Upper Woburn Pl, WC1H 0HT,   ℰ (020) 7943 4500, *info@euston-plaza-h otel.com, Fax (020) 7943 4501*
🛋, ⇌s – |≑|, ↪ rm, ▤ 📺 ℰ ♿ – 🔬 150. ⓂⓈ AE � *VISA* JCB. ⧚
Three Crowns : **Meals** *(closed Saturday and Sunday lunch)* (dinner only) 19.95 and a la carte 23.40/32.50 **s.** ♀
Terrace : **Meals** a la carte 15.40/18.40 **s.** ♀ – ⌻ 12.95 – **150 rm** 153.00/238.50.
♦ Nearby transport links make this a useful location. Scandinavian owned, which is reflected in the style of the bedrooms. Executive rooms are partic-ularly well-equipped. Three Crowns has smart basement location. Lighter fare in Terrace conservatory.

🏠 **London Euston Travel Inn Capital**   18 SZD   s
141 Euston Rd, WC1H 9PJ,   ℰ (0870) 2383301, *Fax (020) 7554 3419*
|≑|, ↪ rm, ▤ rest, 📺 ♿. ⓂⓈ AE � *VISA*. ⧚
Meals (grill rest.) (dinner only) – **220 rm** 79.95.
♦ Budget accommodation with clean and spacious bedrooms, all with a large workspace. Double glazed but still ask for a quieter room at the back.

Hampstead *Gtr London* – ✉ *NW3.*

🔓 *Winnington Rd, Hampstead ℘ (020) 8455 0203.*

🏨 **Holiday Inn**   11 PZA **r**
215 Haverstock Hill, NW3 4RB, ℘ (0870) 4009037, *reservations-hampstead@6 c.com, Fax (020) 7435 5586*
🏠 – 🛗, 🚭 rm, 📺 🕻 🅿️. ⓪ ⒶⒺ ⓪ 𝐕𝐈𝐒𝐀 𝐉𝐂𝐁
Meals 15.00 (lunch) and a la carte 16.95/22.00 **s.** – ☐ 14.95 – **140 rm** 165.00.
◆ A well-equipped group hotel adjacent to a petrol station. Convenient for the boutiques and cafés of Hampstead. Bright, modern bedrooms. Formula menus.

🏨 **The House**   11 PZA **e**
2 Rosslyn Hill, NW3 1PH, ℘ (020) 7431 8000, *reception@thehousehotel.co.uk, Fax (020) 7433 1775*
without rest. – 🛗 📺 🕻. ⓪ ⒶⒺ ⓪ – ☐ 11.00 – **23 rm** 120.00/165.00.
◆ Large Victorian house close to the shops and not far from Hampstead Heath. Pleasant breakfast room/bar. Invidually styled, well appointed rooms, with smart marbled bathrooms.

🏨 **Langorf**   11 PZA **c**
20 Frognal, NW3 6AG, ℘ (020) 7794 4483, *info@langorfhotel.com, Fax (020) 7435 9055*
without rest. – 🛗 📺. ⓪ ⒶⒺ ⓪ 𝐕𝐈𝐒𝐀. 🍴
41 rm ☐ 82.00/110.00, 5 suites.
◆ Converted Edwardian house in a quiet residential area. Bright breakfast room overlooks secluded walled garden. Fresh bedrooms, many of which have high ceilings.

✕✕ **ZeNW3**   11 PZA **a**
83-84 Hampstead High St, NW3 1RE, ℘ (020) 7794 7863, *Fax (020) 7794 6956*
▤. ⓪ ⓪ 𝐕𝐈𝐒𝐀
closed 25 December – **Meals** - Chinese - 14.50/35.00 and a la carte approx. 22.50.
◆ Contemporary interior provided by the glass topped tables and small waterfall feature on the stairs. Professional service. Carefully prepared Chinese food.

✕ **Cucina**   11 PZA **X**
45a South End Rd, NW3 2QB, ℘ (020) 7435 7814, *postmaster@cucinahampste ad.co.uk, Fax (020) 7435 7815*
▤. ⓪ ⒶⒺ 𝐕𝐈𝐒𝐀
Meals a la carte 21.85/34.85 ☲.
◆ The small deli at the front gives few clues to the large room inside. Eclectic mix of artwork scattered around the room. Modern menu with influences from around the globe.

🍴 **The Wells**   11 PZA **V**
30 Well Walk, NW3 1BX, ℘ (020) 7794 3785, *Fax (020) 7794 6817*
🏠 – ▤. ⓪ ⒶⒺ ⓪ 𝐕𝐈𝐒𝐀
Meals a la carte 23.75/31.00 ☲.
◆ Attractive 18C inn with modern interior. Ground floor bar and a few tables next to open-plan kitchen; upstairs more formal dining rooms. Classically-based French cooking.

🍴 **The Magdala**   11 PZA **S**
2A South Hill Park, NW3 2SB, ℘ (020) 7435 2503, *Fax (020) 7435 6167*
🏠 – ⓪ 𝐕𝐈𝐒𝐀
closed 25 December – **Meals** a la carte 15.70/24.25 ☲.
◆ Located on the edge of the Heath. Two bars popular with locals, one with open-plan kitchen. Upstairs dining room, open at weekends, offers robust cooking. Simpler lunch menu.

Hatton Garden *Gtr London* – ✉ *EC1.*

XX **Bleeding Heart**   32 ANT **e**
Bleeding Heart Yard, EC1N 8SJ, off Greville St, ✆ (020) 7242 8238, *bookings@b leedingheart.co.uk, Fax (020) 7831 1402*
🍴 – 🕭 AE ⓪ VISA
closed 24 December-5 January, Saturday, Sunday and Bank Holidays – **Meals** a la carte 21.40/35.85 ♈.
♦ Wood panelling, candlelight and a heart motif; a popular romantic dinner spot. By contrast, a busy City restaurant at lunchtime. French influenced menu. Weighty wine list.

Holborn *Gtr London* – ✉ *WC2.*

🏨 **Renaissance Chancery Court**   32 AMT **a**
252 High Holborn, WC1V 7EN, ✆ (020) 7829 9888, *sales.chancerycourt@renais sancehotels.com, Fax (020) 7829 9889*
♿, 🕭 – 🛗, ✑ rm, 🖭 TV 📞 ♿ – 🔥 400. 🕭 AE ⓪ VISA JCB, ❄
Meals – (see *QC* below) – ⌓ 17.95 – **354 rm** 311.35/346.60, 2 suites.
♦ Striking building built in 1914. converted to hotel in 2000. Impressive marbled lobby and grand central courtyard. Very large bedrooms with comprehensive modern facilities.

🏨 **Kingsway Hall**   31 ALT **b**
Great Queen St, WC2B 5BX, ✆ (020) 7309 0909, *reservations@kingswayhall.co. uk, Fax (020) 7309 9129*
♿ – 🛗, ✑ rm, 🖭 TV 📞 ♿ – 🔥 150. 🕭 AE ⓪ VISA. ❄
Harlequin : **Meals** *(closed lunch Saturday, Sunday and Bank Holidays)* 14.95/ 17.95 **s.** and dinner a la carte – ⌓ 15.25 – **168 rm** 185.00, 2 suites.
♦ Large, corporate-minded hotel. Striking glass-framed and marbled lobby. Stylish ground floor bar. Well-appointed bedrooms with an extensive array of mod cons. Relaxing restaurant in warm pastel colours.

XXX **QC** (at Renaissance Chancery Court H.)   32 AMT **a**
252 High Holborn, WC1V 7EN, ✆ (020) 7829 7000, *Fax (020) 7829 9889*
🕭 AE ⓪ VISA JCB
closed Saturday lunch and Sunday – **Meals** 21.50 (lunch) and a la carte 31.50/ 47.00 ♈.
♦ Impressive dining room with walls clad in Italian marble; Corinthian columns. Waiters provide efficient service at well-spaced tables; original menus.

XX **Matsuri - High Holborn**   32 AMT **c**
Mid City Pl, 71 High Holborn, WC1V 6EA, ✆ (020) 7430 1970, *eat@matsuri-rest aurant.com, Fax (020) 7430 1971*
✑, 🕭 AE ⓪ VISA JCB
closed 24-26 and 31 December, 1-2 January, Sunday and Bank Holidays – **Meals** - Japanese - 22.00/25.00 and a la carte 23.50/43.00 ♈.
♦ Spacious, airy Japanese restaurant. Authentic menu served in main dining room, in basement teppan-yaki bar and at large sushi counter, where chefs demonstrate their skills.

Primrose Hill *Gtr London* – ✉ *NW1.*

XX **Odette's**   11 QZB **b**
130 Regent's Park Rd, NW1 8XL, ✆ (020) 7586 5486, *Fax (020) 7586 0508*
🕭 AE ⓪ VISA
closed Saturday lunch and Sunday dinner – **Meals** 14.50 (lunch) and a la carte 35.00/45.00.
♦ Identified by the pretty hanging baskets outside. A charming interior with mirrors of various sizes covering the walls. Detailed service. Contemporary cuisine.

🏠 **The Queens**　　　　　　　　　　　　　　　　　　11 QZB **a**
49 Regent's Park Rd, NW1 8XD, 📞 (020) 7586 0408, *Fax (020) 7586 5677*
🛋 – **⬤❸** **VISA**
Meals a la carte 16.90/21.90 ♀.
　◆ One of the original "gastropubs". Very popular balcony overlooking Primrose Hill and the high street. Robust and traditional cooking from the blackboard menu.

🏠 **The Engineer**　　　　　　　　　　　　　　　　11 QZB **z**
65 Gloucester Ave, NW1 8JH, 📞 (020) 7722 0950, *info@the-eng.com,*
Fax (020) 7483 0592
🛋 – **⬤❸** **VISA**
closed 25-26 December and 1 January – **Meals** a la carte 25.25/29.25 ♀.
　◆ Busy pub that boasts a warm, neighbourhood feel. Dining room, decorated with modern pictures, has modish appeal. Informal, chatty service. Modern cuisine.

Swiss Cottage *Gtr London* – ✉ *NW3.*

🏨 **Marriott Regents Park**　　　　　　　　　　　11 PZB **a**
128 King Henry's Rd, NW3 3ST, 📞 (020) 7722 7711, *Fax (020) 7586 5822*
🎱, 🏋, 🔲 – 📱, ✋ rm, 🔲 📺 🛁 📶 – 🔼 300. **⬤❸ AE ⬤** **VISA**. 🛇
Meals (bar lunch)/dinner a la carte 18.00/31.50 **s.** ♀ – ☕ 16.45 – **298 rm** 143.75, 5 suites.
　◆ Large writing desks and technological extras attract the corporate market to this purpose-built group hotel. The impressive leisure facilities appeal to weekend guests. Large, open-plan restaurant and bar.

🏨 **Swiss Cottage**　　　　　　　　　　　　　　11 PZB **n**
4 Adamson Rd, NW3 3HP, 📞 (020) 7722 2281, *reservations@swisscottagehotel.co.uk, Fax (020) 7483 4588*
without rest. – 📱 ✋ 📺 – 🔼 35. **⬤❸ AE ⬤** **VISA**. 🛇
53 rm ☕ 66.00/120.00, 6 suites.
　◆ Made up of four Victorian houses in a residential conservation area. Bedrooms vary in size and shape, reflecting the age of the house. Basement breakfast room.

🍴🍴 **Bradley's**　　　　　　　　　　　　　　　　11 PZB **e**
25 Winchester Rd, NW3 3NR, 📞 (020) 7722 3457, *Fax (020) 7435 1392*
🍽. **⬤❸ AE** **VISA** **JCB**
closed 25 December-1 January and Saturday lunch – **Meals** 16.00 (lunch) and a la carte 25.50/36.50 ♀.
　◆ Warm pastel colours and modern artwork add a Mediterranean touch to this neighbourhood restaurant. The theme is complemented by the cooking of the chef patron.

🍴🍴 **Benihana**　　　　　　　　　　　　　　　　11 PZB **s**
100 Avenue Rd, NW3 3HF, 📞 (020) 7586 9508, *benihana@dircon.co.uk, Fax (020) 7586 6740*
🍽. **⬤❸ AE ⬤** **VISA**
closed 25 December – **Meals** - Japanese (Teppan-Yaki) - 19.25/25.50.
　◆ An entertaining experience where Japanese chefs chop, juggle and cook in front of you. Be prepared to talk with strangers as guests are seated in groups around the counters.

🍴 **Globe**　　　　　　　　　　　　　　　　　　11 PZB **v**
100 Avenue Rd, NW3 3HF, 📞 (020) 7722 7200, *globerella@aol.com, Fax (020) 7722 2772*
🍽. **⬤❸** **VISA**
closed Saturday lunch and Sunday dinner – **Meals** a la carte 19.00/25.50 🍷 ♀.
　◆ Next to the Hampstead Theatre, which opened in 2003, so this airy, conservatory establishment tends to be busier earlier and later in the evening. Stylish upstairs bar.

Tufnell Park *Gtr London* – ✉ *NW5.*

Samphire — 12 RZA n
135 Fortess Rd, NW5 2HR, ☎ (020) 7482 4855, *Fax (020) 7482 4856*
▤. MC VISA
closed 25-26 December and 1 January – **Meals** (dinner only and Sunday lunch) a la carte 19.40/24.85 ♀.
◆ Modern decor in grey and burgundy; smoking upstairs. Well chosen menu of dishes made of good quality ingredients and served in generous portions by friendly staff. Good value.

Junction Tavern — 12 RZA x
101 Fortess Rd, NW5 1AG, ☎ (020) 7485 9400, *Fax (020) 7485 9401*
– MC VISA JCB
closed 24-26 December – **Meals** a la carte 16.50/25.00 ♀.
◆ Typical Victorian pub with wood panelling. Eat in the bar or in view of the open plan kitchen. Robust cooking using good fresh ingredients, served in generous portions.

CITY OF LONDON *Gtr London.*

Great Eastern — 34 ART t
Liverpool St, EC2M 7QN, ☎ (020) 7618 5000, *sales@great-eastern-hotel.co.uk, Fax (020) 7618 5011*
– rm, ▤ TV – 250. MC AE VISA
Fishmarket : **Meals** - Seafood - *(closed Saturday, Sunday and Bank Holidays)* a la carte 24.55/47.00 ♀
Miyabi : **Meals** - Japanese - *(closed Saturday, Sunday and Bank Holidays)* (booking essential) 23.50 (lunch) and a la carte 21.50/39.50 – (see also ***Aurora*** below) – ☕ 22.00 – **264 rm** 264.30/370.10, 3 suites.
◆ A contemporary and stylish interior hides behind the classic Victorian façade of this railway hotel. Bright and spacious bedrooms with state-of-the-art facilities. Fishmarket based within original hotel lobby. Miyabi is compact Japanese restaurant.

Grange City — 34 ASU s
8-10 Coopers Row, EC3N 2BD, ☎ (020) 7863 3700, *city@grangehotel.com, Fax (020) 7863 3701*
≤, , , , – , rm, ▤ TV – 450. MC AE VISA JCB
Forum : **Meals** - Italian - *(closed lunch Saturday and Sunday)* 25.00 and a la carte 18.20/32.00 **s.** ♀
Koto II : **Meals** - Sushi - a la carte approx. 14.00 **s.** – ☕ 16.00 – **234 rm** 280.00, 5 suites.
◆ Smart commercial hotel with splendid view of the Tower of London. Well-appointed wood furnished rooms. Superb leisure centre with large pool. Striking and colourful Forum with Italian menus. Informal Koto II has Japanese theme and sushi conveyor belt.

Threadneedles — 34 ARU y
5 Threadneedle St, EC2R 8AY, ☎ (020) 7657 8080, *res_threadneedles@etontownhouse.com, Fax (020) 7657 8100*
▤ TV – 35. MC AE VISA JCB.
Meals – (see ***Bonds*** below) – ☕ 17.95 – **69 rm** 311.40/364.25, 1 suite.
◆ A converted bank, dating from 1856, with a stunning stained-glass cupola in the lounge. Rooms are very stylish and individual featuring CD players and Egyptian cotton sheets.

The Chamberlain

34 ASU **n**

130-135 Minories, EC3 1NU, ℰ (020) 7680 1500, *thechamberlain@fullers.co.uk,
Fax (020) 7702 2500*

🛗, ⇆ rm, 🖵 📺 ✆ ⅙ – 🛎 40. ⦿ 🖭 ⦿ *VISA*. ✆

closed 24 December-3 January **Meals** (in bar Saturday and Sunday) a la carte
14.20/16.20 ♈ – ⌁ 10.95 – **64 rm** 159.00.

◆ Modern hotel aimed at business traveller, two minutes from the Tower of
London. Warmly decorated bedrooms with writing desks. All bathrooms have
inbuilt plasma TVs.

Novotel London Tower Bridge

34 ASU **b**

10 Pepys St, EC3N 2NR, ℰ (020) 7265 6000, *h3107@accor-hotels.com,
Fax (020) 7265 6060*

🖼, ⇑ – 🛗, ⇆ rm, 🖵 📺 ✆ ⅙ – 🛎 95. ⦿ 🖭 ⦿ *VISA*. ✆

The Garden Brasserie : **Meals** 18.95 (lunch) and a la carte 20.00/28.00 **s.** ♈ –
⌁ 12.95 – **199 rm** 155.00/175.00, 4 suites.

◆ Modern, purpose-built hotel with carefully planned, comfortable bedrooms. Useful City location and close to Tower of London which is visible from
some of the higher rooms. Informally styled brasserie.

Travelodge

34 AST **s**

1 Harrow Pl, E1 7DB, ℰ (08700) 850950, *Fax (020) 7626 1105*

without rest. – 🛗 ⇆ 📺 ✆ ⅙. ⦿ 🖭 ⦿ *VISA* *JCB*. ✆ – **142 rm** 79.95.

◆ Suitable for both corporate travellers and families alike. Spacious, carefully
designed, bright and modern rooms with sofa beds and ample workspace.

Aurora (at Great Eastern H.)

34 ART **t**

Liverpool St, EC2M 7QN, ℰ (020) 7618 7000, *restaurants@great-eastern-hotel.
co.uk, Fax (020) 7618 7001*

🖵. ⦿ 🖭 ⦿ *VISA*

closed Saturday, Sunday and Bank Holidays – **Meals** 28.00/45.00 and a la carte
32.50/52.50 ♈♈ ♈.

◆ Vast columns, ornate plasterwork and a striking glass dome feature in this
imposing dining room. Polished and attentive service of an elaborate and
modern menu.

Rhodes Twenty Four

34 ART **v**

24th floor, Tower 42, 25 Old Broad St, EC2N 1HQ, ℰ (020) 7887 7703, *reservati
ons@rhodes24.co.uk, Fax (020) 7877 7725*

≼ London – 🛗 🖵. ⦿ 🖭 ⦿ *VISA*

closed Christmas-New Year, Saturday, Sunday and Bank Holidays – **Meals**
a la carte 25.00/40.00 ♈.

◆ Modern restaurant on the 24th floor of the former Natwest building with
panoramic views of the city. Extensive menu of classic British dishes. Attentive
service.

Whites

27 NU **u**

1 New Street Sq, EC4A 3BF, ℰ (020) 7583 1313, *sales@wslrestaurants.co.uk,
Fax (020) 7353 1662*

🖵. ⦿ 🖭 ⦿ *VISA* *JCB*

closed Saturday, Sunday and Bank Holidays – **Meals** 34.00 (dinner) and a la carte 34.00/42.50 ♈.

◆ Up a spiral staircase to this first floor open plan restaurant with linen-clad
tables, chairs and banquettes. Very busy at lunch time. Good sized classical
menu.

Coq d'Argent

33 AQU **c**

No.1 Poultry, EC2R 8EJ, ℰ (020) 7395 5000, *Fax (020) 7395 5050*

🌤 – 🛗 🖵. ⦿ 🖭 ⦿ *VISA*

closed Saturday lunch and Sunday dinner – **Meals** - French - (booking essential) 25.00 (lunch) and a la carte 29.50/41.00 ♈♈ ♈.

◆ Take the dedicated lift to the top of this modern office block. Tables on the
rooftop terrace have city views; busy bar. Gallic menus highlighted by popular
shellfish dishes.

XXX **Tatsuso**   34 ART **u**
32 Broadgate Circle, EC2M 2QS, ℰ (020) 7638 5863, *Fax (020) 7638 5864*
▤. ⓜⓢ ⒶⒺ ⓞ *VISA* ⌨
closed Christmas-New Year, Saturday, Sunday and Bank Holidays –
Meals - Japanese - (booking essential) 38.00/97.00 and a la carte 50.00/
100.00 **s.**
◆ Dine in the busy teppan-yaki bar or in the more formal restaurant. Approachable staff in traditional costume provide attentive service of authentic and precise dishes.

XXX **1 Lombard Street (Restaurant)**   33 AQU **r**
⚙ 1 Lombard St, EC3V 9AA, ℰ (020) 7929 6611, *hb@1lombardstreet.com,*
Fax (020) 7929 6622
▤. ⓜⓢ ⒶⒺ ⓞ *VISA* ⌨
closed Saturday, Sunday and Bank Holidays – **Meals** (lunch booking essential)
32.00/34.00 and a la carte ♀.
◆ A haven of tranquillity behind the forever busy brasserie. Former bank provides the modern and very comfortable surroundings in which to savour the accomplished cuisine.
Spec. Carpaccio of tuna with Oriental spices, ginger and lime vinaigrette. Fillet of lamb, tomato and mint velouté. Strawberries in Sauternes with black pepper, crème fraîche sorbet.

XXX **Prism**   34 ARU **u**
147 Leadenhall, EC3V 4QT, ℰ (020) 7256 3875, *prism@harveynichols.co.uk,*
Fax (020) 7256 3876
▤. ⓜⓢ ⒶⒺ ⓞ *VISA*
closed 24 December-5 January, Saturday and Sunday – **Meals** 25.00 (dinner) and a la carte 34.00/41.00 ♀.
◆ Enormous Corinthian pillars and a busy bar feature in this capacious and modern restaurant. Efficient service of an eclectic menu. Quieter tables in covered courtyard.

XXX **Bonds** (at Threadneedles H.)   34 ARU **y**
5 Threadneedle St, EC2R 8AY, ℰ (020) 7657 8088, *bonds@theetongroup.com,*
Fax (020) 7657 8089
▤. ⓜⓢ ⒶⒺ ⓞ *VISA* ⌨
closed Saturday, Sunday and Bank Holidays – **Meals** a la carte 33.95/
46.00 ♀.
◆ Modern interior juxtaposed with the grandeur of a listed city building. Vast dining room with high ceiling and tall pillars. Attentive service of hearty, contemporary food.

XX **Club Gascon** (Aussignac)   33 APT **z**
⚙ 57 West Smithfield, EC1A 9DS, ℰ (020) 7796 0600, *Fax (020) 7796 0601*
▤. ⓜⓢ ⒶⒺ *VISA*
closed 23 December-3 January, Saturday lunch, Sunday and Bank Holidays –
Meals - French (Gascony specialities) - (booking essential) 35.00/55.00 and a la carte 27.00/45.50 ♀.
◆ Intimate and rustic restaurant on the edge of Smithfield Market. Specialises in both the food and wines of Southwest France. Renowned for the foie gras tasting dishes.
Spec. Variations of duck, creamed caviar and sardine sorbet. Glazed veal sweetbreads, rosemary and mousserons. Lamb fritto, spicy vegetables.

XX **Boisdale of Bishopgate**   34 ART **a**
Swedland Court, 202 Bishopgate, EC2M 4NR, ℘ (020) 7283 1763, *info@boisdal
e-city.co.uk, Fax (020) 7283 1664*
🍽. **MO AE VISA**
closed 25 December-2 January, Saturday, Sunday and Bank Holidays – **Meals** -
Scottish - a la carte 22.95/40.00 ⬨.
◆ Through ground floor bar, serving oysters and champagne, to brick vault-
ed basement with red and tartan décor. Menu featuring Scottish produce.
Live jazz most evenings.

XX **Searcy's**   33 AQT **n**
Barbican Centre, Level 2, Silk St, EC2Y 8DS, ℘ (020) 7588 3008, *searcys@barbic
an.org.uk, Fax (028) 7382 7247*
🍽. **MO AE VISA**
closed Saturday lunch and Sunday – **Meals** 22.00/32.00 ⬨.
◆ Stylish modern surroundings, smooth effective service and seasonal modern British cooking. Unique location ideal for visitors to Barbican's multi-arts
events.

XX **Kasturi**   34 ASU **a**
57 Aldgate High St, EC3N 1AL, ℘ (020) 7480 7402, *reservation@kasturi-restaur
ant.co.uk, Fax (020) 7702 0256*
🍽. **MO AE VISA**
closed 24 December-1 January, Saturday lunch, Sunday and Bank Holidays –
Meals - Indian - a la carte 17.65/23.90.
◆ Spacious wooden floored restaurant enhanced by mirrors; modern art on
walls. Good service. Varied menu with original and authentic dishes.

XX **Imperial City**   34 ARU **a**
Royal Exchange, Cornhill, EC3V 3LL, ℘ (020) 7626 3437, *enquiries@orgplc.co.u
k, Fax (020) 7338 0125*
🍽. **MO AE ① VISA**
closed 25-26 December, Saturday, Sunday and Bank Holidays – **Meals** - Chinese - 17.00/32.95 and a la carte 18.00/29.50 ⬨.
◆ Vaulted basement restaurant with large water feature; originally Royal
Exchange wine cellars. Smart, friendly service of an authentic menu covering
all regions of China.

XX **Chamberlain's**   34 ARU **V**
23-25 Leadenhall Market, EC3V 1LR, ℘ (020) 7648 8690, *info@chamberlains.or
g, Fax (020) 7648 8691*
MO AE ① VISA
closed Christmas, Saturday, Sunday and Bank Holidays – **Meals** - Seafood -
15.95 (dinner) and a la carte 25.95/39.45 ⬨.
◆ Bright, modern restaurant in ornate Victorian indoor market. Top quality
seafood from fish and chips to mousse of lobster. There's even a fish tank in
the lavatories!

*Write to us...
If you have any comments on the contents of this Guide.
Your praise as well as your criticisms will receive careful
consideration and, with your assistance, we will be able to add
to our stock of information and, where necessary, amend
our judgments.
Thank you in advance!*

CROYDON *Gtr London.*

Addington – ✉ *Surrey.*

⟜₁₈, ⟜₁₈, ⟜₉ *Addington Court, Featherbed Lane* ℘ *(020) 8657 0281* GZ – ⟜₁₈ *The Addington, 205 Shirley Church Rd* ℘ *(020) 8777 1055* GZ.

XX Planet Spice   7   GZ **C**
88 Selsdon Park Rd, CR2 8JT, ℘ *(020) 8651 3300, Fax (020) 8651 4400*
▤ **P**. ◍ **AE** ◉ **VISA** **JCB**
closed 25-26 December and Friday lunch – **Meals** - Indian - a la carte 18.20/ 21.60 ♀.
♦ Brasserie style Indian restaurant with fresh, vibrant décor and a modern feel. Attentive and helpful service. Traditional cooking with some innovative touches.

Coulsdon *Surrey* – ✉ *Surrey.*

⛫ Coulsdon Manor
Coulsdon Court Rd, via Stoats Nest Rd (B 2030), CR5 2LL, ℘ *(020) 8668 0414, coulsdonmanor@marstonhotels.com, Fax (020) 8668 3118*
⮠, ≼, ⌨, ⥱s, ⟜₁₈, XX, squash – ⫯ ⭲ **TV** ℂ **P**. – ⚭ 180. ◍ **AE** ◉ **VISA**. ⅗
Manor House : **Meals** 16.50/29.00 and a la carte 32.40/44.50 ♀ – **35 rm** ⌸ 124.00/178.00.
♦ A secluded Victorian country house, extended over the years. Set in 140 acres, much of which is taken up by the popular golf course. Smart bedrooms, restful sitting room. Softly-lit dining room with cocktail bar.

Croydon *Surrey* – ✉ *Surrey.*

🛈 *Croydon Clocktower, Katharine St* ℘ *(020) 8253 1009.*

⛫ Hilton Croydon   7   FZ **e**
Waddon Way, Purley Way, CR9 4HH, ℘ *(020) 8680 3000, res_croydon@hilton.com, Fax (020) 8681 6171*
⌨, ⥱s, ▨ – ⫯ ⭲ ▤ **TV** ℂ ⅙ **P**. – ⚭ 400. ◍ **AE** ◉ **VISA** **JCB**. ⅗
closed 1-3 January – **Meals** *(closed Sunday lunch)* a la carte 17.95/29.20 **s**. ♀ – ⌸ 14.25 – **168 rm** 120.00.
♦ A modern hotel where the relaxing café in the open-plan lobby is open all day. Internet access is available in all bedrooms, which are decorated to a good standard. Open-plan dining room; informal char-grill concept.

⛫ Jurys Inn   7   FZ **v**
Wellesley Road, CR0 9XY, ℘ *(020) 8448 6000, jurysinncroydon@jurysdoyle.com, Fax (020) 8448 6111*
⫯, ⭲ rm, ▤ **TV** ℂ ⅙ – ⚭ 120. ◍ **AE** ◉ **VISA**
Meals (bar lunch)/dinner 15.95 and a la carte – ⌸ 9.00 – **240 rm** 80.00.
♦ Along main dual carriageway in town centre. Informal coffee bar in foyer. Conference facilities on first and second floors. Bright, modern rooms with good facilities. Restaurant near foyer; very relaxed informality.

⌂ Travel Inn Metro   7   GZ **s**
104 Coombe Rd, CR0 5RB, on A 212, ℘ *(0870) 1977069, Fax (020) 8686 6435*
⇴ – ⭲ rm, **TV** ⅙ **P**. ◍ **AE** ◉ **VISA**. ⅗
Meals (grill rest.) – **39 rm** 54.95.
♦ Surprisingly pleasant country setting for this purpose-built lodge-style hotel; surrounded by woodland with an adjacent mock-rustic pub serving traditional cuisine.

⌂ Premier Lodge   7   FZ **e**
619 Purley Way, CR0 4RJ, ℘ *(020) 8225 1909, Fax (0870) 7001435*
⫯ ⭲, ▤ rest, ℂ ⅙ **P**. ◍ **AE** ◉ **VISA**. ⅗
Meals (grill rest.) a la carte approx. 16.00 – **82 rm** 56.00.
♦ Located in an out-of-town leisure park with assorted fast food outlets and children's play area. Uniform lodge accommodation, competitively priced. Bright, popular dining room.

✗ **Mario**　　　　　　　　　　　　　　　　　　　　　7　FZ　**S**
299 High St, CR0 1QL, ☎ (020) 8686 5624
🏧 AE VISA JCB
closed 25 December, last 2 weeks August, Saturday lunch, Sunday, Monday and Bank Holidays – **Meals** - Italian - 17.00 (lunch) and a la carte 15.75/35.50.
◆ Guests can be in no doubt as to the nationality of this cosy, personally run establishment; walls are adorned with Italian pictures and knick-knacks. Traditional menu.

EALING *Gtr London.*

Ealing *Gtr London* – ✉ *W5.*

🏌 *West Middlesex, Greenford Rd, Southall* ☎ *(020) 8574 3450* BV – 🏌 *Horsenden Hill, Woodland Rise, Greenford* ☎ *(020) 8902 4555* BU.

🏨 **Ramada Jarvis London West**　　　　　　　　　　2　CV　**V**
Ealing Common, W5 3HN, ☎ (020) 8896 8400, *sales.londonwest@ramadajarvis .co.uk, Fax (020) 8992 7082*
|≑|, ⇆ rm, ▤ rest, 📺 ☎ P – 🛗 250. 🏧 AE ⓞ VISA JCB. ✻
Meals (buffet lunch Monday-Friday) (bar lunch Saturday) a la carte 19.95/25.30 ⚐ – ⚏ 11.95 – **189 rm** 140.00.
◆ On the edge of the Common, a commercial hotel refurbished in 2000. Smart, modern interior in eye-catchingly bold colours. Well-equipped bedrooms. Restaurant or bar dining options.

🏨 **Travel Inn Metro**　　　　　　　　　　　　　　　1　BU　**c**
Western Ave, Greenford, UB6 8TE, off A 40, ☎ (020) 8998 8820, *Fax (020) 8998 8823*
⇆ rm, ▤ rest, 📺 ₺ P. 🏧 AE ⓞ VISA JCB. ✻
Meals (grill rest.) – **39 rm** 56.95.
◆ Modern, purpose-built lodge offering good value accommodation with bright and carefully planned bedrooms. Children's play area and popular grill restaurant adjacent.

🏨 **Travelodge**　　　　　　　　　　　　　　　　　6　CV　**X**
Western Ave, W3 0TE, ☎ (08700) 850950, *Fax (020) 8752 1134*
without rest. – |≑| ⇆ 📺 ₺ P. 🏧 AE ⓞ VISA. ✻
64 rm 79.95.
◆ Modern lodge-style accommodation with clean and spacious bedrooms at an affordable price. Convenient for the A40. All rooms double glazed but those at the back are quieter.

✗✗ **Maxim**　　　　　　　　　　　　　　　　　　　1　BV　**a**
153-155 Northfield Ave, W13 9QT, ☎ (020) 8567 1719, *Fax (020) 8932 0717*
▤. 🏧 AE VISA JCB
closed 25 to 28 December and Sunday lunch – **Meals** - Chinese (Peking) - 12.00/30.00 and a la carte 17.00/30.00.
◆ Decorated with assorted oriental ornaments and pictures. Well-organised service from smartly attired staff. Authentic Chinese cooking from the extensive menu.

South Ealing *Gtr London* – ✉ *W5.*

🏠 **Ealing Park Tavern**　　　　　　　　　　　　　1　BV　**e**
222 South Ealing Rd, W5 4RL, ☎ (020) 8758 1879, *Fax (020) 8560 5269*
🍴 – 🏧 AE VISA
closed 25 December, 1 January and Monday lunch – **Meals** a la carte 18.50/22.00 ⚐.
◆ Victorian building with an atmospheric, cavernous interior. Characterful beamed dining room and an open-plan kitchen serving modern dishes from a daily changing menu.

ENFIELD *Gtr London – pop. 566.*

🏌️ *Lee Valley Leisure, Picketts Lock Lane, Edmonton 📞 (020) 8803 3611* GT.

Enfield *Middx – ✉ Middx.*

🏌️ *Whitewebbs, Beggars Hollow, Clay Hill 📞 (020) 8363 2951, N : 1 m.* FT.

🏨 **Royal Chace** 3 ET **a**
The Ridgeway, EN2 8AR, 📞 (020) 8884 8181, *enquiries@royalchace.hotel.co.
uk, Fax (020) 8884 8150*
🏊 heated, 🌳 – ⇌✕ 📺 ᓌ. ꔪ – 🛁 270. 🐵 AE ⓪ VISA. ✖
closed 25-26 December and 1 January – **Meals** *(closed Sunday dinner)* (bar
lunch Monday-Saturday)/dinner a la carte 21.75/30.50 – **92 rm** ⊊ 99.00/
115.00.
◆ A corporate-minded hotel, privately owned and convenient for the M25.
Many of the uniformly decorated bedrooms look out over the large gardens
and parkland at the rear. Restaurant is popular for private functions.

🏛 **Oak Lodge** 3 FT **a**
80 Village Rd, Bush Hill Park, EN1 2EU, 📞 (020) 8360 7082, *oaklodge@fsmail.
net*
🏠, 🌳 – ⇌✕ 📺 ᓌ. 🐵 AE ⓪ VISA JCB
Meals (dinner only) a la carte 17.50/24.50 – **6 rm** ⊊ 69.50/89.50.
◆ An Edwardian house personally run by the hospitable owner and located in
a residential area. Individually decorated bedrooms are compact but well-
equipped. Cosy dining room overlooks secluded rear garden.

Hadley Wood *Herts. – ✉ Herts.*

🏨 **West Lodge Park** 3 ET **i**
off Cockfosters Rd, EN4 0PY, 📞 (020) 8216 3900, *westlodgepark@bealeshotel
s.co.uk, Fax (020) 8216 3937*
🏊, ≤, 🏠, ≋s, 🌳, ᵭ – 🛗 ⇌✕ 📺 📞 ᓌ. ꔪ – 🛁 80. 🐵 AE ⓪ VISA JCB. ✖
The Cedar : **Meals** *closed Saturday lunch* 18.50/32.50 and a la carte 26.75/
34.65 – ⊊ 13.50 – **59 rm** 108.00/180.00.
◆ Family owned for over half a century, a country house in sweeping
grounds with arboretum. Comfortable sitting rooms; neat, spacious bedrooms. Use of nearby leisure centre. Dining room boasts large windows and
exposed brick walls.

Winchmore Hill *Gtr London – ✉ N21.*

🏠 **The Kings Head** 3 ET **e**
1 The Green, N21 1BB, 📞 (020) 8886 1988, *Fax (020) 8882 3881*
ꔪ. 🐵 VISA
Meals a la carte 16.90/23.90 ⊊.
◆ Large scrubbed pine tables, leather sofas and wall tapestries decorate this
contemporary inn. Modern, eclectic cooking with supplementary blackboard
specials.

GREENWICH *Gtr London.*

Blackheath *Gtr London – ✉ SE3.*

🍴🍴 **Chapter Two** 8 HX **c**
43-45 Montpelier Vale, SE3 0TJ, 📞 (020) 8333 2666, *fiona.chapter2@talk21.co
m, Fax (020) 8355 8399*
⇌✕ ▤. 🐵 AE ⓪ VISA JCB
Meals 18.50/22.50 ⊊.
◆ Smart and contemporary interior. Decorated in primary colours, with pine
flooring. Formal service of a well-priced, well-judged European-influenced
modern menu.

Greenwich *Gtr London* – ✉ *SE10*.

🛈 *Pepys House, 2 Cutty Sark Gardens* ℰ *(0870) 6082000.*

✕✕ Spread Eagle
7 GV **C**

1-2 Stockwell St, SE10 9JN, ℰ (020) 8853 2333, *goodfood@spreadeagle.org*, *Fax (020) 8305 0447*

▤, ⓩⓞ AE ⓞ VISA JCB

closed 25-26 December, Tuesday lunch and Monday – **Meals** 13.00/16.75 (lunch) and a la carte 23.50/27.25 ♈.

♦ This converted pub is something of an institution. Cosy booth seating, wood panelling and a further upstairs room. Traditional French-influenced menu with attentive service.

✕ North Pole
7 GV **U**

131 Greenwich High Rd, SE10 8JA, ℰ (020) 8853 3020, *northpoleozzy@hotmai l.com, Fax (020) 8853 3501*

ⓩⓞ AE ⓞ VISA

closed 25 December – **Meals** 17.50 and a la carte 20.00/28.00 ♈.

♦ Former corner pub with popular ground floor bar. Upstairs dining room benefits from high ceilings, large windows and bright colours. Relaxed service, robust cooking.

If you are held up on the road - from 6pm onwards -
confirm your hotel booking by telephone.
It is safer and quite an accepted practice.

HACKNEY *Gtr London*.

Hoxton *Gtr London* – ✉ *N1*.

🏨 Express by Holiday Inn
20 XZC **a**

275 Old St, EC1V 9LN, ℰ (020) 7300 4300, *reservationsfc@holidayinnlondon.c om, Fax (020) 7300 4400*

🛗, ⇄ rm, ▤ rest, 📺 ℰ ⅙ – ♨ 80. ⓩⓞ AE ⓞ VISA JCB ⅜

Meals (dinner only) a la carte 18.40/22.00 **s.** – **224 rm** 110.00.

♦ Large purpose-built property close to the tube and the financial district. Brightly decorated bedrooms are all generously sized and offer good value accommodation. Open-plan dining room.

✕✕ Real Greek
20 XZC **V**

15 Hoxton Market, N1 6HG, ℰ (020) 7739 8212, *admin@therealgreek.co.uk, Fax (020) 7739 4910*

ⓩⓞ VISA

closed Christmas, Sunday and Bank Holidays – **Meals** - Greek - 13.50 (lunch) and a la carte approx. 29.50 ♈.

♦ A former Victorian pub in a pleasant square. Plain wooden tables with open-plan kitchen. Very tasty, wholly Greek menu and wine list with un-affected and pleasant service.

✕ Fifteen
13 VZC **C**

15 Westland Pl, N1 7LP, ℰ (020) 7251 1515, *Fax (020) 7251 2749*

▤, ⓩⓞ AE VISA JCB

closed 25-26 December, Sunday dinner and Bank Holiday Mondays – **Meals** a la carte 41.50/46.50 ♈.

♦ Jamie Oliver's TV restaurant. Open plan kitchen showing the trainee chefs at work. Typical menu of robust earthy flavours using carefully-sourced ingredients.

※ **Cru**   20 XZC **m**
2-4 Rufus St, N1 6PE, ℘ (020) 7729 5252
▦. **⑩⑥** Ⓐ **①** **VISA**
closed 25-26 December and 1 January – **Meals** 18.50 (lunch) and a la carte
19.50/30.40 ♀.
♦ Converted 19C warehouse trendily located with artwork for sale. Bar and
delicatessen leading past open kitchen to restaurant. Modern menu with
Asian influences. Good value.

※ **Mezedopolio**   20 XZC **v**
15 Hoxton Market, N1 6HG, ℘ (020) 7739 8212, *admin@therealgreek.demon.c
o.uk, Fax (020) 7739 4910*
⑩⑥ **VISA**
closed Christmas, Sunday and Bank Holidays – **Meals** - Greek meze - (bookings
not accepted) a la carte 15.00/20.00.
♦ Greek meze bar, part of The Real Greek, though with a more informal style.
High ceilings, marble memorials. Large menu of authentic dishes from Greece
and the Aegean.

Stoke Newington *Gtr London* – ✉ *N16.*

※ **Rasa**   14 XZA **e**
55 Stoke Newington Church St, N16 0AR, ℘ (020) 7249 0344
▦. **⑩⑥** Ⓐ **VISA** J̲C̲B̲
Meals - Indian Vegetarian - (booking essential)(dinner only and lunch Saturday
and Sunday) 15.50 and a la carte 10.25/13.75.
♦ Busy Indian restaurant, an unpretentious environment in which to sample
authentic, sometimes unusual, dishes. The "Feast" offers a taste of the range
of foods on offer.

In this guide
a symbol or a character,
printed in red *or* **black**, *in light or bold type*
does not have the same meaning.
Pay particular attention to the explanatory pages.

HAMMERSMITH and FULHAM *Gtr London.*

Fulham *Gtr London* – ✉ *SW6.*

🏨 **London Putney Bridge Travel Inn Capital**   22 MZH **c**
3 Putney Bridge Approach, SW6 3JD, ℘ (020) 7471 8300, *Fax (020) 7471 8315*
‖⁑‖, ⇆ rm, ▤ rest, ⅏ ⅍. **⑩⑥** Ⓐ **①** **VISA**. ⅍
Meals (grill rest.) (dinner only) – **154 rm** 74.95.
♦ A longer name for a larger lodge. Converted office block offering clean,
well-priced accommodation. All rooms have sofa beds and large worktops.

※※ **Blue Elephant**   22 NZG **z**
4-6 Fulham Broadway, SW6 1AA, ℘ (020) 7385 6595, *london@blueelephant.co
m, Fax (020) 7386 7665*
▦. **⑩⑥** Ⓐ **①** **VISA**
Closed 24-26 December, 1 January and Saturday lunch – **Meals** - Thai -
(booking essential) 15.00/33.00 and a la carte 20.50/43.50 ⅌.
♦ Elaborately ornate, unrestrained décor: fountains, bridges, orchids and
ponds with carp. Authentic Thai food served by attentive staff in national
costumes.

XX **Mao Tai**   22 NZH e
58 New Kings Rd, Parsons Green, SW6 4LS, ℘ (020) 7731 2520, *info@maotai.c
o.uk, Fax (020) 7471 8994*
📧. ⓜⓔ ⒶⒺ ⓞ 𝑽𝑰𝑺𝑨
closed 25-26 December – **Meals** - Chinese (Szechuan) - 12.50/24.70
and a la carte 25.05/38.20 ℥.
♦ A light and modern interior with wood flooring and framed artwork with
an eastern theme. Well organised service. Chinese cuisine with Szechuan
specialities.

X **Zinc**   22 NZG a
Fulham Island, 1 Farm Lane, SW6 1BE, ℘ (020) 7386 2250, *Fax (020) 7386 2260*
🌳 – 📧. ⓜⓔ ⒶⒺ ⓞ 𝑽𝑰𝑺𝑨
closed 25-26 December – **Meals** 15.00 (lunch) and a la carte 23.50/30.50 ℥.
♦ Bright modern bar; informal chic restaurant. Grills, seafood and modern
international fare. No booking so arrive early for a table on the canopied and
heated terrace.

🍷 **The Salisbury Tavern**   22 MZG e
21 Sherbrooke Rd, SW6 7HX, ℘ (020) 7381 4005, *thesalisburytavern@longsho
tplc.com, Fax (020) 7381 1002*
📧. ⓜⓔ ⒶⒺ 𝐉𝐂𝐁
closed 25 December – **Meals** (live jazz Monday evening) 17.50
(lunch) and a la carte 21.40/26.70 ℥.
♦ Its residential location attracts a local crowd to the stylish bar. Separate,
and equally à la mode, dining room with pleasant young staff. Wide ranging
traditional menu.

Hammersmith *Gtr London* – ✉ *W6/W12/W14.*

XX **River Café** (Ruth Rogers/Rose Gray)   21 LZG r
🕄 Thames Wharf, Rainville Rd, W6 9HA, ℘ (020) 7386 4200, *info@rivercafe.co.uk,
Fax (020) 7386 4201*
🌳 –ⓜⓔ ⒶⒺ ⓞ 𝑽𝑰𝑺𝑨
closed Christmas-New Year, Sunday dinner and Bank Holidays – **Meals** - Italian
- (booking essential) a la carte 41.00/54.00 ℥.
♦ Warehouse conversion with full length windows on one side, open plan
kitchen the other. Canteen-style atmosphere. Accomplished rustic Italian
cooking, uses the finest produce.
Spec. Pasta parcels with roast pigeon, pork and pancetta. Wood-roasted
turbot with capers and marjoram. Lemon and pine nut cake.

X **Snows on the Green**   15 LZF X
166 Shepherd's Bush Rd, Brook Green, W6 7PB, ℘ (020) 7603 2142, *sebastian
@snowsonthegreen.freeserve.co.uk, Fax (020) 7602 7553*
📧. ⓜⓔ ⒶⒺ ⓞ 𝑽𝑰𝑺𝑨
*closed 24-28 December, last 2 weeks August, Saturday lunch, Sunday and
Bank Holiday Mondays* – **Meals** 12.50/16.50 (lunch) and a la carte 22.00/28.00
℥.
♦ Name refers to the chef patron, not the inclement weather found in west
London. Mediterranean influenced decoration matched by the style of the
cooking.

X **The Brackenbury**   15 LZE a
129-131 Brackenbury Rd, W6 0BQ, ℘ (020) 8748 0107, *Fax (020) 8741 0905*
🌳 –ⓜⓔ ⒶⒺ 𝑽𝑰𝑺𝑨
closed Easter, 25-26 December, 1 January, Saturday lunch and Sunday dinner –
Meals 15.00 (lunch) and a la carte 21.00/27.50 **s**. ℥.
♦ The closely set wooden tables, pavement terrace and relaxed service add
to the cosy, neighbourhood feel. Cooking is equally unfussy; modern yet
robust.

※ **Azou** 21 KZG **U**

375 King St, W6 9NJ, ℰ (020) 8536 7266, *azourestaurant@artserve.net,*
Fax (020) 8748 1009

▤. **🕼🕼 ⓞ** **VISA**

closed lunch Saturday and Sunday and Bank Holidays – **Meals** - North African -
(lunch booking essential) a la carte 16.40/23.50.

♦ The North African theme is not confined to the menu; the room is decorated with hanging lanterns, screens and assorted knick-knacks. Friendly
service and well priced dishes.

🕼 **Anglesea Arms** 15 LZE **C**

35 Wingate Rd, W6 0UR, ℰ (020) 8749 1291, *Fax (020) 8749 1254*

🕼 **-🕼🕼** **VISA**

closed 1 week Christmas and 1 January – **Meals** (bookings not accepted)
12.95 (lunch) and a la carte 14.95/21.95 ℤ.

♦ The laid-back atmosphere and local feel make this pub a popular venue.
Worth arriving early as bookings are not taken. Modern cooking from blackboard menu.

Olympia *Gtr London* – ✉ *W14.*

✖✖ **Cotto** 16 MZE **f**

44 Blythe Rd, W14 0HA, ℰ (020) 7602 9333, *bookings@cottorestaurant.co.uk,*
Fax (020) 7602 5003

▤. **🕼🕼 AE** **VISA** **JCB**

closed 1 week Christmas, Saturday lunch, Sunday and Bank Holidays – **Meals**
15.00/18.00 ℤ.

♦ On two floors, with vivid abstract paintings on white walls, chrome-framed
chairs and music. Efficient service from black-clad staff. Modern cooking with
some originality.

Shepherd's Bush *Gtr London* – ✉ *W12/W14.*

🏨 **K West** 16 MZE **C**

Richmond Way, W14 0AX, ℰ (020) 7674 1000, *Fax (020) 7674 1050*

I₅, **⊠s** **– |⧉| ⇔ ▤ TV** ✆ **& – ▲** 60. **🕼🕼 AE** **VISA**. ✖

Meals a la carte 27.00/41.00 ℤ **–** � 18.00 **– 222 rm** 276.00/411.25.

♦ Former BBC offices, the interior now decorated in smart, contemporary
style. Bedrooms in understated modern style, deluxe rooms with work desks
and DVD and CD facilities.

✖✖ **Chez Moi** 16 MZE **S**

23 Richmond Way, W14 0AS, ℰ (020) 7602 6004, *chezmoi_rest@hotmail.com,*
Fax (020) 7602 8147

🕼🕼 AE ⓞ **VISA**

closed Saturday lunch, Sunday dinner and Bank Holidays – **Meals** - French -
12.50/17.50 (lunch) a la carte 22.50/31.50 ℤ.

♦ Friendly neighbourhood restaurant with window onto garden. Red and
black décor. Classic French menu of popular traditional dishes.

🕼 **Havelock Tavern** 16 MZE **e**

57 Masbro Rd, W14 0LS, ℰ (020) 7603 5374, *Fax (020) 7602 1163*

🕼 **– ▤**

closed 22-26 December – **Meals** (bookings not accepted) a la carte approx.
19.50/23.50 **s**. ℤ.

♦ Typical new wave London pub where the kitchen produces generously
portioned modern food. Pine tables and chairs, and a large central bar.
Privately owned.

HARINGEY *Gtr London.*

Crouch End *Gtr London* – ✉ *N8.*

⌂ **Mountview** 3 EU **r**
31 Mount View Rd, N4 4SS, ☏ (020) 8340 9222, *mountviewbb@aol.com*
without rest., ☞ – ⅙ ✕ TV. ⓜⓢ VISA. ⅍
closed 25 December – **3 rm** ☲ 40.00/70.00.
♦ Redbrick Victorian house with a warm and stylish ambience engendered by
the homely décor. One bedroom features an original fireplace and two overlook the quiet rear garden.

✕✕ **Les Associés** 3 EU **e**
172 Park Rd, N8 8JT, ☏ (020) 8348 8944, *Fax (020) 8340 7499*
ⓜⓢ VISA
closed 1-15 January, 2 weeks August, Sunday dinner and Monday – **Meals** -
French - (dinner only and Sunday lunch)/dinner a la carte 21.50/26.20.
♦ Its relaxed ambience and polite, friendly service make this a popular local
spot. Traditional and reliable French cooking in comfortable surroundings.

✕ **Florians** 3 EU **c**
4 Topsfield Par, Middle Lane, N8 8RP, ☏ (020) 8348 8348, *Fax (020) 8292 2092*
☆ – ☰. VISA
closed 25-26 December and 1-2 January – **Meals** - Italian - a la carte 18.95/
24.00 ♀.
♦ Light room with tiled flooring and large paintings, nestling behind a busy
front bar. Italian menu with blackboard daily specials. Efficient and obliging
service.

✕ **Bistro Aix** 3 EU **v**
54 Topsfield Parade, Tottenham Lane, N8 8PT, ☏ (020) 8340 6346
ⓜⓢ AE ⓞ VISA
closed 25 December and Monday – **Meals** a la carte 15.50/28.50.
♦ The simple wood furniture is complemented by plants and pictures. The
owner chef's experience in France is reflected in the menu and the robust
and hearty cooking.

HARROW *Gtr London.*

Harrow Weald *Middx* – ✉ *Middx.*

🏨 **Grim's Dyke** 1 BT **a**
Old Redding, HA3 6SH, ☏ (020) 8385 3100, *reservations@grimsdyke.com*,
Fax (020) 8954 4560
�, 🛋 – ⅙ ✕ rm, TV P – 🛋 100. ⓜⓢ AE ⓞ VISA
Gilberts : **Meals** *closed Saturday lunch* 24.50 and a la carte 29.50/40.50 ♀ –
44 rm ☲ 125.00/170.00.
♦ Victorian mansion, former country residence of W.S.Gilbert. Rooms divided between main house and lodge, the former more characterful. Over 40
acres of garden and woodland. Restaurant with ornately carved fireplace.

Kenton *Middx* – ✉ *Middx.*

🏨 **Travel Inn Metro** 1 BU **e**
Kenton Rd, HA3 8AT, ☏ (020) 8907 4069, *Fax (020) 8909 1604*
🛗, ⅙ ✕ rm, TV 🛠 P. ⓜⓢ AE ⓞ VISA. ⅍
Meals (grill rest.) – **70 rm** 54.95.
♦ Lodge hotel providing clean, comfortable and affordable accommodation.
Adjacent Beefeater pub offers a menu specialising in popular grill-based
dishes.

Pinner *Middx* – ✉ *Middx.*

🍴🍴 Friends 1 BU **a**
11 High St, HA5 5PJ, ✆ (020) 8866 0286, *info@friendsrestaurant.co.uk,*
Fax (020) 8866 0286
🍴✕ ▤, 🆖 AE ① VISA JCB
closed Sunday dinner, Monday and Bank Holidays – **Meals** 17.50/26.50 ♀.
◆ Pretty beamed cottage, with some parts dating back 400 years. Inside, a welcoming glow from the log fire; personal service from owners and a fresh, regularly-changing menu.

HAVERING *Gtr London.*

Romford *Essex* – ✉ *Essex.*

🏌18, 🏌9 *Risebridge, Risebridge Chase, Lower Bedfords Rd* ✆ (01708) 741429, **JT**.

🏛 Travel Inn Metro 4 JU **a**
Mercury Gdns, RM1 3EN, ✆ (01708) 760548, *Fax (01708) 760456*
⬗, 🍴✕ rm, 📺 ⅙ 🅿, 🆖 AE ① VISA
Meals (grill rest.) – **40 rm** 54.95.
◆ Clean and well-maintained lodge-style accommodation, with the nearby M25 providing easy road links. Adjacent pub-restaurant specialises in popular, grilled dishes.

In this guide
a symbol or a character,
printed in red or black, in light or bold type
does not have the same meaning.
Pay particular attention to the explanatory pages.

HILLINGDON *Gtr London.*

🏌18 *Haste Hill, The Drive, Northwood* ✆ (01923) 825224 **AU**.

Heathrow Airport *Middx.*

🏨 Radisson Edwardian 5 AX **e**
140 Bath Rd, Hayes, UB3 5AW, ✆ (020) 8759 6311, *resre@radisson.com,*
Fax (020) 8759 4559
🛐, 🈁 – ⬗, 🍴✕ rm, ▤ 📺 ✆ 🅿 – ♨ 550. 🆖 AE ① VISA JCB, ✀
Henleys : Meals *(closed Saturday-Sunday)* 25.00 and a la carte 33.00/41.00 **s.**
– ▭ 15.00 – **442 rm** 233.80/276.10, 17 suites.
◆ Capacious group hotel with a huge atrium over the leisure facilities. Plenty of comfortable lounges, well-appointed bedrooms and attentive service. Henleys boasts oil paintings and cocktail bar. Informal, slim leather-chaired Brasserie.

🏨 Crowne Plaza London Heathrow 1 AV **v**
Stockley Rd, West Drayton, UB7 9NA, ✆ (01895) 445555, *reservations.cplhr@ic hotelsgroup.com, Fax (01895) 445122*
🛐, 🈁, ⬛, 🏌9 – ⬗, 🍴✕ rm, ▤ 📺 ✆ ⅙ 🅿 – ♨ 200. 🆖 AE ① VISA JCB, ✀
Concha Grill : Meals 18.50/25.50 **s.** and a la carte ♀ – (see also **Simply Nico Heathrow** below) – ▭ 16.00 – **457 rm** 195.00, 1 suite.
◆ Extensive leisure, aromatherapy and beauty salons make this large hotel a popular stop-over for travellers. Club bedrooms are particularly well-equipped. Bright, breezy Concha Grill with juice bar.

London Heathrow Marriott

5   AX   Z

Bath Rd, Hayes, UB3 5AN, ℰ (020) 8990 1100, *reservations.heathrow@marriot thotels.co.uk, Fax (020) 8990 1110*

[⅃₆, ⇆s, 🔲 – ⬧, ⅄⇐ rm, 🖭 TV 📞 ⅃ 🅿 – 🥢 540. ⓂⓈ AE ⓞ VISA. ⚂]

Tuscany : **Meals** - Italian -*(closed Sunday)* (dinner only) a la carte 22.90/ 40.95 ⏃

Allie's grille : **Meals** a la carte 22.75/33.50 ⏃ – ⊆ 16.45 – **388 rm** 149.20/ 223.25, 2 suites.

♦ Built at the end of 20C, this modern, comfortable hotel is centred around a large atrium, with comprehensive business facilities: there is an exclusive Executive floor. Tuscany's is bright and convivial.

Sheraton Skyline

5   AX   u

Bath Rd, Hayes, UB3 5BP, ℰ (020) 8759 2535, *res268_skyline@sheraton.com, Fax (020) 8750 9150*

[⅃₆, 🔲 – ⬧ ⅄⇐ 🖭 TV 📞 ⅃ 🅿 – 🥢 500. ⓂⓈ AE ⓞ VISA JCB]

Sage : **Meals** a la carte 23.50/41.00 ⏃ – ⊆ 17.00 – **348 rm** 199.00, 2 suites.

♦ Well known for its unique indoor swimming pool surrounded by a tropical garden which is overlooked by many of the bedrooms. Business centre available. Classically decorated dining room.

Hilton London Heathrow Airport

5   AX   n

Terminal 4, TW6 3AF, ℰ (020) 8759 7755, *gm_heathrow@hilton.com, Fax (020) 8759 7579*

[⅃₆, ⇆s, 🔲 – ⬧, ⅄⇐ rm, 🖭 TV 📞 ⅃ 🅿 – 🥢 250. ⓂⓈ AE ⓞ VISA JCB]

Brasserie : **Meals** a la carte 23.40/42.95 **s.** ⏃

Zen Oriental : **Meals** - Chinese - a la carte 14.40/59.80 **s.** – ⊆ 18.50 – **390 rm** 229.12, 5 suites.

♦ Group hotel with a striking modern exterior and linked to Terminal 4 by a covered walkway. Good sized bedrooms, with contemporary styled suites. Spacious Brasserie in vast atrium. Zen Oriental offers formal Chinese experience.

Holiday Inn London Heathrow

1   AV   C

Sipson Rd, West Drayton, UB7 0JU, ℰ (0870) 4008595, *rmheathrowm4@ichot elsgroup.com, Fax (020) 8897 8659*

[⅃₆ – ⬧, ⅄⇐ rm, 🖭 TV 📞 ⅃ 🅿 – 🥢 140. ⓂⓈ AE ⓞ VISA JCB. ⚂]

Sampans : **Meals** - Asian - *(closed Sunday dinner)* (dinner only) 18.95/29.95 and a la carte 22.90/35.45

Rotisserie : **Meals** (buffet meals) 15.95/19.50 **s.** – ⊆ 15.00 – **610 rm** 179.00, 4 suites.

♦ Busy group hotel where the Academy conference suite attracts the business community. Bedrooms come in a variety of styles. Popular Irish bar. Sampans offers regional Chinese dishes. Spacious Rotisserie with chef carving to order. Pizzas and pasta at Fresca.

Renaissance London Heathrow

5   AX   C

Bath Rd, TW6 2AQ, ℰ (020) 8897 6363, *lhrrenaissance@aol.com, Fax (020) 8897 1113*

[⅃₆, ⇆s – ⬧, ⅄⇐ rm, 🖭 TV 📞 ⅃ 🅿 – 🥢 520. ⓂⓈ AE ⓞ VISA. ⚂]

Meals 18.50/22.00 and a la carte 20.00/38.50 **s.** ⏃ – ⊆ 15.95 – **643 rm** 139.00, 6 suites.

♦ Low level façade belies the size of this easily accessible hotel. Large lounge and assorted shops in the lobby. Some of the soundproofed bedrooms have views of the runway. Open-plan restaurant with buffet or à la carte.

🏨 **Holiday Inn Heathrow Ariel** 5 AX **i**
118 Bath Rd, Hayes, UB3 5AJ, ℘ (0870) 400 9040, *reservations-heathrow@ich otelsgroup.com, Fax (020) 8564 9265*
|⇕|, ⇔ rm, ▤ rest, 📺 ✆ 🅿 – 🛁 55. 🆖 🆎 ⓪ 𝘝𝘐𝘚𝘈
Meals (bar lunch Saturday) (buffet lunch) a la carte 17.15/29.15 **s.** – ⊆ 14.95 –
186 rm 159.00.
◆ Usefully located hotel in a cylindrical shape. Modern bedrooms with warm colours. Third floor executive rooms particularly impressive. Conference rooms available. Subtly-lit, relaxing restaurant.

🏨 **Travel Inn Heathrow Capital** 5 AX **x**
15 Bath Rd, TW6 2AB, ℘ (0870) 6075075, *Fax (0870) 2419000*
|⇕|, ⇔ rm, ▤ 📺 ✆ & 🅿 – 🛁 30. 🆖 🆎 ⓪ 𝘝𝘐𝘚𝘈 𝐉𝐂𝐁. ✼
Meals (grill rest.) – **590 rm** 69.95.
◆ Well-priced Travel Inn with modern, wood-panelled exterior and huge atrium. Well-equipped meeting rooms. Bedrooms are of good quality with triple glazing. Bright, airy, informal grill restaurant.

🍴🍴 **Simply Nico Heathrow** (at Crowne Plaza London Heathrow H.) 5 AV **v**
Stockley Rd, West Drayton, UB7 9NA, ℘ (01895) 437564, *heathrow.simplynico @corushotels.com, Fax (01895) 437565* – ▤ 🅿. 🆖 🆎 ⓪ 𝘝𝘐𝘚𝘈
closed Saturday lunch and Sunday – **Meals** a la carte 25.00/42.90 �.
◆ Located within the hotel but with its own personality. Mixes modern with more classically French dishes. Professional service in comfortable surroundings.

Ickenham *Middx.*

🍴 **Jospens** 8 AU **a**
15 Long Lane, UB10 8QU, ℘ (01895) 632519, *Fax (01895) 272284*
▤. 🆖 🆎 ⓪ 𝘝𝘐𝘚𝘈
closed 25-26 December, 1 week January, 1 week July and Sunday and Monday – **Meals** 13.50 (lunch) and a la carte 23.50/29.00.
◆ Neighbourhood restaurant with window boxes, set amidst neat, trimmed trees. Smart interior boasts deep lilac ceiling. Simple, well executed dishes with modern influences.

HOUNSLOW *Gtr London.*

🏌18 *Wyke Green, Syon Lane, Isleworth* ℘ (020) 8560 8777 **BV** – 🏌 *Airlinks, Southall Lane* ℘ (020) 8561 1418 **ABV** – 🏌 *Hounslow Heath, Staines Rd* ℘ (020) 8570 5271 **BX**.
🅳 *24 The Treaty Centre, High St* ℘ (020) 8572 8279 (closed Sunday).

Chiswick *Middx* – ✉ *W4.*

🍴🍴 **La Trompette** 21 KZG **y**
5-7 Devonshire Rd, W4 2EU, ℘ (020) 8747 1836, *latrompette@btconnect.com, Fax (020) 8995 8097*
� – ▤. 🆖 🆎 𝘝𝘐𝘚𝘈
closed 24-26 December – **Meals** 21.50/30.00 �.
◆ Terraced property on smart residential street. Open-plan restaurant with linen laid tables and a bustling atmosphere. Daily menus of French influenced robust modern dishes.

🍴 **Fish Hoek** 21 KZG **r**
W4 1PE, ℘ (020) 8742 0766, *info@fishhoek.co.uk, Fax (020) 8742 3374*
🆖 𝘝𝘐𝘚𝘈
closed 22 December-6 January and Monday – **Meals** - Seafood - a la carte 21.00/50.50 �.
◆ Smart interior with tiled floor and fishing photos on the walls. Menu offers a wide selection of seafood from around the world, prepared with care and competence.

Fishworks
21 KZG **X**

6 Turnham Green Terr, W4 1QP, ℰ (020) 8994 0086

☆ – ✂. ⓪⑩ ᴀᴇ 𝙑𝙄𝙎𝘼

closed Sunday except lunch in summer, Christmas, Bank Holidays, Tuesday following Bank Holidays and Monday – **Meals** - Seafood - (booking essential) a la carte 21.20/37.70 ℤ.

◆ Well-run branded restaurant opening onto delightful rear terrace with olive trees. Daily blackboard menu of grills and popular seafood dishes.

Pug
21 KZG **n**

68 Chiswick High Rd, W4 1SY, ℰ (020) 8987 9988, *Fax (020) 8987 9911*

☆ – ▤. ⓪⑩ ᴀᴇ 𝙑𝙄𝙎𝘼

Meals 9.95 and a la carte 21.50/24.00 ℤ.

◆ Wood-floored restaurant with simple décor and dark wood tables, adjoins leather furnished bar and lounge area. Daily changing modern menus with Mediterranean influences.

The Devonshire House
21 KZG **a**

126 Devonshire Rd, W4 2JJ, ℰ (020) 8987 2626, *Fax (020) 8995 0152*

☆ –⓪⑩ ᴀᴇ 𝙑𝙄𝙎𝘼

closed Monday lunch – **Meals** 17.85 (lunch) and dinner a la carte 17.95/27.70 ℤ.

◆ Period pub conversion retaining original features. Leather banquettes and chairs; bare tables. Daily menu of modern cooking, slightly simpler at lunchtime. Attentive service.

The Bollo
6 CV. **Z**

13-15 Bollo Lane, W4 5LS, ℰ (020) 8994 6037, *Fax (020) 8995 9854*

☆ –⓪⑩ ᴀᴇ 𝙑𝙄𝙎𝘼

closed 25 December – **Meals** 14.50 (lunch) and a la carte 19.50/28.50 ℤ.

◆ Attractive period brick pub with dining area under a domed glass rotunda. Daily changing menu - mixture of traditional and eclectic dishes - served throughout the pub.

ISLINGTON *Gtr London.*

Archway – ✉ N19.

The Parsee
3 EU **a**

34 Highgate Hill, N19 5NL, ℰ (020) 7272 9091, *dining@theparsee.co.uk, Fax (020) 7687 1139*

▤. ⓪⑩ ᴀᴇ ⓪ 𝙑𝙄𝙎𝘼 ᴊᴄʙ

closed 25 December-1 January and Sunday – **Meals** - Indian (Parsee) - (dinner only) a la carte 19.40/22.70 ℤ.

◆ Two brightly painted rooms, one non smoking and featuring a painting of a Parsee Angel. Good value, interesting, carefully spiced cuisine, Persian and Indian in inspiration.

St John's
12 RZA **S**

91 Junction Rd, N19 5QU, ℰ (020) 7272 1587, *stjohnsarchway@virgin.net, Fax (020) 7687 2247*

⓪⑩ ᴀᴇ 𝙑𝙄𝙎𝘼

closed 25-26 December and Monday lunch – **Meals** a la carte 15.50/25.00 ℤ.

◆ Busy front bar enjoys a lively atmosphere; dining room in a large rear room. Log fire at one end, open hatch into kitchen the other. Blackboard menu; rustic cooking.

Barnsbury *Gtr London* – ⊠ *N1.*

XX **Morgan M** 13 UZA **a**
489 Liverpool Rd, N7 8NS, ℰ (020) 7609 3560, *Fax (020) 8292 5699*
✻⊁ ▤. ◍◍ ⓪ *VISA*
closed 24-30 December, Saturday lunch, Sunday dinner and Monday – **Meals**
19.50/27.50 ⚍.
♦ Simple restaurant in a converted pub. Smartly-laid tables complemented
by formal service. Modern dishes based on classical French combinations.

X **The Dining Room** 13 UZB **a**
169 Hemingford Rd, N1 1DA, ℰ (020) 7609 3009
✿ –◍◍ *VISA*
closed 1 week Christmas, last 2 weeks August, Sunday dinner and Monday –
Meals *(dinner only and Sunday lunch)* a la carte 20.50/24.00 ⚍.
♦ Simple, attractive and cosy neighbourhood restaurant with fawn colours
and mirrors. Open hatch into kitchen. Asian-influenced cooking at a fair
price.

Canonbury *Gtr London* – ⊠ *N1.*

🏠 **Centuria** 13 VZB **V**
100 St Paul's Rd, N1 2QP, ℰ (020) 7704 2345, *Fax (020) 7704 2204*
◍◍ *VISA*
closed lunch Monday-Friday – **Meals** a la carte 20.25/23.50 ⚍.
♦ Large pub in a residential area, with the dining room separate from the
busy bar. Open-plan kitchen produces a modern menu, with influences ranging from Italy to Morocco.

Clerkenwell *Gtr London* – ⊠ *EC1.*

🏛 **The Rookery** 33 AOT **p**
12 Peters Lane, Cowcross St, EC1M 6DS, ℰ (020) 7336 0931, *reservations@roo
kery.co.uk, Fax (020) 7336 0932*
without rest. – ✻⊁ 📺 📞. ◍◍ ᴀᴇ ⓪ *VISA* ᴊᴄʙ. ✿
closed 24-26 December – ⚌ 9.75 **32 rm** 252.60/323.10, 1 suite.
♦ A row of charmingly restored 18C houses. Wood panelling, stone-flagged
flooring, open fires and antique furniture. Highly individual bedrooms, with
Victorian bathrooms.

XX **Smiths of Smithfield** 33 AOT **S**
Top Floor, 67-77 Charterhouse St, EC1M 6HJ, ℰ (020) 7251 7950, *smiths@smit
hfield.co.uk, Fax (020) 7236 5666*
≼, ✿ – 📶 ▤. ◍◍ ᴀᴇ ⓪ *VISA*
closed 25-26 December and 1 January – **Meals** a la carte 19.25/24.25 ⚍:
The Dining Room : **Meals** *(closed Saturday lunch, Sunday and Bank Holidays)*
a la carte 20.75/25.25 ⚍.
♦ On three floors where the higher you go the more formal it becomes.
Busy, bustling atmosphere and modern menu. Good views of the market
from the top floor terrace. The Dining Room with mirrors and dark blue walls.

X **St John** 33 APT **C**
26 St John St, EC1M 4AY, ℰ (020) 7251 0848, *reservations@stjohnrestaurant.c
om, Fax (020) 7251 4090*
▤. ◍◍ ᴀᴇ ⓪ *VISA* ᴊᴄʙ
closed Christmas-New Year, Easter, Saturday lunch and Sunday – **Meals**
a la carte 24.90/28.00 ⚍.
♦ Deservedly busy converted 19C former smokehouse. Popular bar, simple
comforts. Menu specialises in offal and an original mix of traditional and
rediscovered English dishes.

Finsbury *Ctr London –* ✉ *WC1/EC1/EC2.*

XX **The Clerkenwell Dining Room**   19 UZD h
69-73 St John St, EC1M 4AN, ℰ (020) 7253 9000, *zak@theclerkenwell.com,*
Fax (020) 7253 3322
▤. ⓜⓞ ⒜⒠ ⓞ *VISA* ⒿⒸⒷ
closed 25-26 December, 1 January, Saturday lunch and Sunday – **Meals** 16.00
(lunch) and a la carte 26.75/30.75 ♀.

* Former pub, now a stylish modern restaurant with etched glass façade.
Three adjoining dining areas with bar provide setting for contemporary British cooking.

X **Café Lazeez City**   19 UZD r
88 St John St, EC1M 4EH, ℰ (020) 7253 2224, *clerkenwell@cafelazeez.com,*
Fax (020) 7253 2112
▤. ⓜⓞ ⒜⒠ ⓞ *VISA*
closed Saturday lunch, Sunday and Bank Holidays – **Meals** - North Indian -
a la carte approx. 18.00 ⓥⓖ.

* Past the busy bar into this modern Indian restaurant. Has a certain warehouse feel, with a high ceiling and wood flooring. North Indian cooking from
the open-plan kitchen.

X **Quality Chop House**   19 UZD n
94 Farringdon Rd, EC1R 3EA, ℰ (020) 7837 5093, *qualitychophouse@clara.co.*
uk, Fax (020) 7833 8748
⚡╪ ▤. ⓜⓞ ⒜⒠ *VISA*
closed 24 December-1 January and Saturday lunch – **Meals** a la carte 17.75/
28.00.

* On the window is etched "Progressive working class caterers". This is borne
out with the individual café-style booths and a menu ranging from jellied eels
to caviar.

X **Moro**   19 UZD b
34-36 Exmouth Market, EC1R 4QE, ℰ (020) 7833 8336, *info@moro.co.uk,*
Fax (020) 7833 9338
▤. ⓜⓞ ⒜⒠ ⓞ *VISA* ⒿⒸⒷ
closed 2 weeks Christmas, Saturday lunch, Sunday and Bank Holidays – **Meals**
(booking essential) a la carte 25.50/28.00 ⓥⓖ ♀.

* Daily changing menu an eclectic mix of Mediterranean, Moroccan and
Spanish. Friendly T-shirted staff. Informal surroundings with bare tables and a
large zinc bar.

🛏 **The Peasant**   19 UZD e
240 St John St, EC1V 4PH, ℰ (020) 7336 7726, *eat@thepeasant.co.uk,*
Fax (020) 7490 1089
ⓜⓞ ⒜⒠ *VISA*
closed 1 week after Christmas, Saturday lunch and Sunday – **Meals** (booking
essential) a la carte 21.00/27.00 ♀.

* Large, busy pub with half of the ground floor given over as a bar. Dining
continues in the high-ceilinged room upstairs. Robust and rustic cooking
with generous portions.

Highbury *Ctr London –* ✉ *N5.*

X **Au Lac**   13 VZA a
82 Highbury Park, N5 2XE, ℰ (020) 7704 9187, *Fax (0207) 704 9187*
▤. ⓜⓞ ⓞ *VISA*
closed lunch Saturday, Sunday and Bank Holidays – **Meals** - Vietnamese -
16.00 and a la carte 8.20/20.00.

* Cosy Vietnamese restaurant, with brightly coloured walls and painted fans.
Large menus with authentic dishes usefully highlighted. Fresh flavours; good
value.

Islington *Ctr London –* ⊠ *N1.*

🏨 **Hilton London Islington** 13 UZB **s**
53 Upper St, N1 0UY, ℘ (020) 7354 7700, *res_islington@hilton.com,* *Fax (020) 7354 7711*
🛎, ƒ₅, ⊜s – 🛗, ⇔ rm, 🖵 📺 ℂ & – 🛗 35. 🅼🅾 🄰🄴 🅾 *VISA* 🄹🄲🄱. ✳
Meals a la carte 22.90/31.65 **s.** ⊊ – ⊊ 16.00 – **178 rm** 186.80, 6 suites.
♦ Benefits from its location adjacent to the Business Design Centre. A purpose-built hotel with all bedrooms enjoying the appropriate creature comforts. Open-plan brasserie with small bar.

🏨 **Jurys Inn London** 13 UZB **g**
60 Pentonville Rd, N1 9LA, ℘ (020) 7282 5500, *jurysinnlondon@jurysdoyle.com, Fax (020) 7282 5511*
🛗, ⇔ rm, 🖵 📺 ℂ & – 🛗 55. 🅼🅾 🄰🄴 🅾 *VISA*. ✳
closed 24-26 December – **Meals** (bar lunch)/dinner 18.00 **s.** and a la carte – ⊊ 8.50 – **229 rm** 104.00.
♦ A corporate group hotel with good local transport links. Large lobby leads off the characterful Irish themed pub. Uniform-sized bedrooms, all well-equipped.

🍴🍴 **Lola's** 13 UZB **n**
The Mall, 359 Upper St, N1 0PD, ℘ (020) 7359 1932, *lolas@lolas.co.uk, Fax (020) 7359 2209*
🖵. 🅼🅾 🄰🄴 🅾 *VISA*
closed 25-26 December and 1 January – **Meals** 18.75 (lunch) and a la carte 27.75/37.00 ⊊.
♦ On the first floor of a converted tram shed above the antique shops. Bright and airy, with glass ceiling and assorted artwork: an ideal setting to enjoy modern British dishes.

🍴🍴 **Frederick's** 13 UZB **c**
Camden Passage, N1 8EG, ℘ (020) 7359 2888, *eat@fredericks.co.uk, Fax (020) 7359 5173*
🛎, 🌿 – 🖵. 🅼🅾 🄰🄴 *VISA* 🄹🄲🄱
closed 24 December-2 January, Sunday and Bank Holidays – **Meals** 15.50 (lunch) and a la carte 23.50/34.50 ⊊.
♦ Long-standing restaurant among the antique shops of Camden Passage. Attractive garden and al fresco dining; main room with large, plant-filled conservatory.

🍴🍴 **Almeida** 13 UZB **r**
30 Almeida St, N1 1AD, ℘ (020) 7354 4777, *oliviere@conran-restaurants.co.uk, Fax (020) 7354 2777*
🖵. 🅼🅾 🄰🄴 🅾 *VISA* 🄹🄲🄱
closed 25-26 December and 1-2 January – **Meals** - French - 17.50 (lunch) and a la carte 19.50/37.50 ⊛ ⊊.
♦ Spacious, open plan restaurant with pleasant contemporary styling adjacent to Almeida Theatre. Large à la carte: a collection of classic French dishes.

🍴🍴 **Metrogusto** 13 UZB **e**
🔗 13 Theberton St, N1 0QY, ℘ (020) 7226 9400, *Fax (020) 7226 9400*
⇔ 🖵. 🅼🅾 🄰🄴 *VISA* 🄹🄲🄱
closed Christmas, Bank Holidays and lunch Monday-Thursday – **Meals** - Italian - 18.50 (lunch) and a la carte 22.50/28.50 ⊛ ⊊.
♦ Stylish and smart with a contemporary feel. Dining in two rooms with striking modern art on the walls and a relaxed atmosphere. Modern, carefully prepared Italian food.

🏨 **Drapers Arms**   13 UZB X
44 Barnsbury St, N1 1ER, ℘ (020) 7619 0348, *Fax (020) 7619 0413*
🛋 –📶⑤ **VISA**
closed 26-28 December, 1-2 January and Sunday dinner – **Meals** a la carte
18.50/29.00 ♀.
◆ Real presence to the the façade of this Georgian pub tucked away in a
quiet residential area. Spacious modern interior where competent, contemporary dishes are served.

🏨 **The Northgate**   13 VZB a
113 Southgate Rd, N1 3JS, ℘ (020) 7359 7392, *Fax (020) 7359 7393*
🛋 –📶⑤ **VISA** **JCB**
closed 24-26 December and 1 January – **Meals** (dinner only and lunch Saturday and Sunday) a la carte 20.00/25.00 ♀.
◆ Corner pub with wood flooring and modern art on display. Rear dining
area with a large blackboard menu offering a cross section of internationally
influenced modern dishes.

🏨 **The Social**   13 VZB C
33 Linton St, N1 7DU, ℘ (020) 7354 5809, *Fax (020) 7354 8087*
📶⑤ **AE** **VISA** **JCB**
closed 25-31 December and lunch Monday-Friday – **Meals** (booking essential)
a la carte 15.50/25.00.
◆ The former Hanbury Arms has a youthful clientele attracted by the DJ and
music in the bar. The open plan kitchen and restaurant serve from a modern,
sensibly priced menu.

🏨 **The Barnsbury**   13 UZB V
209-211 Liverpool Rd, N1 1LX, ℘ (020) 7607 5519, *info@thebarnsbury.co.uk,*
Fax (020) 7607 3256
🛋 –📶⑤ **VISA**
closed 25-26 December and 1 January – **Meals** a la carte 17.50/26.45 ♀.
◆ Former public house with pine tables and chairs arranged round central
counter bar; art work for sale on the walls. Robust and hearty food in
generous portions.

KENSINGTON and CHELSEA (Royal Borough of) *Gtr London.*

Chelsea *Gtr London –* ✉ *SW1/SW3/SW10.*

🏨🏨🏨 **The Carlton Tower**   37 AGX n
Cadogan Pl, SW1X 9PY, ℘ (020) 7235 1234, *contact@carltontower.com,*
Fax (020) 7235 9129
≤, 🝙, ⇔s, 🔲, 🌡, ✍ – 🛗, ✟ rm, 🖩 📺 ✆ ⅙ ⇔ – 🔏 400. 📶⑤ **AE** ⓪
VISA. ✍
Rib Room *:* **Meals** 26.00 (lunch) and a la carte 38.00/61.00 ♀ – ⇆ 22.50 –
190 rm 381.80, 30 suites.
◆ Imposing international hotel overlooking a leafy square. 'The Peak' health
club is particularly well-equipped. Generously proportioned rooms have every
conceivable facility. Rib Room restaurant has a clubby atmosphere.

🏨🏨 **Conrad London**   23 PZG j
Chelsea Harbour, SW10 0XG, ℘ (020) 7823 3000, *lonch_rs@hilton.com,*
Fax (020) 7351 6525
≤, 🝙, ⇔s, 🔲 – 🛗, ✟ rm, 🖩 📺 ✆ ⅙ ⇔ – 🔏 250. 📶⑤ **AE** ⓪ **VISA** **JCB**
Meals – (see *Aquasia* below) – ⇆ 18.75, **160 suites** 229.00/259.00.
◆ Modern, all-suite hotel within an exclusive marina and retail development.
Many of the spacious and well-appointed rooms have balconies and views
across the Thames.

Sheraton Park Tower
37 AGX t
101 Knightsbridge, SW1X 7RN, ℘ (020) 7235 8050, *central.london.reservations@sheraton.com, Fax (020) 7235 8231*
≼, ₤₆ – |≣|, ✦ rm, 🖳 📺 ℃ ⅍ ⟺ – ♨ 100. 🆗 AE ⓪ VISA JCB, ✷
Meals – (see *One-O-One* below) – ⊑ 20.75 – **258 rm** 446.50/470.00, 22 suites.
♦ Built in the 1970s in a unique cylindrical shape. Well-equipped bedrooms are all identical in size. Top floor executive rooms have commanding views of Hyde Park and City.

Capital
37 AFX a
⁂⁂ 22-24 Basil St, SW3 1AT, ℘ (020) 7589 5171, *reservations@capitalhotel.co.uk, Fax (020) 7225 0011*
|≣|, ✦ rm, 🖳 📺 ℃ ⟺ – ♨ 25. 🆗 AE ⓪ VISA JCB
Meals (booking essential) 28.50/55.00 ♀ – ⊑ 16.50 – **48 rm** 223.25/440.00.
♦ Discreet and privately owned town house with distinct English charm. Individual, opulently decorated rooms with plenty of thoughtful touches. Elegant and intimate restaurant.
Spec. Seared tiger prawns, scallops and calamari. Pot-roast pigeon, potato and bacon galette, truffle jus. Apple consommé with liquorice ravioli and gingerbread.

The Cadogan
37 AGY b
75 Sloane St, SW1X 9SG, ℘ (020) 7235 7141, *info@cadogan.com, Fax (020) 7245 0994*
🚗, ✸ – |≣|, ✦ rm, 🖳 rest, 📺 ℃ – ♨ 40. 🆗 AE ⓪ VISA JCB
Meals *(closed Saturday lunch)* 18.90/29.50 **s.** ♀ – ⊑ 16.50 – **61 rm** 170.30/346.60, 4 suites.
♦ A true English hotel retaining many Edwardian features: Oscar Wilde was arrested here! Charming wood panelled drawing room. Smart bedrooms in a country house style. Discreet, cosy wood panelled restaurant.

Basil Street
37 AGX d
8 Basil St, SW3 1AH, ℘ (020) 7581 3311, *info@thebasil.com, Fax (020) 7581 3693*
|≣|, ✦ rm, 📺 ℃ – ♨ 30. 🆗 AE ⓪ VISA JCB, ✷
Meals 22.00/27.00 **s.** – ⊑ 16.50 – **80 rm** 170.30/240.80.
♦ Classic English hotel in a pleasant residential road between Harrods and Harvey Nichols. Exclusive ladies only lounge. Traditionally furnished rooms with modern amenities. Dining room boasts rich style of a bygone era.

Draycott
37 AGY c
26 Cadogan Gdns, SW3 2RP, ℘ (020) 7730 6466, *reservations@draycotthotel.com, Fax (020) 7730 0236*
🚗 – |≣| ✦, 🖳 rm, 📺 ℃. 🆗 AE ⓪ VISA
Meals (room service only) – ⊑ 18.50 – **31 rm** 129.25/340.75, 4 suites.
♦ Charming Victorian house in an exclusive residential area. Elegant sitting room overlooks the tranquil communal garden. Individually decorated rooms in a country house style.

Millennium Knightsbridge
37 AGX r
17-25 Sloane St, SW1X 9NU, ℘ (020) 7235 4377, *reservations.knightsbridge@mill-cop.com, Fax (020) 7235 3705*
|≣| ✦ 🖳 📺 ⅍ – ♨ 120. 🆗 AE ⓪ VISA JCB, ✷
Meals – (see *Mju* below) – ⊑ 19.00 – **218 rm** 270.25/329.00, 4 suites.
♦ Modern, corporate hotel in the heart of London's most fashionable shopping district. Executive bedrooms are well-appointed and equipped with the latest technology.

Franklin
37 AEY e

22-28 Egerton Gdns, SW3 2DB, ☎ (020) 7584 5533, *bookings@franklinhotel.co.uk, Fax (020) 7584 5449*

🚗 – 🛗 ⊁ 🗐 TV 📞 🐶 AE ⓪ VISA. ⅍

Meals 29.50 (dinner) and a la carte 23.00/34.50 **s.** ♀ – ⬜ 16.50 – **47 rm** 188.00/293.75.

◆ Attractive Victorian town house in an exclusive residential area. Charming drawing room overlooks a tranquil communal garden. Well-furnished rooms in a country house style.

Knightsbridge
37 AFX s

10 Beaufort Gdns, SW3 1PT, ☎ (020) 7584 6300, *knightsbridge@firmdale.com, Fax (020) 7584 6355*

🛗 🗐 TV 📞 🐶 AE VISA. ⅍

Meals (room service only) – ⬜ 14.50 – **44 rm** 170.30/300.00.

◆ Attractively furnished town house with a very stylish, discreet feel. Every bedroom is immaculately appointed and has an individuality of its own; fine detailing throughout.

The London Outpost of the Carnegie Club
37 AGY r

69 Cadogan Gdns, SW3 2RB, ☎ (020) 7589 7333, *info@londonoutpost.co.uk, Fax (020) 7581 4958*

without rest., 🚗 – 🛗 ⊁ 🗐 TV. 🐶 AE ⓪ VISA JCB – ⬜ 16.95 – **11 rm** 188.00/317.25.

◆ Classic town house in a most fashionable area. Relaxed and comfy lounges full of English charm. Bedrooms, named after local artists and writers, full of thoughtful touches.

The Sloane
37 AFY c

29-31 Draycott Pl, SW3 2SH, ☎ (020) 7581 5757, *reservations@sloanehotel.com, Fax (020) 7584 1348*

🛗 ⊁ rm, 🗐 TV 📞 🐶 AE ⓪ VISA JCB. ⅍

Meals (room service) – ⬜ 12.00 – **22 rm** 193.80/293.70.

◆ Intimate and discreet Victorian town house with an attractive rooftop terrace. Individually styled and generally spacious rooms with antique furniture and rich fabrics.

Eleven Cadogan Gardens
37 AGY u

11 Cadogan Gdns, SW3 2RJ, ☎ (020) 7730 7000, *reservations@number-eleven.co.uk, Fax (020) 7730 5217*

🛋, 🚠, 🚗 – 🛗 TV 📞 🐶 AE ⓪ VISA JCB. ⅍

Meals a la carte 21.50/31.50 – ⬜ 13.00 – **55 rm** 145.00/295.00, 4 suites.

◆ Occupying four Victorian houses, one of London's first private town house hotels. Traditionally appointed bedrooms vary considerably in size. Genteel atmosphere.

Egerton House
37 AFY y

17-19 Egerton Terrace, SW3 2BX, ☎ (020) 7589 2412, *bookings@egertonhousehotel.co.uk, Fax (020) 7584 6540*

🛗 ⊁ 🗐 TV 📞 🐶 AE ⓪ VISA JCB. ⅍

Meals (room service only) – ⬜ 16.00 – **29 rm** 188.00/293.75.

◆ Stylish redbrick Victorian town house close to the exclusive shops. Relaxed drawing room popular for afternoon tea. Antique furnished and individually decorated rooms.

🏨 **Beaufort**   37 AFX **n**
33 Beaufort Gdns, SW3 1PP, ℰ (020) 7584 5252, *enquiries@thebeaufort.co.uk,*
Fax (020) 7589 2834
without rest. – 🛗 ⇤ 🖭 📺 📞 . 🆓 AE ① VISA JCB . ⚘
29 rm 182.00/305.50.
   ◆ English floral watercolours adorn the walls throughout this elegant Victorian town house. Modern and co-ordinated rooms. Tariff includes all drinks and continental breakfast.

🏨 **Parkes**   37 AFX **X**
41 Beaufort Gdns, SW3 1PW, ℰ (020) 7581 9944, *reception@parkeshotel.com,*
Fax (020) 7581 1999
without rest. – 🛗 🖭 📺 📞 . 🆓 AE ① VISA JCB . ⚘ – ⬛ 10.00 – **19 rm**
229.00/282.00, 14 suites 381.00/487.00.
   ◆ Behind the portico entrance one finds a well-kept private hotel. The generally spacious and high ceilinged rooms are pleasantly decorated. Friendly and personally run.

🏨 **Myhotel Chelsea**   37 AFY **Z**
35 Ixworth Pl, SW3 3QX, ℰ (020) 7225 7500, *mychelsea@myhotel.co.uk,*
Fax (020) 7225 7555
ʃ๑ – 🛗 🖭 📺 📞 – 🏋 60. 🆓 AE ① VISA JCB
Meals a la carte 21.00/25.00 – ⬛ 16.00 – **43 rm** 205.60/240.87, 2 suites.
   ◆ Restored Victorian property in a fairly quiet and smart side street. Conservatory breakfast room. Modern and well-equipped rooms are ideal for the corporate traveller.

🏨 **Sydney House**   36 ADY **S**
9-11 Sydney St, SW3 6PU, ℰ (020) 7376 7711, *info@sydneyhousechelsea.com,*
Fax (020) 7376 4233
🛗 ⇤ 🖭 📺 📞 . 🆓 AE ① VISA JCB . ⚘
Meals (room service only) – ⬛ 12.00 – **21 rm** 175.00/250.00.
   ◆ Two usefully located Victorian town houses. Basement breakfast room; small lounge near entrance. Compact contemporary style bedrooms; one on top floor with own roof terrace.

🏨 **57 Pont Street**   37 AFY **a**
57 Pont St, SW1X 0BD, ℰ (020) 7590 1090, *no57@no57.com,*
Fax (020) 7590 1099
without rest. – 🛗 ⇤ 🖭 📺 📞 – 🏋 30. 🆓 AE ① VISA JCB . ⚘
closed 24 December-1 January – ⬛ 10.00 – **20 rm** 146.00/264.00.
   ◆ Small, friendly, modern townhouse with discreet plaque at the end of Pont Street. Basement breakfast room and sitting room with deep brown suede chairs. Snug, modern rooms.

🏨 **L'Hotel**   37 AFX **b**
28 Basil St, SW3 1AS, ℰ (020) 7589 6286, *reservations@lhotel.co.uk,*
Fax (020) 7823 7826
🛗 , ▤ rest, 📺 ➡ . 🆓 AE ① VISA JCB . ⚘
Le Metro : **Meals** *(closed Sunday dinner)* a la carte 19.50/21.50 ⬛ – **12 rm**
116.30/188.00.
   ◆ Discreet town house a short walk from Harrods. Wooden shutters, pine furniture and stencilled walls provide a subtle rural theme. Well-appointed, comfy and informally run. Basement café dining.

XXXX ఊఊఊఊ
ఴఴఴ **Gordon Ramsay** 37 AFZ **C**

68-69 Royal Hospital Rd, SW3 4HP, ℘ (020) 7352 4441, *Fax (020) 7352 3334*

▤. ⬛Ⓢ ᴀᴇ ⓞ *VISA* ᴊᴄв

closed 2 week Christmas, Saturday, Sunday and Bank Holidays – **Meals** (booking essential) 35.00/65.00 ♀.

◆ Elegant and sophisticated room. The eponymous chef creates some of Britain's finest, classically inspired cooking. Detailed and attentive service. Book one month in advance.

Spec. Caramelised pig's trotter with veal sweetbreads and celeriac rémoulade. Fillet of sea bass, crushed new potatoes and sautéed langoustine. Chocolate and hazelnut soufflé, milk ice cream.

XXX ఊఊఊ
ఴ **Aubergine** 36 ACZ **ᴦ**

11 Park Walk, SW10 0AJ, ℘ (020) 7352 3449, *Fax (020) 7351 1770*

▤. ⬛Ⓢ ᴀᴇ ⓞ *VISA*

closed 24 December-2 January, Saturday lunch, Sunday and Bank Holidays – **Meals** (booking essential) 32.00/50.00 ♀.

◆ Intimate, refined restaurant where the keen staff provide well drilled service. French influenced menu uses top quality ingredients with skill and flair. Extensive wine list.

Spec. Galette of pig's head with langoustine. Veal sweetbread with artichoke, lemon and mustard cream. Warm cherries with beignet, vanilla ice cream.

XXX ఊఊఊ
ఴ **Tom Aikens** 37 AFY **n**

43 Elystan St, SW3 3NT, ℘ (020) 7584 2003, *info@tomaikens.co.uk, Fax (020) 7584 2001*

▤. ⬛Ⓢ ᴀᴇ *VISA* ᴊᴄв

closed 2 weeks August, 2 weeks Christmas-New Year, Saturday, Sunday and Bank Holidays – **Meals** 24.50/49.00 ♀.

◆ Smart restaurant; minimalist style decor with chic tableware. Highly original menu of individual and inventive dishes; smooth service. Book one month in advance.

Spec. Rabbit confit with carrot and Sauternes jelly. John Dory with langoustine beignet and apricot purée. Caramel parfait with almond mousse.

XXX ఊఊఊ
 Drones 37 AGX **C**

1 Pont St, SW1X 9EJ, ℘ (020) 7235 9555, *sales@whitestarline.org.uk, Fax (020) 7235 9566*

▤. ⬛Ⓢ ᴀᴇ ⓞ *VISA*

closed 1 January, dinner 25 December, Saturday lunch and Sunday dinner – **Meals** 17.95 (lunch) and a la carte 24.50/43.50 ♀.

◆ Smart exterior with etched plate-glass window. L-shaped interior with moody film star photos on walls. French and classically inspired tone to dishes.

XXX ఊఊఊ
 Bibendum 37 AEY **S**

Michelin House, 81 Fulham Rd, SW3 6RD, ℘ (020) 7581 5817, *manager@bibendum.co.uk, Fax (020) 7823 7925*

▤. ⬛Ⓢ ᴀᴇ ⓞ *VISA*

closed 25-26 December – **Meals** 25.00 (lunch) and dinner a la carte 32.50/46.50 ♀.

◆ A fine example of Art Nouveau architecture; a London landmark. 1st floor restaurant with striking stained glass 'Michelin Man'. Attentive service of modern British cooking.

XXX **Floriana** 37 AFX d
15 Beauchamp Pl, SW3 1NQ, ✆ (020) 7838 1500, *Fax (020) 7584 1464*
▤. MC AE ⓓ VISA JCB
closed 25-26 December, 1 January, Easter and Sunday – **Meals** - Italian - 19.50 (lunch) and a la carte 19.50/35.00 ♀.
◆ Behind the busy bar is a refined and contemporary restaurant. Approachable service of an elaborate, modern Italian menu. 1st floor room, with atrium roof, is more relaxing.

XXX **Fifth Floor** (at Harvey Nichols) 37 AGX s
Knightsbridge, SW1X 7RJ, ✆ (020) 7235 5250, *Fax (020) 7235 7856*
⇕ ▤. MC AE ⓓ VISA
closed 25-26 December, 1 January and Sunday dinner – **Meals** 25.00 (lunch) and dinner a la carte 29.00/42.50 ♀.
◆ Wander through this famous store or take the lift straight to the top floor. Chic restaurant with comfy tub chairs overlooks a busy bar and the impressive delicatessen.

XXX **One-O-One** (at Sheraton Park Tower H.) 37 AGX t
William St, SW1X 7RN, ✆ (020) 7290 7101, *Fax (020) 7235 6196*
▤. MC AE ⓓ VISA JCB
Meals - Seafood - 25.00 (lunch) and a la carte 39.50/55.50 ♀.
◆ Modern and very comfortable restaurant overlooking Knightsbridge decorated in cool blue tones. Predominantly seafood menu offers traditional and more adventurous dishes.

XXX **Toto's** 37 AFY x
Walton House, Walton St, SW3 2JH, ✆ (020) 7589 0075, *Fax (020) 7581 9668*
MC AE ⓓ VISA JCB
closed 3 days Christmas – **Meals** - Italian - a la carte 26.50/46.00 ♀.
◆ Converted mews house in tucked away location. Ornately decorated and bright restaurant with additional balcony area. Professional service of an extensive Italian menu.

XXX **Chutney Mary** 22 OZG v
535 King's Rd, SW10 0SZ, ✆ (020) 7351 3113, *mw@realindianfood.com, Fax (020) 7351 7694*
▤. MC AE ⓓ VISA
Meals - Indian - (dinner only and lunch Saturday and Sunday) 16.50 (lunch) and a la carte 23.00/44.50 ♀.
◆ Striking murals of British India adorn the walls of this forever popular restaurant. Extensive menu of specialities from all corners of India. Complementary wine list.

XX **Aquasia** (at Conrad London H.) 23 PZG j
Chelsea Harbour, SW10 0XG, ✆ (020) 7300 8443, *Fax (020) 7351 6525*
≤, 🏠 – ▤ P. MC AE ⓓ VISA JCB
closed Saturday lunch and Sunday dinner – **Meals** a la carte 25.00/40.00 ♀.
◆ Modern restaurant located within Conrad International hotel. Views over Chelsea Harbour. Cuisine captures the essence of the Mediterranean and Asia.

XX **Bluebird** 23 ZGP e
350 King's Rd, SW3 5UU, ✆ (020) 7559 1000, *Fax (020) 7559 1111*
⇕ ▤. MC AE ⓓ VISA
Meals a la carte 26.00/43.75 🎭 ♀.
◆ A foodstore, café and homeware shop also feature at this impressive skylit restaurant. Much of the modern British food is cooked in wood-fired ovens. Lively atmosphere.

XX **Poissonnerie de l'Avenue**   37 AFY u
82 Sloane Ave, SW3 3DZ, ℘ (020) 7589 2457, *info@poissonnerie.co.uk,*
Fax (020) 7581 3360
🍽️. ⓜⓢ ᴬᴱ ⓞ *VISA*
closed dinner 24 December-3 January, Sunday and Bank Holidays – **Meals** -
French Seafood - 22.00 (lunch) and a la carte 26.00/32.00.
♦ Long-established and under the same ownership since 1965. Spacious and
traditional French restaurant offering an extensive seafood menu. An institution favoured by locals.

XX **English Garden**   37 AFY y
10 Lincoln St, SW3 2TS, ℘ (020) 7584 7272, *Fax (020) 7584 1961*
🍽️. ⓜⓢ ᴬᴱ ⓞ *VISA* ᴶᶜᴮ
closed Monday lunch – **Meals** 19.50/30.00 ⚏.
♦ Attractive mid-19C house in a stylish residential area. Relaxed restaurant
with British slate covered walls. Conservatory to the rear. Detailed service,
modern cooking.

XX **Racine**   37 AEY t
239 Brompton Rd, SW3 2EP, ℘ (020) 7584 4477, *Fax (020) 7584 4900*
🍽️. ⓜⓢ ᴬᴱ *VISA*
closed 25-26 December – **Meals** - French - 16.50 (lunch) and a la carte 21.25/
34.75 ⚏.
♦ Dark leather banquettes, large mirrors and wood floors create the atmosphere of a genuine Parisienne brasserie. Good value, well crafted, regional
French fare.

XX **Mao Tai**   37 AFY f
96 Draycott Ave, SW3 3AD, ℘ (020) 7225 2500, *info@maotai.co.uk,*
Fax (020) 7225 1965
🍽️. ⓜⓢ ᴬᴱ ⓞ *VISA*
closed 24-25 December – **Meals** - Chinese (Szechuan) - 12.50/24.70
and a la carte 25.05/38.20 ⚏.
♦ Spacious Chinese restaurant in the heart of Chelsea. Modern, stylish décor
with distinctive Eastern feel. Unique Szechuan menus, boasting some highly
original dishes.

XX **Chez Max**   37 AFX c
3 Yeoman's Row, SW3 2AL, ℘ (020) 7590 9999, *sales@whitestarline.org.uk,*
Fax (020) 7590 9900
🍽️. ⓜⓢ ᴬᴱ ⓞ *VISA*
closed 25-26 December – **Meals** - French - 17.50 and a la carte 21.50/32.50 ⚏.
♦ Warm welcome guaranteed: colourful posters and deep burgundy walls
embrace diners. Competent Gallic staff serve well priced, assured dishes from
the classic French repertoire.

XX **The Painted Heron**   23 PZG d
112 Cheyne Walk, SW10 0DJ, ℘ (020) 7351 5232, *Fax (020) 7351 5313*
🍽️. ⓜⓢ *VISA*
closed 25-26 December and Saturday lunch – **Meals** - Indian - a la carte
23.00/26.50 ⚏.
♦ Just off Cheyne Walk near the river. Contemporary in style, exemplified by
oil paintings. Modern Indian dishes with eclectic ingredients drawn from
around the sub-continent.

XX Pellicano

37 AFY d

19-21 Elystan St, SW3 3NT, ℘ (020) 7589 3718, *pellicanor@aol.com*, *Fax (020) 7584 1789*

📷 – ▤, 🔟 AE ⓪ VISA JCB

closed 24 December-2 January and 9-13 April – **Meals** - Italian - 15.00 (lunch) and a la carte 20.00/32.50 ♈.

♦ Attractive neighbourhood restaurant with dark blue canopy over pavement terrace. Contemporary interior with wood floors. Tasty and interesting modern Italian dishes.

XX Mju (at Millennium Knightsbridge H.)

37 AGX r

17-25 Sloane St, SW1X 9NU, ℘ (020) 7201 6330, *mju@mill-cop.com*, *Fax (020) 7235 3705*

✦ ▤, 🔟 AE ⓪ VISA JCB

closed Sunday and Bank Holidays – **Meals** 24.95/40.00 and dinner a la carte 19.00/36.00 ♈.

♦ On the first floor of the Millennium Knightsbridge Hotel, a large glass ceiling provides plenty of light. Original mix of flavours underpinned by a classical French base.

XX Brasserie St Quentin

37 AEY a

243 Brompton Rd, SW3 2EP, ℘ (020) 7589 8005, *reservations@brasseriestque ntin.co.uk, Fax (020) 7584 6064*

▤. 🔟 AE ⓪ VISA

closed 1 week Christmas and 2 weeks August – **Meals** 16.50 (lunch) and a la carte 18.95/36.85 🗇 ♈.

♦ Authentic Parisien brasserie, with rows of closely set tables, banquettes and ornate chandeliers. Attentive service and a lively atmosphere. French classics aplenty.

XX Benihana

37 AFZ e

77 King's Rd, SW3 4NX, ℘ (020) 7376 7799, *benihana@dircon.co.uk*, *Fax (020) 7376 7377*

▤. 🔟 AE ⓪ VISA

closed 25 December – **Meals** - Japanese (Teppan-Yaki) - 19.25/25.50.

♦ Vast basement restaurant. Be prepared to share your table with other guests; teppan-yakis sit up to eight. Theatrical preparation and service of modern Japanese cooking.

XX Caraffini

37 AGZ a

61-63 Lower Sloane St, SW1W 8DH, ℘ (020) 7259 0235, *info@caraffini.co.uk*, *Fax (020) 7259 0236*

📷 – ▤. 🔟 AE VISA

closed Sunday and Bank Holidays – **Meals** - Italian - a la carte 24.10/32.95.

♦ The omnipresent and ebullient owner oversees the friendly service in this attractive neighbourhood restaurant. Authentic and robust Italian cooking; informal atmosphere.

XX Vama

23 PZG e

438 King's Rd, SW10 0LJ, ℘ (020) 7351 4118, *andy@vama.co.uk*, *Fax (020) 7565 8501*

🔟 AE ⓪ VISA JCB

closed 25-26 December and 1 January – **Meals** - Indian - (booking essential) 13.00/20.00 and a la carte 19.95/35.20 ♈.

♦ Adorned with traditional artefacts, a modern and bright restaurant. Keen and eager service of an elaborate and seasonally changing menu of Northwest Indian specialities.

XX **Le Colombier** 36 ADZ **e**
145 Dovehouse St, SW3 6LB, ℰ (020) 7351 1155, *Fax (020) 7351 0077*
☆ –⓪ⓐ ᴀᴇ 𝘝𝘐𝘚𝘈
Meals - French - 17.50 (lunch) and a la carte 20.20/37.90 ⊠ ♀.
♦ Proudly Gallic corner restaurant in an affluent residential area. Attractive
enclosed terrace. Bright and cheerful surroundings and service of traditional
French cooking.

XX **The Collection** 37 AEY **V**
264 Brompton Rd, SW3 2AS, ℰ (020) 7225 1212, *office@thecollection.co.uk,*
Fax (020) 7225 1050
▤. ⓪ⓐ ᴀᴇ 𝘝𝘐𝘚𝘈
closed 25 December and Bank Holidays – **Meals** (dinner only and lunch
Saturday and Sunday) 35.00 and a la carte ♀.
♦ Beyond the impressive catwalk entrance one will find a chic bar and a vast
split level, lively restaurant. The eclectic and global modern menu is enjoyed
by the young crowd.

XX **Eight over Eight** 23 PZG **n**
392 King's Rd, SW3 5UZ, ℰ (020) 7349 9934, *Fax (020) 7351 5157*
▤. ⓪ⓐ ᴀᴇ 𝘝𝘐𝘚𝘈 ᴊᴄʙ
closed Christmas – **Meals** - South East Asian - a la carte 22.00/26.50 ♀.
♦ Lively modern restaurant in converted theatre pub; bar in front and dining
room at rear. Enthusiastic service. Eclectic Asian menu: strong flavours and
unusual combinations.

XX **Good Earth** 37 AFY **h**
233 Brompton Rd, SW3 2EP, ℰ (020) 7584 3658, *goodearthgroup@aol.com,*
Fax (020) 7823 8769
▤. ⓪ⓐ ᴀᴇ 𝘝𝘐𝘚𝘈 ᴊᴄʙ
Meals - Chinese - 25.00/35.00 (dinner) and a la carte 9.95/25.10 ♀.
♦ Ornately decorated, long-established and comfortable restaurant. Polite
and efficient service. Extensive and traditional Chinese menu.

XX **Dan's** 37 AEZ **s**
119 Sydney St, SW3 6NR, ℰ (020) 7352 2718, *Fax (020) 7352 3265*
☆ –⓪ⓐ ᴀᴇ 𝘝𝘐𝘚𝘈
closed Sunday dinner – **Meals** 19.50 (lunch) and a la carte 25.50/33.40.
♦ The eponymous owner oversees the operation in this long established
neighbourhood restaurant. Eclectic menu with global influences. Private dining available.

XX **Haandi** 37 AFX **V**
136 Brompton Rd, SW3 1HY, ℰ (020) 7823 7373, *haandirestaurant@btconnec*
t.com, Fax (020) 7823 9696
▤. ⓪ⓐ ᴀᴇ ⓪ 𝘝𝘐𝘚𝘈 ᴊᴄʙ
Meals - Indian - a la carte 16.82/35.40 ♀.
♦ Spacious basement restaurant, though with natural light in some sections.
Live jazz in the bar and chefs very much on display. Flavoursome, succulent
north Indian food.

X **Thierry's** 36 ADZ **c**
342 King's Rd, SW3 5UR, ℰ (020) 7352 3365, *eat@thierrys-restaurant.co.uk,*
Fax (020) 7352 3365
▤. ⓪ⓐ ᴀᴇ ⓪ 𝘝𝘐𝘚𝘈
closed 24 December-3 January, last 2 weeks August, Sunday dinner and
Monday – **Meals** - French - a la carte 17.70/35.95 ♀.
♦ Keen service at this cosy and friendly French bistro. Favoured by local
residents, the traditional menu features many of the classics.

✗ Bibendum Oyster Bar   37 AEY **S**
Michelin House, 81 Fulham Rd, SW3 6RD, ☏ (020) 7589 1480, *manager@biben dum.co.uk, Fax (020) 7823 7148*

MC AE ① VISA

closed 25-26 December – **Meals** - Seafood specialities - (bookings not accepted) a la carte 19.00/29.00.

♦ Dine in either the busy bar, or in the light and relaxed foyer of this striking landmark. Concise menu of mainly cold dishes focusing on fresh seafood and shellfish.

✗ itsu   37 AFY **j**
118 Draycott Ave, SW3 3AE, ☏ (020) 7590 2400, *cebsonetcomuk.co.uk, Fax (020) 7590 2403*

≣. MC AE VISA

closed 25 December – **Meals** - Japanese - (bookings not accepted) a la carte 15.00/20.00 ♈.

♦ Sit at the conveyor belt and select your dishes from it. Cosmopolitan 'euro sushi' selection with Asian specialities. Fashionable and willing staff. Busy bar upstairs.

⛶ Admiral Codrington   37 AFY **V**
17 Mossop St, SW3 2LY, ☏ (020) 7581 0005, *theadmiralcodrington@longshotp lc.com, Fax (020) 7589 2452*

≣. MC AE VISA JCB

closed 24-26 December – **Meals** a la carte 19.85/27.95 ♈.

♦ Aproned staff offer attentive, relaxed service in this busy gastropub. A retractable roof provides alfresco dining in the modern back room. Cosmopolitan menu of modern dishes.

⛶ Chelsea Ram   23 PZG **r**
32 Burnaby St, SW10 0PL, ☏ (020) 7351 4008, *pint@chelsearam.com, Fax (020) 7349 0885*

MC VISA JCB

closed 25 and 31 December – **Meals** a la carte 17.00/24.00 ♈.

♦ Wooden floors, modern artwork and books galore feature in this forever popular pub. Concise menu of modern British cooking with daily changing specials. Friendly atmosphere.

⛶ Swag and Tails   37 AFX **r**
10-11 Fairholt St, SW7 1EG, ☏ (020) 7584 6926, *swagandtails@mway.com, Fax (020) 7581 9935*

MC AE VISA JCB

closed 10 days Christmas-New Year, Saturday, Sunday and Bank Holidays – **Meals** a la carte 17.90/28.00 ♈.

♦ Attractive Victorian pub close to Harrods and the fashionable Knightsbridge shops. Polite and approachable service of a blackboard menu of light snacks and seasonal dishes.

⛶ Builders Arms   37 AFZ **X**
13 Britten St, SW3 3TY, ☏ (020) 7349 9040, *Fax (020) 7351 3181*

≣. MC VISA

Meals (bookings not accepted) a la carte 18.40/25.00 ♈.

♦ Modern 'gastropub' favoured by the locals. Eclectic menu of contemporary dishes with blackboard specials. Polite service from a young and eager team.

⛶ Lots Road Pub & Dining Room   23 PZG **b**
114 Lots Rd, SW10 0RJ, ☏ (020) 7352 6645, *lotsroad@thespiritgroup.com, Fax (020) 7376 4975*

≣. MC AE VISA

closed 25 December – **Meals** a la carte 16.00/25.00 ♈.

♦ Traditional corner pub with an open-plan kitchen, flowers at each table and large modern pictures on the walls. Contemporary menus change daily.

Earl's Court *Gtr London –* ✉ *SW5/SW10.*

🏨 **K + K George**   35 AAY **S**
1-15 Templeton Pl, SW5 9NB, ✆ (020) 7598 8700, *hotelgeorge@kkhotels.co.u k, Fax (020) 7370 2285*

🚗 – |♿| ⇄ ▤ 🖵 ✆ 🄿 ⓜⓞ 🄰🄴 ⓞ 𝘝𝘐𝘚𝘈 JCB ⚥

Meals (in bar) a la carte 14.10/22.20 ♀ – **154 rm** ⊑ 175.00/210.00.
♦ Converted Victorian house overlooking its own large rear garden. Scandinavian style to the bedrooms with low beds, white walls and light wood furniture. Smart business centre. Informal dining in the bar.

🏨 **Twenty Nevern Square**   35 AAY **u**
Nevern Sq, SW5 9PD, ✆ (020) 7565 9555, *hotel@twentynevernsquare.co.uk, Fax (020) 7565 9444*

|♿| 🖵 ✆ 🄿 ⓜⓞ 🄰🄴 𝘝𝘐𝘚𝘈 JCB ⚥

Meals *(closed Sunday)* (residents only) (dinner only) 16.00 and a la carte 15.95/19.45 **s.** ♀ – ⊑ 9.00 – **19 rm** 110.00/140.00.
♦ In an attractive Victorian garden square, an individually designed, privately owned town house. Original pieces of furniture and some rooms with their own terrace.

🏨 **Mayflower**   35 ABY **n**
26-28 Trebovir Rd, SW5 9NJ, ✆ (020) 7370 0991, *mayflowerhotel@mayflower-group.co.uk, Fax (020) 7370 0994*

without rest., 🚗 – |♿| ⇄ 🖵 ✆ ⓜⓞ 🄰🄴 𝘝𝘐𝘚𝘈 JCB – ⊑ 9.00 **48 rm** 69.00/99.00.
♦ Two white houses combined into a stylish establishment with secluded rear garden, juice bar and breakfast room. Highly individual bedrooms with Indian and Asian décor.

🏨 **Henley House**   35 ABY **e**
30 Barkston Gdns, SW5 0EN, ✆ (020) 7370 4111, *reservations@henleyhouseh otel.com, Fax (020) 7370 0026*

without rest. – |♿| 🖵 ⓜⓞ 🄰🄴 ⓞ 𝘝𝘐𝘚𝘈 JCB ⚥ – ⊑ 3.40 – **21 rm** 74.00/89.00.
♦ Located in a pleasant redbricked square, just yards from the high street. Bedrooms all styled similarly, with floral designs and good extras. Conservatory breakfast room.

🏨 **Amsterdam**   35 ABY **c**
7 and 9 Trebovir Rd, SW5 9LS, ✆ (020) 7370 2814, *reservations@amsterdam-h otel.com, Fax (020) 7244 7608*

without rest., 🚗 – |♿| ⇄ 🖵 ⓜⓞ 🄰🄴 ⓞ 𝘝𝘐𝘚𝘈 JCB ⚥

19 rm ⊑ 72.00/86.00, 8 suites.
♦ Basement breakfast room and a small secluded garden. The boldly decorated bedrooms dazzle with vivid colour schemes; some boast their own balcony.

🏨 **Rushmore**   35 ABY **a**
11 Trebovir Rd, SW5 9LS, ✆ (020) 7370 3839, *rushmore-reservations@london. com, Fax (020) 7370 0274*

without rest. – ⇄ 🖵 ⓜⓞ 🄰🄴 ⓞ 𝘝𝘐𝘚𝘈 JCB ⚥

22 rm ⊑ 59.00/79.00.
♦ Behind its Victorian façade lies an hotel popular with tourists. Individually decorated bedrooms in a variety of shapes and sizes. Piazza-styled conservatory breakfast room.

╳╳ Langan's Coq d'Or
35 ABZ **e**

254-260 Old Brompton Rd, SW5 9HR, ℘ (020) 7259 2599, *admin@langansresta urant.co.uk, Fax (020) 7370 7735*

🛱 – 🔳. **⑩ 盃 ⑩ VISA JCB**

closed Monday and Bank Holidays – **Meals** (dinner only and lunch Saturday and Sunday) 16.50.

♦ Formal reception area leads into a modern, open-plan restaurant. Walls adorned with photographs of assorted celebrities. Smooth service and traditional British food.

╳╳ Sticklebackpink
35 ABZ **a**

168 Ifield Rd, SW10 9AF, ℘ (020) 7835 0874, *info@stickleback-restaurant.com*
🔳. **⑩ 盃 VISA**

closed Monday – **Meals** - Indian - a la carte 20.00/41.00 ℤ.

♦ Basement and conservatory restaurant reached by a spiral stair from the bar. Elegantly-laid tables and friendly service. Menu of modern Indian dishes.

▯▯ Hollywood Arms
36 ACZ **c**

45 Hollywood Rd, SW10 9HX, ℘ (020) 7349 7840, *Fax (020) 7349 7841*
🔳. **⑩ 盃 ⑩ VISA**

closed 25 December – **Meals** a la carte 19.50/24.00 ℤ.

♦ Period pub in smart residential area with stylish interior furnished in rich autumnal colours. Efficient service. Concise menu with Mediterranean influences and flavours.

Kensington *Gtr London* – ✉ *SW7/W8/W11/W14.*

▦▦ Royal Garden
35 ABX **c**

2-24 Kensington High St, W8 4PT, ℘ (020) 7937 8000, *sales@royalgarden.co.u k, Fax (020) 7361 1991*

≼, 🖪, ⬚s – |⬚|, ⇌ rm, 🔳 📺 ✆ ♿ 🅿 – ⚒ 600. **⑩ 盃 ⑩ VISA JCB**. ⬚
Park Terrace : Meals 21.00 (lunch) and a la carte 26.75/47.75 – (see also **The Tenth** below) – ⬚ 18.00 – **376 rm** 287.80/393.60, 20 suites.

♦ A tall, modern hotel with many of its rooms enjoying enviable views over the adjacent Kensington Gardens. All the modern amenities and services, with well-drilled staff. Bright, spacious, large-windowed restaurant.

▦▦ Hilton London Kensington
16 MZE **x**

179-199 Holland Park Ave, W11 4UL, ℘ (020) 7603 3355, *sales_kensington@hil ton.com, Fax (020) 7602 9397*

|⬚|, ⇌ rm, 🔳 📺 ✆ ♿ 🅿 – ⚒ 200. **⑩ 盃 ⑩ VISA JCB**. ⬚
Imbue : Meals *(closed lunch Saturday and Sunday)* 20.00/22.00 and a la carte 25.00/29.00 ℤ
Zen Oriental : Meals - Chinese- a la carte 12.50/24.00 – ⬚ 15.00 – **602 rm** 210.30/233.80.

♦ The executive bedrooms and the nearby exhibition centres make this a popular business hotel. Equally useful spot for tourists; it has all the necessary amenities. Warm, pastel coloured Market. Zen Oriental serving authentic classic Chinese cooking.

▦▦ Hilton London Olympia
16 MZF **a**

380 Kensington High St, W14 8NL, ℘ (020) 7603 3333, *rm_olympia@hilton.co m, Fax (020) 7603 4846*

🖪 – |⬚|, ⇌ rm, 🔳 📺 ✆ ♿ 🅿 – ⚒ 250. **⑩ 盃 ⑩ VISA JCB**
Meals *(closed Saturday lunch)* 20.00 and a la carte 16.00/29.50 ℤ – ⬚ 16.50 –
395 rm 128.00, 10 suites.

♦ Busy, corporate hotel, benefiting from being within walking distance of Olympia. Bedrooms of a good size, with light wood furniture and fully tiled bathrooms. Bright dining room with large windows.

🏛 The Milestone   35 ABX u

1-2 Kensington Court, W8 5DL, ℘ (020) 7917 1000, *Fax (020) 7917 1010*

Ĺ₆, ⬡ – |♦|, ⇌ rm, ▤ �📺 ✆, ◍ⓐ ⒜Ⓔ ⓞ **VISA** JCB, ✄

Meals (booking essential to non-residents) 19.95 (lunch) and a la carte 35.00/
55.00 ⚲ – ⚲ 17.00 – **52 rm** 340.75, 5 suites.

◆ Elegant 'boutique' hotel with decorative Victorian façade and English feel.
Charming oak panelled lounge and snug bar. Meticulously decorated bedrooms with period detail. Panelled dining room with charming little oratory
for privacy seekers.

🏛 Holland Court   16 MZE d

31-33 Holland Rd, W14 8HJ, ℘ (020) 7371 1133, *reservations@hollandcourt.co
m, Fax (020) 7602 9114*

without rest., ☞ – |♦| ⇌ �📺, ◍ⓐ ⒜Ⓔ ⓞ **VISA** JCB, ✄

22 rm ⚲ 95.00/125.00.

◆ Privately owned and run terraced house. Pretty little garden next to the
conservatory extension of the breakfast room. Well-kept bedrooms benefit
from the large windows.

XXX The Tenth (at Royal Garden H.)   35 ABX c

2-24 Kensington High St, W8 4PT, ℘ (020) 7361 1910, *Fax (020) 7361 1921*

≼ Kensington Palace and Gardens – ▤ P, ◍ⓐ ⒜Ⓔ ⓞ **VISA** JCB

*closed last week December, first week January, last 2 weeks August, Saturday
lunch, Sunday and Bank Holidays* – **Meals** (live music Saturday) 21.00
(lunch) and a la carte 26.75/36.20 ⚲.

◆ Named after the hotel's top floor where this stylish yet relaxed room is
situated. Commanding views of Kensington Palace and the Park. Well-struc-
tured service; modern menu.

XXX Belvedere   16 MZE u

Holland House, off Abbotsbury Rd, W8 6LU, ℘ (020) 7602 1238, *sales@whitest
arline.org.uk, Fax (020) 7610 4382*

☂, ♨ – ▤, ◍ⓐ ⒜Ⓔ ⓞ **VISA**

closed Sunday dinner in winter – **Meals** 24.50/32.50 ⏱ ⚲.

◆ Former 19C orangery in a delightful position in the middle of the Park. On
two floors with a bar and balcony terrace. Huge vases of flowers. Modern take
on classic dishes.

XX Zaika   35 ABX r

1 Kensington High St, W8 5NP, ℘ (020) 7795 6533, *info@zaika-restaurant.co.u
k, Fax (020) 7937 8854*

▤, ◍ⓐ ⒜Ⓔ ⓞ **VISA** JCB

closed 25-26 December, 1 January and Saturday lunch – **Meals** - Indian - 17.95
(lunch) and a la carte 30.25/46.25 ⚲.

◆ A converted bank, sympathetically restored, with original features and
Indian artefacts. Well organised service; careful and accomplished modern
Indian cooking.

Spec. Imli Bateyer (quail glazed with tamarind and cumin). Karara Kekda
Khichdi (soft shell crab and scallops with lentils). Zaika chocolate platter.

XX Clarke's   27 ABV c

124 Kensington Church St, W8 4BH, ℘ (020) 7221 9225, *restaurant@sallyclark
e.com, Fax (020) 7229 4564*

⇌ ▤, ◍ⓐ ⒜Ⓔ ⓞ **VISA**

closed 10 days Christmas-New Year, Sunday and Bank Holidays – **Meals** (set
menu only at dinner) 28.50/40.00 ⚲.

◆ Open-plan kitchen, personally overseen by the owner, provides modern
British cooking. No choice, set menu at dinner. Comfortable and bright, with
a neighbourhood feel.

XX **Babylon** (at The Roof Gardens)   35 ABX **n**
99 Kensington High St (entrance on Derry St), W8 5SA, ✆ (020) 7368 3993, *bab ylon@roofgardens.virgin.co.uk, Fax (020) 7938 2774*

⇐, 🌣 – 🖃. **🕥** **AE** **①** **VISA**

closed 25 December, 1 January, Saturday lunch and Sunday dinner – **Meals** 21.50 and a la carte 24.00/37.50 ♈.

◆ Situated on the roof of this pleasant London building affording attractive veiws of the London skyline. Stylish modern décor in keeping with the contemporary, British cooking.

XX **Launceston Place**   35 ACX **a**
1a Launceston Pl, W8 5RL, ✆ (020) 7937 6912, *LPR@place-restaurants.co.uk, Fax (020) 7938 2412*

🖃. **🕥** **AE** **①** **VISA**

closed 24-26 December, 1 January and Saturday lunch – **Meals** 18.50 (lunch) and a la carte 27.00/38.00 ♈.

◆ Divided into a number of rooms, this corner restaurant is lent a bright feel by its large windows and gilded mirrors. Chatty service and contemporary cooking.

XX **Memories of China**   35 AAY **V**
353 Kensington High St, W8 6NW, ✆ (020) 7603 6951, *Fax (020) 7603 0848*

🖃. **🕥** **AE** **①** **VISA**

closed 25 December and 1 January – **Meals** - Chinese - (booking essential) a la carte 23.50/40.00 ♈.

◆ Subtle lighting and brightly coloured high-back chairs add to the modern feel of this Chinese restaurant. Screens separate the tables. Plenty of choice from extensive menu.

XX **Timo**   35 AAY **c**
343 Kensington High St, W8 6NW, ✆ (020) 7603 3888, *Fax (020) 7603 8111*

🖃. **🕥** **AE** **①** **VISA**

closed 25 December and 1 January – **Meals** - Italian - 19.50/31.50 ♈.

◆ Modern restaurant with unadorned lime green walls and comfortable seating in brown suede banquettes. Italian menus of contemporary dishes and daily changing specials.

XX **The Ark**   27 ABV **r**
122 Palace Gardens Terr, W8 4RT, ✆ (020) 7229 4024, *mail@thearkrestaurant.c o.uk, Fax (020) 7792 8787*

🌣 – 🖃. **🕥** **AE** **①** **VISA**

closed 25-26 December, Sunday dinner and Monday lunch – **Meals** - Italian - 15.00 (lunch) and a la carte 27.00/31.50 ♈.

◆ The hut-like external appearance belies the contemporary interior of this Italian restaurant. Comfortable, bright feel with bar and lounge. Smoothly run, rustic cooking.

X **Kensington Place**   27 AAV **z**
201 Kensington Church St, W8 7LX, ✆ (020) 7727 3184, *kpr@placerestaurants. co.uk, Fax (020) 7229 2025*

🖃. **🕥** **AE** **①** **VISA**

closed 25-26 December – **Meals** (booking essential) 16.50/24.50 and a la carte 26.00/42.00 ♈.

◆ A cosmopolitan crowd still head for this establishment that set the trend for large, bustling and informal restaurants. Professionally run with skilled modern cooking.

※ **Cibo**   16 MZE **b**
3 Russell Gdns, W14 8EZ, ℰ (020) 7371 6271, *Fax (020) 7602 1371*
◍◍ AE ◐ VISA
closed 10 days Christmas, Saturday lunch and Sunday dinner – **Meals** - Italian -
a la carte 20.75/34.75.
 ♦ Smoothly run Italian restaurant that combines style with the atmosphere
of a neighbourhood favourite. Unaffected service with robust and tasty
food.

※ **Malabar**   27 AAV **e**
27 Uxbridge St, W8 7TQ, ℰ (020) 7727 8800, *feedback@malabar-restaurant.co*
.uk
◍◍ VISA
Meals - Indian - (booking essential) (buffet lunch Sunday) 14.75/20.00
and a la carte 20.60/28.50.
 ♦ Indian restaurant in a residential street. Three rooms with individual per-
sonalities and informal service. Extensive range of good value dishes, particularly vegetarian.

※ **Wódka**   35 ABX **c**
12 St Albans Grove, W8 5PN, ℰ (020) 7937 6513, *john@wodka.demon.co.uk,*
Fax (020) 7937 8621
◍◍ AE ◐ VISA
closed lunch Saturday and Sunday – **Meals** - Polish - 13.50 (lunch)
and a la carte 18.00/30.00 ♀.
 ♦ Unpretentious Polish restaurant with rustic, authentic menu. Assorted
blinis and flavoured vodkas a speciality. Simply decorated, with wooden tables
and paper napkins.

North Kensington – ✉ *W2/W10/W11.*

🏠 **Pembridge Court**   27 AAU **n**
34 Pembridge Gdns, W2 4DX, ℰ (020) 7229 9977, *reservations@pemct.co.uk,*
Fax (020) 7727 4982
without rest. – |‡| ▤ TV 📞. ◍◍ AE ◐ VISA
20 rm ⌷ 125.00/195.00.
 ♦ Privately owned 19C town house; very charmingly run, with comfortable
sitting room, small lounge and flowery breakfast room. Bright, light bedrooms, some particularly large.

🏠 **Abbey Court**   27 AAV **u**
20 Pembridge Gdns, W2 4DU, ℰ (020) 7221 7518, *info@abbeycourthotel.co.u*
k, Fax (020) 7792 0858
without rest. – ⇥ TV 📞. ◍◍ AE ◐ VISA JCB. ⌘
22 rm 105.00/155.00.
 ♦ Five-storey Victorian town house with individually decorated bedrooms,
with many thoughtful touches. Breakfast served in a pleasant conservatory.
Friendly service.

🏠 **Portobello**   16 NZE **n**
22 Stanley Gdns, W11 2NG, ℰ (020) 7727 2777, *info@portobello-hotel.co.uk,*
Fax (020) 7792 9641
without rest. – |‡| TV 📞. ◍◍ AE VISA – ⌷ 10.00 **24 rm** 120.00/275.00.
 ♦ An attractive Victorian town house in an elegant terrace. Original and
theatrical décor. Circular beds, half-testers, Victorian baths: no two bedrooms
are the same.

XX **Notting Hill Brasserie**   27 AAU a
92 Kensington Park Rd, W11 2PN, ✆ (020) 7229 4481, *enquiries@nottinghillbr*
asserie.com, Fax (020) 7221 1246
▤. **M©** **AE** **VISA** **JCB**

closed Sunday – **Meals** 18.50 (lunch) and dinner a la carte 25.50/34.50 ⵛ.
♦ Modern, comfortable restaurant with quiet, formal atmosphere set over
four small rooms. Authentic African artwork on walls. Contemporary dishes
with European influence.

XX **Edera**   16 MZE n
148 Holland Park Ave, W11 4VE, ✆ (020) 7221 6090, *Fax (020) 7313 9700*
▤. **M©** **AE** **①** **VISA**

Meals - Italian - 19.50/22.50 ⵛ.
♦ Split level restaurant with 4 outdoor tables. Attentive service by all Italian
staff. Set-price menus of modern Italian cooking with some unusual ingredients and combinations.

X **Manor**   16 NZD S
6-8 All Saints Rd, W11 1HH, ✆ (020) 7243 6363, *mail@manorw11.com,*
Fax (020) 7243 6360
▤. **M©** **AE** **VISA**

Meals (dinner only and lunch Saturday and Sunday) a la carte 22.50/32.50
☼⥈ ⵛ.
♦ Bustling, vibrant restaurant in the heart of Notting Hill. Wood-floored with
banquette seating. Good sized menus: the cuisine is modern with Spanish
influences.

X **Notting Grill**   16 MZE Z
123A Clarendon Rd, W11 4JG, ✆ (020) 7229 1500, *nottinggrill@aol.com,*
Fax (020) 7229 8889
✿ -**M©** **AE** **①** **VISA** **JCB**

closed 25-26 December, Good Friday and August Bank Holiday – **Meals** - Steak
specialities - (dinner only and lunch Saturday and Sunday) a la carte 29.50/
40.00 ⵛ.
♦ Converted pub that retains a rustic feel, with bare brick walls and wooden
tables. Specialises in well sourced, quality meats.

South Kensington *Gtr London* – ✉ *SW5/SW7/W8.*

🏛 **Millennium Gloucester**   36 ACY r
4-18 Harrington Gdns, SW7 4LH, ✆ (020) 7373 6030, *gloucester@mill-cop.com,*
Fax (020) 7373 0409
⛫ – ▐, ✖ rm, ▤ **TV** ✆ & **P** – ▲ 650. **M©** **AE** **①** **VISA** **JCB**

Bugis Street : **Meals** - Singaporean - 7.95/20.00 and a la carte 17.45/35.90 –
⌷ 15.50 – **604 rm** 250.00, 6 suites.
♦ A large international group hotel. Busy marbled lobby and vast conference
facilities. Smart and well-equipped bedrooms are generously sized, especially
the 'Club' rooms. Informal, compact Bugis Street.

🏛 **The Pelham**   36 ADY Z
15 Cromwell Pl, SW7 2LA, ✆ (020) 7589 8288, *pelham@firmdale.com,*
Fax (020) 7584 8444
▐, ✖ rm, ▤ **TV** ✆, **M©** **AE** **VISA**. ✾

Kemps : **Meals** a la carte 20.00/33.00 ⵛ – ⌷ 17.50 – **48 rm** 176.20/293.70,
3 suites.
♦ Attractive Victorian town house with a discreet and comfortable feel.
Wood panelled drawing room and individually decorated bedrooms with
marble bathrooms. Detailed service. Warm basement dining room.

Blakes 36 ACZ n
33 Roland Gdns, SW7 3PF, ℰ (020) 7370 6701, *blakes@blakeshotels.com*, *Fax (020) 7373 0442*
🕮 – |♯|, ▤ rest, TV 📞 🕮 AE ⓞ VISA JCB ✖
Meals a la carte 50.00/70.00 **s.** – 😑 25.00 – **36 rm** 190.00/393.00, 5 suites.
♦ Behind the Victorian façade lies one of London's first 'boutique' hotels. Dramatic, bold and eclectic décor, with oriental influences and antiques from around the globe. Fashionable restaurant with bamboo and black walls.

Harrington Hall 36 ACY n
5-25 Harrington Gdns, SW7 4JW, ℰ (020) 7396 9696, *sales@harringtonhall.co.uk, Fax (020) 7396 9090*
f₆, ⇌s – |♯|, ⬆ rm, ▤ TV 📞 – ♨ 260. 🕮 AE ⓞ VISA JCB ✖
Wetherby's : **Meals** 22.50/27.50 and a la carte 25.00/29.00 **s.** ⴺ – 😑 15.50 – **200 rm** 195.00/260.00.
♦ A series of adjoined terraced houses, with an attractive period façade that belies the size. Tastefully furnished bedrooms, with an extensive array of facilities. Classically decorated dining room.

Millennium Bailey's 36 ACY a
140 Gloucester Rd, SW7 4QH, ℰ (020) 7373 6000, *baileys@mill-cop.com, Fax (020) 7370 3760*
|♯|, ⬆ rm, ▤ TV 📞 – ♨ 460. 🕮 AE ⓞ VISA JCB ✖
Olives : **Meals** (bar lunch)/dinner 20.00 and a la carte approx. 25.00 ⴺ – 😑 15.50 – **211 rm** 135.00/250.00.
♦ Elegant lobby, restored to its origins dating from 1876, with elaborate plasterwork and a striking grand staircase. Victorian feel continues through into the bedrooms. Modern, pastel shaded restaurant.

Vanderbilt 36 ACY Z
68-86 Cromwell Rd, SW7 5BT, ℰ (020) 7761 9013, *resvand@radisson.com, Fax (020) 7761 9003*
f₆ – |♯|, ⬆ rm, ▤ TV 📞 – ♨ 120. 🕮 AE ⓞ VISA JCB ✖
Meals 27.50 and a la carte 30.00/36.00 ⴺ – 😑 13.50 – **215 rm** 229.10/298.45.
♦ A Victorian town house, once home to the Vanderbilt family. Retains many original features such as stained glass windows and fireplaces. Now a modern, group hotel. Restaurant has unusual objets d'art and striking cracked glass bar.

Rembrandt 36 ADY X
11 Thurloe Pl, SW7 2RS, ℰ (020) 7589 8100, *rembrandt@sarova.co.uk, Fax (020) 7225 3476*
f₆, ⇌s, ⬚ – |♯|, ⬆ rm, ▤ rest, TV – ♨ 200. 🕮 AE ⓞ VISA JCB ✖
Meals (carving lunch) 18.95 and a la carte 14.70/27.40 **s.** ⴺ – **195 rm** 😑 190.00/240.00.
♦ Built originally as apartments in the 19C, now a well-equipped hotel opposite the VA museum and a short walk from Harrods. Comfortable lounge, adjacent leisure club. Spacious dining room.

London Marriott Kensington 35 ABY n
147 Cromwell Rd, SW5 0TH, ℰ (020) 7973 1000, *events.kensington@marriotthotels.co.uk, Fax (020) 7370 1685*
f₆, ⇌s, ⬚ – |♯| ⬆ ▤ TV 📞 ⅙ – ♨ 200. 🕮 AE ⓞ VISA JCB ✖
Fratelli : **Meals** - Italian - 18.00 (lunch) and a la carte 23.50/33.50 ⴺ – 😑 14.95 – **216 rm** 233.80.
♦ Modern seven-storey hotel around atrium with good leisure centre. Coffee bar and Spanish tapas bar. Spacious, comfortable, well-equipped bedrooms with many extras. Informal Italian restaurant with open kitchen and wide ranging menu.

🏨 **Jurys Kensington** 36 ADY **g**
109-113 Queen's Gate, SW7 5LR, ☎ (020) 7589 6300, *kensington@jurydoyle.co m, Fax (020) 7581 1492*
|≣|, ✻ rm, ▤ 📺 ☎ ♿, – 🏛 80. 💳 AE ① VISA JCB. ✼
Meals *(dinner only)* 18.50 and a la carte 15.00/18.50 – ☲ 16.00 – **173 rm** 130.00/230.00.
◆ A row of 18C town houses that were converted into a hotel in the 1920s. Spacious lobby lounge and busy basement Irish pub. Well-equipped, comfortable bedrooms. Dining room exudes a traditional appeal.

🏨 **Regency** 36 ADY **e**
100 Queen's Gate, SW7 5AG, ☎ (020) 7373 7878, *info@regency-london.co.uk, Fax (020) 7370 5555*
ऌ, ☎s – |≣|, ✻ rm, ▤ 📺 ☎ – 🏛 100. 💳 AE ① VISA JCB. ✼
Meals *(closed lunch Saturday and Sunday)* (carvery lunch)/dinner a la carte 11.00/24.00 **s**. ♈ – ☲ 15.00 – **199 rm** 187.00/234.00, 11 suites.
◆ Impressive Regency house in an elegant tree lined street and close to the museums. Bedrooms vary from rather compact singles to spacious duplex suites. Basement restaurant with cocktail bar.

🏨 **Gore** 36 ACX **n**
189 Queen's Gate, SW7 5EX, ☎ (020) 7584 6601, *reservations@gorehotel.co.u k, Fax (020) 7589 8127*
|≣|, ✻ rm, 📺 ☎. 💳 AE ① VISA JCB. ✼
closed 24-25 December –
Bistrot 190 : **Meals** (booking essential) a la carte 23.00/48.50 ♈ – ☲ 15.95 – **53 rm** 182.10/228.25.
◆ Opened its doors in 1892; has retained its individual charm. Richly decorated with antiques, rugs and over 4,000 pictures that cover every inch of wall. Seafood menu with global twists at The Restaurant at One Ninety. Bistrot 190 boasts French-inspired décor.

🏨 **John Howard** 36 ACX **g**
4 Queen's Gate, SW7 5EH, ☎ (020) 7808 8400, *info@johnhowardhotel.co.uk, Fax (020) 7808 8402*
|≣|, ✻ rm, ▤ 📺 ☎. 💳 AE ① VISA JCB. ✼
Meals *(closed Sunday)* (dinner only) 15.00 and a la carte 15.25/20.00 **s**. – ☲ 12.50 – **45 rm** 99.00/129.00, 7 suites.
◆ Occupies the site of three mid-19C houses, just a short walk from Kensington Palace. Some rooms with floor to ceiling windows and balconies, others look onto a quiet mews. Candlelit basement dining room.

🏨 **Number Sixteen** 36 ADY **d**
16 Sumner Pl, SW7 3EG, ☎ (020) 7589 5232, *sixteen@firmdale.com, Fax (020) 7584 8615*
without rest., ☞ – |≣| ▤ 📺 ☎. 💳 AE VISA – ☲ 14.50 **41 rm** 111.60/264.30.
◆ Four Victorian town houses in a smart part of town. Discreet entrance, comfortable sitting room and charming breakfast terrace. Bedrooms in English country house style.

🏨 **The Cranley** 36 ACY **c**
10 Bina Gdns, SW5 0LA, ☎ (020) 7373 0123, *info@thecranley.com, Fax (020) 7373 9497*
|≣|, ✻ rm, ▤ 📺 ☎. 💳 AE ① VISA JCB. ✼
Meals (room service only) – ☲ 9.95 – **36 rm** 182.10/258.50, 3 suites.
◆ Attractive Regency town house that artfully combines charm and period details with modern comforts and technology. Individually styled bedrooms; some with four-posters.

🏠 **Five Sumner Place**   36 ADY **u**

5 Sumner Pl, SW7 3EE, ☎ (020) 7584 7586, *reservations@sumnerplace.com,*
Fax (020) 7823 9962
without rest. – 📶 ✕ 📺, 🐵 AE ① *VISA* JCB. ✗
13 rm ☐ 100.00/152.00.

♦ Part of a striking white terrace built in 1848 in this fashionable part of
town. Breakfast served in bright conservatory. Good sized bedrooms.

🏠 **Aster House**   36 ADY **t**

3 Sumner Pl, SW7 3EE, ☎ (020) 7581 5888, *asterhouse@btinternet.com,*
Fax (020) 7584 4925
without rest., 🌫 – ✕ 🖃 📺 📞, 🐵 *VISA* JCB. ✗
14 rm ☐ 100.00/190.00.

♦ End of terrace Victorian house with a pretty little rear garden and first
floor conservatory. Ground floor rooms available. A wholly non-smoking
establishment.

XXX **Bombay Brasserie**   36 ACY **y**

Courtfield Rd, SW7 4QH, ☎ (020) 7370 4040, *bombay1brasserie@aol.com,*
Fax (020) 7835 1669
🖃, 🐵 AE ① *VISA* JCB
closed 25-26 December – **Meals** - Indian - (buffet lunch) 18.95 and dinner a la carte 27.25/33.25 ☎.

♦ Something of a London institution: an ever busy Indian restaurant with
Raj-style décor. Ask to sit in the brighter plant-filled conservatory. Popular
lunchtime buffet.

XX **Lundum's**   36 ACZ **p**

119 Old Brompton Rd, SW7 3RN, ☎ (020) 7373 7774, *Fax (020) 7373 4472*
🌫 – 🖃, 🐵 AE ① *VISA*
closed 22 December-4 January and Sunday dinner – **Meals** - Danish - 15.50/
21.50 and a la carte 23.00/36.50.

♦ A family run Danish restaurant offering an authentic, traditional lunch with
a more expansive dinner menu. Comfortable room, with large windows.
Charming service.

XX **L'Etranger**   35 ACX **c**

36 Gloucester Rd, SW7 4QT, ☎ (020) 7584 1118, *etranger36@aol.com,*
Fax (020) 7584 8886
🖃, 🐵 AE *VISA*
closed 25-26 December, Saturday lunch and Sunday dinner – **Meals** (booking
essential) 16.50 (lunch) and a la carte 27.50/41.50.

♦ Corner restaurant with mosaic entrance floor and bay window. Modern
décor. Tables extend into adjoining wine shop. French based cooking with
Asian influences.

XX **Khan's of Kensington**   36 ADY **a**

3 Harrington Rd, SW7 3ES, ☎ (020) 7584 4114, *Fax (020) 7581 2900*
🖃, 🐵 AE ① *VISA*
closed 25 December – **Meals** - Indian - a la carte 14.35/24.75.

♦ Bright room with wood flooring and a large mural depicting scenes from
old India. Basement bar in a colonial style. Authentic Indian cooking with
attentive service.

XX **Cambio de Tercio**   36 ACZ **a**

163 Old Brompton Rd, SW5 0LJ, ☎ (020) 7244 8970, *restaurant@cambiodeter*
cio.co.uk, Fax (020) 7373 8817
🐵 AE *VISA*
closed 2 weeks Christmas – **Meals** - Spanish - a la carte 24.90/30.00 ☎.

♦ The keen young owners have created a vibrant room with rich red walls
decorated with assorted bullfighting accessories. Sophisticated Spanish
cooking.

XX **Pasha**   36 ACX **y**

1 Gloucester Rd, SW7 4PP, *𝒫 (020) 7589 7969, Fax (020) 7581 9996*

🖥, 🕮 AE ⓞ VISA JCB

closed 25-26 December, 1 January and Sunday lunch – **Meals** - Moroccan - a la carte 12.25/29.25 ℥.

◆ A marble fountain, lanterns, spice boxes and silk cushions help create a theatrical Moroccan atmosphere. Service is helpful and able: the menu is more extensive at dinner.

XX **Memories of India**   36 ACX **s**

18 Gloucester Rd, SW7 4RB, *𝒫 (020) 7589 6450, Fax (020) 7584 4438*

🖥, 🕮 AE ⓞ VISA JCB

closed 25 December – **Meals** - Indian - 16.95/34.95 and a la carte 11.85/21.85.

◆ A long-standing local favourite, decorated in traditional style with whicker chairs and pink linen tablecloths. Polite and able service. Authentic Indian cooking.

X **Café Lazeez**   36 ADY **V**

93-95 Old Brompton Rd, SW7 3LD, *𝒫 (020) 7581 9993, southkensington@cafe lazeez.com, Fax (020) 7581 8200*

🖥, 🕮 AE ⓞ VISA

Meals - North Indian - a la carte 14.75/25.00 ℥.

◆ Glass-topped tables and tiled flooring add an air of modernity to this Indian restaurant; reflected in the North Indian cooking. Willing service. Upstairs room more formal.

X **Bangkok**   36 ADY **b**

9 Bute St, SW7 3EY, *𝒫 (020) 7584 8529*

🖥, 🕮 VISA

closed Christmas-New Year and Sunday – **Meals** - Thai Bistro - a la carte 17.70/32.45.

◆ This simple Thai bistro has been a popular local haunt for many years. Guests can watch the chefs at work, preparing inexpensive dishes from the succinct menu.

KINGSTON UPON THAMES *Gtr London.*

🏌 *Home Park, Hampton Wick 𝒫 (020) 8977 6645,* BY.

Chessington *Surrey –* ✉ *Surrey.*

🏨 **Travel Inn Metro**   5   BZ **c**

Leatherhead Rd, KT9 2NE, on A 243, *𝒫 (01372) 744060, Fax (01372) 720889*

⊁ rm, 📺 ♿ P, 🕮 AE ⓞ VISA, ⍋

Meals (grill rest.) – **42 rm** 54.95.

◆ Modern budget accommodation beside 'World of Adventures' theme park. Spacious rooms, many with additional sofa beds. Popular pub adjacent offers a traditional menu.

Kingston *Surrey –* ✉ *Surrey.*

🏨 **Kingston Lodge**   6   CY **u**

Kingston Hill, KT2 7NP, *𝒫 (0870) 4008115, kingstonlodge@macdonald-hotels. co.uk, Fax (020) 8547 1013*

🍴 – ⊁ rm, 🖥 rest, 📺 ☎ ♿ P – 🔏 60. 🕮 AE ⓞ VISA JCB, ⍋

The Atrium : **Meals** (grill rest.) (bar lunch Monday-Saturday)/dinner a la carte 16.25/29.40 ℥ – ⊑ 13.50 – **63 rm** 170.00/180.00.

◆ Well-appointed corporate hotel close to the University and Royal parks. Cosy and traditional lounge with open fires. Quietest rooms overlook an attractive courtyard. Relaxed conservatory restaurant.

Surbiton *Surrey –* ✉ *Surrey.*

XX **The French Table**   6   CY   **a**
85 Maple Rd, KT6 4AW, ✆ (020) 8399 2365, *Fax (020) 8390 5353*
▤. **M©** ***VISA***
closed 25-26 December, 1 week January, last 2 weeks in August, Monday, Sunday dinner and lunch Tuesday and Saturday – **Meals** - French-Mediterranean - 16.50 (lunch) and dinner a la carte 26.95/30.65 ♀.
♦ The lively atmosphere makes this narrow room with wooden tables and modern art a popular local. Attentive and relaxed service of a concise French-Mediterranean menu.

LAMBETH *Gtr London.*

Clapham Common *Gtr London –* ✉ *SW4.*

🏨 **Windmill on the Common**   24 RZH   **e**
Clapham Common South Side, SW4 9DE, ✆ (020) 8673 4578, *windmill@young s.co.uk, Fax (020) 8675 1486*
↝ rm, ▤ **TV** ☏ ⓺ **P**. **M©** **AE** ***VISA***. ⅋
Meals a la carte 12.85/24.90 **s**. ♀ – **29 rm** ⌑ 96.00/120.00.
♦ A former Victorian pub that has been sympathetically extended over the years. Pleasant spot on the Common. Well-kept and comfortable rooms of assorted sizes. Dining room and adjacent log-fired bar.

XX **Thyme**   24 SZH   **V**
14 Clapham Park Rd, SW4 7BB, ✆ (020) 7627 2468, *adam@thymeandspace.co m, Fax (020) 7627 2424*
M© **AE** ***VISA*** **JCB**
closed Sunday and Monday – **Meals** 12.50/40.00 and a la carte 21.50/29.00 ♀.
♦ Distinct neighbourhood feel with bustling but intimate ambience. Modern décor. Three set menus; imaginative cooking.

X **Tsunami**   24 SZH   **a**
Unit 3, 1-7 Voltaire Rd, SW4 6DQ, ✆ (020) 7978 1610, *Fax (020) 7978 1591*
M© ***VISA***
closed 25-27 December, 31 December-2 January and Sunday – **Meals** - Japanese - (dinner only and Saturday lunch) a la carte 12.90/35.40 ♀.
♦ Trendy, mininalist-style restaurant. Interesting Japanese menu with many dishes designed for sharing and plenty of original options. Good Sushi and Sashimi selection.

Herne Hill *Gtr London –* ✉ *SE24.*

XX **3 Monkeys**   7   FX   **r**
136-140 Herne Hill, SE24 9QH, ✆ (020) 7738 5500, *jan@3monkeysrestaurant.c om, Fax (020) 7738 5505*
↝ ▤. **M©** **AE** **①** ***VISA*** **JCB**
closed 25-26 December and 1 January – **Meals** - Indian - (dinner only) a la carte 19.00/30.45 ♀.
♦ 'New wave' Indian restaurant in a converted bank. Dining room in bright white reached via a bridge over the bar and kitchen. Menu uses influences from all over India.

*If you are held up on the road - from 6pm onwards - confirm your hotel booking by telephone.
It is safer and quite an accepted practice.*

Kennington *Gtr London –* ✉ *SE11.*

✗✗ Kennington Lane   40 ANZ S
205-209 Kennington Lane, SE11 5QS, ℰ (020) 7793 8313, *Fax (020) 7793 8323*
🍸 – 🍽, 🆗 🆎 **VISA** ᴊᴄʙ
Meals 13.75 (lunch) and a la carte 23.90/25.90 ♀.
♦ Green-hued entrance with large awning leads into the contemporary interior. Bare wooden tables and fresh white walls. Purposeful staff, modern menu with European influences.

✗ Lobster Pot   40 AOY e
3 Kennington Lane, SE11 4RG, ℰ (020) 7582 5556
🍽, 🆗 🆎 ⓞ **VISA** ᴊᴄʙ
closed 23 December-7 January, Sunday and Monday – **Meals** - French Seafood - 13.50/39.50 and a la carte 26.30/37.30.
♦ A nautical theme so bold you'll need your sea legs: fishing nets, shells, aquariums, portholes, even the sound of seagulls. Classic French seafood menu is more restrained.

Lambeth *Gtr London –* ✉ *SE1.*

🏨 Novotel London Waterloo   40 AMY a
113 Lambeth Rd, SE1 7LS, ℰ (020) 7793 1010, *h1785@accor-hotels.com, Fax (020) 7793 0202*
Ⅰ₆, ≘s – |‡|, ⅔ rm, 🍽 📺 📞 ♿ ⟷ – 🔼 40. 🆗 🆎 ⓞ **VISA** ᴊᴄʙ. ✂
Meals (bar lunch Saturday and Sunday) 19.95 and a la carte 22.20/29.30 **s.** ♀ – ☲ 12.95 – **185 rm** 140.00/160.00, 2 suites.
♦ Modern, group owned purpose-built hotel, convenient for the station. Uniformly decorated bedrooms, with a good level of extras. Secure basement parking. All-day brasserie and buffet lunch option.

Waterloo *Gtr London –* ✉ *SE1.*

Channel Tunnel : Eurostar information and reservations ℰ *(08705) 186186.*

🏨 London Marriott H. County Hall   40 AMX a
SE1 7PB, ℰ (020) 7928 5200, *salesadmin.countyhall@marriotthotels.co.uk, Fax (020) 7928 5300*
≼, Ⅰ₆, ≘s, 🔲 – |‡|, ⅔ rm, 🍽 📺 📞 ♿ – 🔼 70. 🆗 🆎 ⓞ **VISA** ᴊᴄʙ. ✂
County Hall : **Meals** 26.50 (lunch) and a la carte 25.50/43.00 **s.** ♀ – ☲ 18.95 – **195 rm** 292.50, 5 suites.
♦ Occupying the historic County Hall building. Many of the spacious and comfortable bedrooms enjoy river and Parliament outlook. Impressive leisure facilities. Famously impressive views from restaurant.

🏨 London County Hall Travel Inn Capital   32 AMV u
Belvedere Rd, SE1 7PB, ℰ (0870) 2383300, *london.county.hall.mti.@whitbread.com, Fax (020) 7902 1619*
|‡| ⅔, 🍽 rest, 📺 📞 ♿. 🆗 🆎 ⓞ **VISA**. ✂
Meals (grill rest.) (dinner only) – **313 rm** 82.95.
♦ Adjacent to the London Eye and within the County Hall building. Budget accommodation in a central London location that is the envy of many, more expensive, hotels.

🏨 Days   40 ANY X
54 Kennington Rd, SE1 7BJ, ℰ (020) 7922 1331, *Reservations (Freephone)* 0800 0280400, *reservations.waterloo@dayshotel.co.uk, Fax (020) 7922 1441 without rest.* – |‡| ⅔ 📺 📞 ♿. 🆗 🆎 ⓞ **VISA**. ✂ – ☲ 5.95 **162 rm** 84.00.
♦ Useful lodge accommodation, opposite the Imperial War Museum. Identical bedrooms are well-equipped and decorated in warm colours. Competitively priced.

MERTON *Gtr London.*

Colliers Wood *Gtr London –* ✉ *SW19.*

🏠 **Express by Holiday Inn** 7 EY **a**
200 High St, SW19 2BH, on A 24, ✆ (020) 8545 7300, *Fax (020) 8545 7301*
without rest. – |🛗| ✳ 📺 📞 ⅙ 🚗 – 🔒 50. 🆎 ⒶⒺ ⓪ 𝘝𝘐𝘚𝘈 ᴊᴄʙ. ✼
83 rm 92.00.
 ♦ Modern, corporate budget hotel. Spacious and well-equipped bedrooms;
power showers in en suite bathrooms. Ideal for the business traveller. Continental breakfast included.

Wimbledon *Gtr London –* ✉ *SW19.*

🏰 **Cannizaro House** 6 DXY **X**
West Side, Wimbledon Common, SW19 4UE, ✆ (0870) 333 9124, *cannizaroho*
use@thistle.co.uk, Fax (0870) 3339224
 🐾, ≼, 🌡, 🏋, – |🛗|, ✳ rm, 📺 📞 🅿. – 🔒 120. 🆎 ⒶⒺ ⓪ 𝘝𝘐𝘚𝘈 ᴊᴄʙ. ✼
Meals a la carte 21.00/41.00 ♈ – 🍽 14.50 – **43 rm** 259.00, 2 suites.
 ♦ Part Georgian mansion in a charming spot on the Common. Appealing
drawing room popular for afternoon tea. Rooms in original house are antique
furnished, some with balconies. Refined restaurant overlooks splendid formal
garden.

✗ **Light House** 6 DY **n**
75-77 Ridgway, SW19 4ST, ✆ (020) 8944 6338, *lightrest@aol.com,*
Fax (020) 8946 4440
 🆎 ⒶⒺ 𝘝𝘐𝘚𝘈
closed 4 days Christmas, 2 days Easter and Sunday dinner – **Meals** - Italian
influences - 12.50 (lunch) and a la carte 22.00/32.70 ♈.
 ♦ Bright and modern neighbourhood restaurant with open plan kitchen.
Informal service of a weekly changing and diverse menu of progressive
Italian/fusion dishes.

🍴 **The Fire Stables** 6 DX **a**
27-29 Church Rd, SW19 5DQ, ✆ (020) 8946 3197, *thefirestables@thespiritgrou*
p.com, Fax (020) 8946 1101
 ▤. 🆎 ⒶⒺ 𝘝𝘐𝘚𝘈
closed 25 December – **Meals** a la carte 18.25/29.00 ♈.
 ♦ Modern "gastropub" in village centre. Open-plan kitchen. Polished wood
tables and banquettes. Varied modern British dishes. Expect fishcakes, duck
confit salad or risotto.

REDBRIDGE *Gtr London.*

Ilford *Essex –* ✉ *Essex.*

 🏌18 *Wanstead Park Rd* ✆ *(020) 8554 2930,* HU – 🏌18, 🏌9 *Fairlop Waters, Forest Rd,*
Barkingside ✆ *(020) 8500 9911* JT.

🏠 **Travelodge** 4 HU **e**
Beehive Lane, IG4 5DR, ✆ (08700) 850950, *Fax (020) 8550 4248*
 ✳ rm, 📺 ⅙ 🅿. 🆎 ⒶⒺ ⓪ 𝘝𝘐𝘚𝘈 ᴊᴄʙ. ✼
Meals (grill rest.) – **32 rm** 79.95.
 ♦ Just off the main A12, a standard lodge-style hotel with well-maintained
and spacious bedrooms. Harvester pub alongside provides a menu specialising in grilled dishes.

🏠 **Travel Inn Metro**　　　　　　　　　　　　　　　　4　HU　i
Redbridge Lane East, IG4 5BG, ℰ (020) 8550 7909, *Fax (020) 8550 6214*
💲, ✳ rm, ▤ rest, 📺 ⎗ 🅿 – 🛄 40. 🕼 🄰🄴 🕥 *VISA*. ✵
Meals (grill rest.) – **44 rm** 54.95.
   ◆ Convenient for the M11, well-kept lodge accommodation with standard sized bedrooms, all with extra sofa beds. Beefeater adjacent provides a grill-based menu.

South Woodford *Essex –* ✉ *Essex.*

XX **Ho-Ho**　　　　　　　　　　　　　　　　　　　4　HU　C
20 High Rd, E18 2QL, ℰ (020) 8989 1041
▤, 🕼 🄰🄴 🕥 *VISA*
closed 25-26 December and Saturday lunch – **Meals** - Chinese (Peking, Szechuan) - 7.50/27.50 and a la carte 14.40/23.90 **s**.
   ◆ Large room with tiled floor and Chinese decoration. Attentive service from smart team. Menu specialises in Peking and Szechuan dishes, with extensive vegetarian choice.

Woodford *Essex –* ✉ *Essex.*

🏌 *2 Sunset Ave, Woodford Green* ℰ *(020) 8504 0553.*
London 13 – Brentwood 16 – Harlow 16.

🏨 **County H. Woodford**　　　　　　　　　　　　4　HT　C
30 Oak Hill, Woodford Green, IG8 9NY, ℰ (0870) 609 6156, *countyepping@corushotels.com, Fax (020) 8506 0941*
💲 ✳, ▤ rest, 📺 🅿 – 🛄 150. 🕼 🄰🄴 🕥 *VISA*. ✵
Meals *(closed Saturday lunch)* 18.95 (lunch) and a la carte 15.00/25.00 – 🍽 10.95 – **99 rm** 79.00/89.00.
   ◆ Purpose-built redbrick hotel on the edge of historic Epping Forest. Standard sized bedrooms, decorated with pine furniture. Extensive conference facilities.

When looking for a quiet hotel
use the maps in the introduction
or look for establishments with the sign ✺

RICHMOND-UPON-THAMES *Gtr London.*

Barnes *Gtr London –* ✉ *SW13.*

XX **Sonny's**　　　　　　　　　　　　　　　　21　KZH　X
94 Church Rd, SW13 0DQ, ℰ (020) 8748 0393, *barnes@sonnys.co.uk, Fax (020) 8748 2698*
▤, 🕼 🄰🄴 🕥 *VISA*
closed Sunday dinner and Bank Holidays – **Meals** 15.00/21.00 (lunch) and a la carte 20.25/31.50 ♀.
   ◆ Dine in the bright, modern and informal restaurant or the equally relaxed café-bar. Attentive service of imaginative modern dishes.

XX **MVH**　　　　　　　　　　　　　　　　　　21　KZH　e
5 White Hart Lane, SW13 0PX, ℰ (020) 8392 1111, *Fax (0208) 878 1919*
🕼 🄰🄴 🕥 *VISA* 🄹🄲🄱
closed 2 weeks after Christmas and lunch Monday-Wednesday – **Meals** 22.00/29.00 and a la carte 23.50/30.50.
   ◆ Restaurant exuding individuality, Bohemian-style bar area and a dining room that mixes a Louis XIV style and modern elements. Unique food in keeping with the mood.

✕ Riva
21 LZH **a**

169 Church Rd, SW13 9HR, ☏ (020) 8748 0434, *Fax (020) 8748 0434*

⦿ AE VISA

closed last 2 weeks August, 1 week Christmas-New Year, 4 days Easter, Saturday lunch and Bank Holidays – **Meals** - Italian - a la carte 26.50/36.00 ⵙ.

◆ The eponymous owner manages the polite service in this unassuming restaurant. Rustic and robust cooking uses some of Italy's finest produce. Extensive all-Italian wine list.

East Sheen *Gtr London –* ✉ *SW14.*

✕✕ Redmond's
6 CX **V**

170 Upper Richmond Road West, SW14 8AW, ☏ (020) 8878 1922, *pippahaywar d@btconnect.com, Fax (020) 8878 1133*

▤. ⦿ AE VISA

closed Bank Holidays except Good Friday – **Meals** (dinner only and Sunday lunch)/dinner 29.50.

◆ Bright, spacious and relaxed restaurant. Friendly and approachable service of modern British cooking prepared with care. Mid-week set-price menu is good value.

✕✕ Crowther's
6 CX **n**

481 Upper Richmond Rd West, SW14 7PU, ☏ (020) 8876 6372, *Pacrowther@a ol.com, Fax (020) 8876 6372*

▤. ⦿ VISA JCB

closed 2 weeks August, 1 week February, 25-30 December, Sunday and Monday – **Meals** (booking essential) (lunch by arrangement)/dinner 26.50.

◆ This traditional and homely restaurant continues to attract a loyal and local clientele. Concise Anglo-French menu cooked and served by the welcoming owners.

▯ The Victoria
6 CX **u**

10 West Temple Sheen, SW14 7RT, ☏ (020) 8876 4238, *mark@thevictoria.net, Fax (020) 8878 3464*

🌧 – ✖ P. ⦿ AE VISA

closed 1 week Christmas – **Meals** a la carte 17.85/29.85 ⵙ.

◆ Traditional pub near Richmond Park with bright modern décor. Large conservatory, terrace and children's play area. Daily menu of Interesting modern and traditional dishes.

Hampton Court *Surrey –* ✉ *Surrey.*

⛉ Carlton Mitre
5 BY **V**

Hampton Court Rd, KT8 9BN, ☏ (020) 8979 9988, *salesmitre@carltonhotels.co .uk, Fax (020) 8979 9777*

≼, 🌧 – ⧄ ⬧ ✖ TV ☏ P. – ⛶ 50. ⦿ AE VISA. ⁒

Rivers Edge : Meals a la carte approx. 16.95

The Mitre : Meals (dinner only and Sunday lunch) a la carte approx. 22.45 –

⌷ 11.50 – **34 rm** 175.00/195.00, 2 suites.

◆ Attractive hotel in unrivalled position, built in 1665 for guests of the royal household. Some of the well-appointed rooms have Palace or river views. The Mitre restaurant has superb river views. Rivers Edge is an informal café-bar with a riverside terrace.

The rates shown may be revised if the cost of living changes to any great extent. Before making your reservations,
confirm with the hotelier the exact price that will be charged.

Hampton Hill *Middx –* ✉ *Middx.*

XX **Monsieur Max**   5   BY **a**
133 High St, TW12 1NJ, ✆ (020) 8979 5546, *monsieurmax@aol.com,*
Fax (020) 8979 3747
▤. **⑩⑩** **AE** **⑩** **VISA**
closed 25-26 December and Saturday lunch – **Meals** - French - 25.00/37.50 ℉.
♦ An appealing neighbourhood restaurant. Relaxed and attentive service of
modern cooking with some classic French influences. Guests can bring their
own wine, if they prefer.

Hampton Wick *Surrey –* ✉ *Surrey.*

🏠 **Chase Lodge**   5   BY **e**
10 Park Rd, KT1 4AS, ✆ (020) 8943 1862, *info@chaselodgehotel.com,*
Fax (020) 8943 9363
TV. **⑩⑩** **AE** **⑩** **VISA** **JCB**
Meals (lunch by arrangement) 15.00/30.00 – **13 rm** ⌷ 65.00/105.00.
♦ Personally-run small hotel in mid-terrace Victorian property in an area of
outstanding architectural and historical interest. Individually furnished, com-
fortable rooms. Bright, airy conservatory restaurant.

Kew *Surrey –* ✉ *Surrey.*

XX **The Glasshouse**   6   CX **Z**
❀ 14 Station Par, TW9 3PZ, ✆ (020) 8940 6777, *Fax (020) 8940 3833*
▤. **⑩⑩** **AE** **VISA**
closed 3 days at Christmas – **Meals** 17.50/30.00 ℉.
♦ Light pours in through the glass façade of this forever busy and contemporary restaurant. Assured service of original modern British cooking.
Spec. Salad of wood pigeon and truffled egg. Pork belly with apple, sage and
choucroute tart. Vanilla yoghurt with poached rhubarb.

Richmond *Surrey –* ✉ *Surrey.*

🏌, 🏌 *Richmond Park, Roehampton Gate* ✆ (020) 8876 3205 CX – 🏌 *Sudbrook
Park* ✆ (020) 8940 1463 CX.

🛈 *Old Town Hall, Whittaker Ave* ✆ (020) 8940 9125.

🏛 **Petersham**   6   CX **c**
Nightingale Lane, TW10 6UZ, ✆ (020) 8940 7471, *enq@petershamhotel.co.uk,*
Fax (020) 8939 1002
≼, ☞ – 🛗 **TV** 📞 **P** – 🕿 50. **⑩⑩** **AE** **⑩** **VISA**. ❄
Meals –(see **Restaurant** below) – **60 rm** ⌷ 135.00/295.00, 1 suite.
♦ Extended over the years, a fine example of Victorian Gothic architecture.
Impressive Portland stone, self-supporting staircase. Most comfortable
rooms overlook the Thames.

🏛 **Richmond Gate**   6   CX **c**
158 Richmond Hill, TW10 6RP, ✆ 0870 609 6177, *richmondgate@corushotels.
com, Fax (020) 8332 0354*
🏋, ⇔, 🎱, ☞ – ⇌ **TV** 📞 **P** – 🕿 45. **⑩⑩** **AE** **⑩** **VISA** **JCB**. ❄
Gates On The Park : **Meals** *(closed lunch Saturday)* 19.75/31.00 ℉ – **67 rm**
⌷ 150.00/178.00, 1 suite.
♦ Originally four elegant Georgian town houses and now a very comfortable
corporate hotel. Cosy lounges have a period charm. Well-appointed rooms
have thoughtful extras. Small, comfortable, Georgian style restaurant.

⌂ **Doughty Cottage**   6   CX   C
142A Richmond Hill, TW10 6RN, ℰ (020) 8332 9434, *deniseoneill425@aol.co.uk*, Fax *(020) 8948 3716*
without rest., ⌗ – ⇆ 📺 **P.** 🅾🅾 *VISA* JCB. ⌒
closed 24-26 December – ⌑ 5.50 **3 rm** 75.00/103.00.
  ◆ Positioned high above the river, this attractive 18C Regency house is discreetly set behind a picturesque walled garden. Thoughtfully equipped rooms, two with patio gardens.

※※※ **Restaurant** (at Petersham H.)   6   CX   C
Nightingale Lane, TW10 6UZ, ℰ (020) 8939 1084, *Fax (020) 8939 1002*
≤, ⌗ – ⇆ ▤ **P.** 🅾🅾 **AE** ⓞ *VISA*
Meals (closed Sunday dinner) 20.00 (lunch) and a la carte 28.00/43.00 ⓣ.
  ◆ Tables by the window have spectacular views across royal parkland and the winding Thames. Formal surroundings in which to enjoy classic and modern cooking. See the cellars.

Teddington *Middx* – ✉ *Middx.*

※※ **The Wharf**   5   BX   a
22 Manor Rd, TW11 8BG, ℰ (020) 8977 6333, *the.wharf@walk-on-water.co.uk*, Fax *(020) 8977 9444*
≤, ⌗ – ⬇ ▤ **P.** 🅾🅾 **AE** *VISA*
Meals 16.00 (lunch) and a la carte 21.50/33.00 ⓣ.
  ◆ Riverside restaurant with large heated terrace opposite Teddington lock. Modern menu of good value dishes; fixed price menu in the week; modern music.

Twickenham *Middx* – ✉ *Middx.*

※※ **McClements**   5   BX   a
❀ 2 Whitton Rd, TW1 1BJ, ℰ (020) 8744 9610, *johnmac21@aol.com*, Fax *(020) 8744 9598*
⇆ ▤. 🅾🅾 **AE** *VISA*
closed 2 weeks Christmas-New Year, Sunday and Monday – **Meals** 19.50/40.00 ⓣ.
  ◆ An intimate neighbourhood restaurant offering polished service. Accomplished modern British cooking. 'Degustation' menu includes wines. Excellent wine list..
Spec. Baby courgette with asparagus mousse and mushroom cream. Roast loin of venison with cabbage and chocolate sauce. Banana split.

※ **Brula**   5   BX   V
☺ 43 Crown Rd, St Margarets, TW1 3EJ, ℰ (020) 8892 0602, *Fax (020) 8892 7727*
🅾🅾 *VISA*
closed 1 week Christmas, Sunday and Bank Holidays except Good Friday – **Meals** (booking essential) 11.00 (lunch) and a la carte 19.50/25.00.
  ◆ Behind the stained glass windows and the rose arched entrance, you'll find an intimate and cosy bistro. Friendly and relaxed service of a weekly changing, rustic menu.

※ **Ma Cuisine**   5   BX   a
☺ 6 Whitton Rd, TW1 1BJ, ℰ (020) 8607 9849
🅾🅾 **AE** ⓞ *VISA*
closed Sunday dinner – **Meals** - French - 9.50/15.00.
  ◆ Small neighbourhood bistro style restaurant offering good value. Classic French country cooking with blackboard specials; concise wine list.

🛈 *London Bridge, 6 Tooley St* ℰ *(020) 7403 8299.*

Bermondsey *Gtr London –* ✉ *SE1.*

🏨 **London Bridge**   33 AQV **a**
8-18 London Bridge St, SE1 9SG, ℰ (020) 7855 2200, *sales@london-bridge-hotel.co.uk, Fax (020) 7855 2233*
ǀ₅ – 🛗, ✲ rm, 🖥 📺 ✆ ᕕ – 🔼 100. 🐼 🖭 ⓪ 𝘝𝘐𝘚𝘈 JCB. 🛇
Georgetown : Meals 12.50/15.00 (lunch) and a la carte 17.50/21.75 **s.** – ⬚ 13.95 – **135 rm** 150.00/190.00, 3 suites.
♦ In one of the oldest parts of London, independently owned with an ornate façade dating from 1915. Modern interior with classically decorated bedrooms and an impressive gym. Restaurant echoing the colonial style serving Malaysian dishes.

🏨 **London Tower Bridge Travel Inn Capital**   20 XZE **a**
159 Tower Bridge Rd, SE1 3LP, ℰ (020) 7940 3700, *Fax (020) 7940 3719*
🛗, ✲ rm, 📺 ᕕ 🅿. 🐼 🖭 ⓪ 𝘝𝘐𝘚𝘈. 🛇
Meals (grill rest.) (dinner only) – **195 rm** 74.95.
♦ Ideal for tourists by being next to a tube station and the famous bridge. Clean and spacious budget accommodation, with uniform-sized bedrooms.

XXX **Le Pont de la Tour**   34 ASV **c**
36d Shad Thames, Butlers Wharf, SE1 2YE, ℰ (020) 7403 8403, *Fax (020) 7403 0267*
≼, 🏠 –🐼 🖭 ⓪ 𝘝𝘐𝘚𝘈
Meals 29.50 (lunch) and dinner a la carte 32.50/43.00 ⬚.
♦ Elegant and stylish room commanding spectacular views of the Thames and Tower Bridge. Formal and detailed service. Modern menu with an informal bar attached.

XX **Bengal Clipper**   34 ASV **e**
Cardamom Building, Shad Thames, Butlers Wharf, SE1 2YR, ℰ (020) 7357 9001, *clipper@bengalrestaurants.co.uk, Fax (020) 7357 9002*
🖥. 🐼 🖭 𝘝𝘐𝘚𝘈
Meals - Indian - a la carte 12.25/17.25.
♦ Housed in a Thames-side converted warehouse, a smart Indian restaurant with original brickwork and steel supports. Menu features Bengali and Goan dishes. Evening pianist.

XX **Tentazioni**   20 XZE **x**
2 Mill St, Lloyds Wharf, SE1 2BD, ℰ (020) 7237 1100, *tentazioni@aol.com, Fax (020) 7237 1100*
🐼 🖭 ⓪ 𝘝𝘐𝘚𝘈 JCB
closed 25 December, Sunday, lunch Saturday and Monday – **Meals** - Italian - 26.00 and a la carte 25.00/34.00 ⬚.
♦ Former warehouse provides a bright and lively environment. Open staircase between the two floors. Keenly run, with a menu offering simple, carefully prepared Italian food.

X **Blueprint Café**   34 ASV **u**
Design Museum, Shad Thames, Butlers Wharf, SE1 2YD, ℰ (020) 7378 7031, *Fax (020) 7357 8810*
≼ Tower Bridge –🐼 🖭 ⓪ 𝘝𝘐𝘚𝘈
Meals a la carte 22.50/39.50 ⬚.
♦ Above the Design Museum, with impressive views of the river and bridge: handy binoculars on tables. Eager and energetic service, modern British menus: robust and rustic.

✗ **Cantina Del Ponte**   34 ASV **C**
36c   Shad   Thames,   Butlers   Wharf,   SE1   2YE,   ✆ (020) 7403 5403,
Fax (020) 7403 4432
≤, 斎 –⨶ ᴀᴇ ⓪ 𝗩𝗜𝗦𝗔
Meals - Italian - 13.50 (lunch) and a la carte 16.20/27.40 ♀.
♦ Quayside setting with a large canopied terrace. Terracotta flooring; modern rustic style décor, simple and unfussy. Tasty, refreshing Mediterranean-
influenced cooking.

✗ **Butlers Wharf Chop House**   34 ASV **n**
36e   Shad   Thames,   Butlers   Wharf,   SE1   2YE,   ✆ (020) 7403 3403,
Fax (020) 7403 3414
≤ Tower Bridge, 斎 –⨶ ᴀᴇ ⓪ 𝗩𝗜𝗦𝗔
closed Sunday dinner – **Meals** 23.75 (lunch) and dinner a la carte 23.00/33.75
♀.
♦ Book the terrace in summer and dine in the shadow of Tower Bridge.
Rustic feel to the interior, with obliging service. Menu focuses on traditional
English dishes.

Dulwich *Gtr London* – ✉ *SE21*.

✗✗ **Belair House**   7 FX **e**
Gallery Rd, Dulwich Village, SE21 7AB, ✆ (020) 8299 9788, *info@belairhouse.co*
.uk, Fax (020) 8299 6793
斎, 🌳 –**P**, ⨶ ᴀᴇ ⓪ 𝗩𝗜𝗦𝗔
closed Sunday dinner and Monday lunch – **Meals** 22.00/32.00 ♀.
♦ A striking Georgian summer house, floodlit at night, and surrounded by
manicured lawns. By contrast, interior is bright and modern with summery
colours. Eclectic menu.

Rotherhithe *Gtr London* – ✉ *SE16*.

🏨 **Hilton London Docklands**   7 GV **r**
265   Rotherhithe   St,   Nelson   Dock,   SE16   5HW,   ✆ (020) 7231 1001,
Fax (020) 7231 0599
≤, 斎, 𝐼₆, ⤢, ◪ – ⧣, ⤢ rm, ▤ 🆃🆅 ✆ ᵭ **P** – ⬥ 350. ⨶ ᴀᴇ 𝗩𝗜𝗦𝗔. ⌘
closed 23-29 December –
***Traders Bistro* :** Meals *(closed Sunday)* (dinner only) a la carte 20.00/30.00 ♀
***Terrace* :** **Meals** (dinner only) 25.00 **s**. ♀ – ⌑ 15.00 – **361 rm** 125.00,
4 suites.
♦ Redbrick group hotel with glass façade. River-taxi from the hotel's own
pier. Extensive leisure facilities. Standard size rooms with all mod cons. Eat on
board Traders Bistro, a reconstructed galleon moored in dry dock. The Terrace for buffet style dining.

Southwark *Gtr London* – ✉ *SE1*.

🏨 **Novotel London City South**   34 AQV **C**
53-61 Southwark Bridge Rd, SE1 9HH, ✆ (020) 7089 0400, *h3269@accor-hotel*
s.com, Fax (020) 7089 0410
𝐼₆, ⤢ – ⧣, ⤢ rm, ▤ 🆃🆅 ✆ ᵭ – ⬥ 100. ⨶ ᴀᴇ ⓪ 𝗩𝗜𝗦𝗔 ᴊᴄʙ
***The Garden Brasserie* :** Meals 18.95 and a la carte 15.45/30.90 **s**. ♀ – ⌑
12.95 – **178 rm** 140.00/160.00, 4 suites.
♦ The new style of Novotel with good business facilities. Triple glazed bedrooms, furnished in the Scandinavian with keyboard and high speed internet.
Brasserie style dining room with windows all down one side.

🏨 **Mercure**   33 APV r
71-79 Southwark St, SE1 0JA, ✆ (020) 7902 0800, *h2814@accor-hotels.com,*
Fax (020) 7902 0810
📠 – 🛗, ⇔ rm, 🖥 📺 ✆ 🕭. – 🏋 60. 🅾🅾 🄰🄴 ⓞ 𝕍𝕀𝕊𝔸 𝙹𝙲𝙱. ⌘
The Loft : **Meals** (bar lunch Saturday and Sunday) 14.50/18.00 and a la carte ♀
– ☲ 12.95 – **144 rm** 140.00/160.00.
 ◆ Newly converted office block, providing bright and spacious accommodation. Modern, open-plan lobby leads to well-equipped and comfortable bedrooms. Split-level dining room with tiled flooring.

🏨 **Premier Lodge**   33 AQV b
Anchor, Bankside, 34 Park St, SE1 9EF, ✆ (0870) 7001456, *Fax (0870)*
7001457
🛗, ⇔ rm, 📺 ✆ 🕭. 🅾🅾 🄰🄴 ⓞ 𝕍𝕀𝕊𝔸. ⌘
Meals (grill rest.) a la carte approx. 14.50 – **56 rm** 72.00.
 ◆ A good value lodge with modern, well-equipped bedrooms which include
a spacious desk area, ideal for the corporate and leisure traveller.

🏨 **Express by Holiday Inn**   33 APV e
103-109 Southwark St, SE1 0JQ, ✆ (020) 7401 2525, *stay@expresssouthwark.c*
o.uk, Fax (020) 7401 3322
without rest. – 🛗 ⇔ 🖥 📺 ✆ 🕭 🅿. 🅾🅾 🄰🄴 ⓞ 𝕍𝕀𝕊𝔸. ⌘
88 rm 98.00.
 ◆ Useful location, just ten minutes from Waterloo. Purpose-built hotel
with modern bedrooms in warm pastel shades. Fully equipped business
centre.

🏨 **Southwark Rose**   34 AQV c
43-47 Southwark Bridge Rd, SE1 9HH, ✆ (020) 7015 1480, *info@southwarkros*
ehotel.co.uk, Fax (020) 7015 1481
without rest. – 🛗 ⇔ 🖥 📺 ✆ 🕭 🅿. 🅾🅾 🄰🄴 𝕍𝕀𝕊𝔸
☲ 7.95 – **78 rm** 105.00, 6 suites.
 ◆ Purpose built budget hotel south of the City, near the Globe Theatre. Top
floor breakfast room with bar. Uniform style, reasonably spacious bedrooms
with writing desks.

XXX **Oxo Tower**   32 ANV a
(8th floor), Oxo Tower Wharf, Barge House St, SE1 9PH, ✆ (020) 7803 3888, *ox*
o.reservations@harveynichols.co.uk, Fax (020) 7803 3838
≼ London skyline and River Thames, 🏛 – 🛗 🖥. 🅾🅾 🄰🄴 ⓞ 𝕍𝕀𝕊𝔸
closed 25-26 December – **Meals** 28.50 (lunch) and dinner a la carte 27.50/
43.50 ♀ – (see also **Oxo Tower Brasserie** below).
 ◆ Top of a converted factory, providing stunning views of the Thames and
beyond. Stylish, minimalist interior with huge windows. Smooth service of
modern cuisine.

XX **Baltic**   33 AOV e
74 Blackfriars Rd, SE1 8HA, ✆ (020) 7928 1111, *info@balticrestaurant.co.uk,*
Fax (020) 7928 8487
🅾🅾 🄰🄴 ⓞ 𝕍𝕀𝕊𝔸
closed Saturday lunch – **Meals** - East European with Baltic influences - 13.50
(lunch) and a la carte 18.00/30.00 ♀.
 ◆ Set in a Grade II listed 18C former coach house. Enjoy authentic and hearty
east European and Baltic influenced food. Interesting vodka selection and live
jazz on Sundays.

✗ Oxo Tower Brasserie   32 ANV a
(8th floor), Oxo Tower Wharf, Barge House St, SE1 9PH, ✆ (020) 7803 3888,
Fax (020) 7803 3838
≼ London skyline and River Thames, 🏠 – 🛗 ▤. 🆖 ᴀᴇ ⓪ 𝚅𝙸𝚂𝙰 ᴊᴄʙ .
closed 25-26 December – **Meals** 18.50 (lunch) and a la carte 21.50/31.50 ♀.
♦ Same views but less formal than the restaurant. Open-plan kitchen, relaxed service and the modern menu is slightly lighter. In summer, try to
secure a table on the terrace.

✗ Cantina Vinopolis   33 AQV z
No.1 Bank End, SE1 9BU, ✆ (020) 7940 8333, *cantina@vinopolis.co.uk,*
Fax (020) 7940 8334
▤. 🆖 ᴀᴇ ⓪ 𝚅𝙸𝚂𝙰 ᴊᴄʙ
closed Christmas, New Year and Sunday dinner – **Meals** 26.95 and a la carte
20.95/33.70 ♀.
♦ Large, solid brick vaulted room under Victorian railway arches, with an
adjacent wine museum. Modern menu with a huge selection of wines by the
glass.

✗ Livebait   32 ANV c
43 The Cut, SE1 8LF, ✆ (020) 7928 7211, *livebaitwaterloo@groupchezgerard.c
o.uk, Fax (020) 7928 2279*
🆖 ᴀᴇ ⓪ 𝚅𝙸𝚂𝙰
closed 25-26 December, 1 January, Sunday and Bank Holidays – **Meals** -
Seafood - 15.95 (lunch) and a la carte 30.00/40.00 ♀.
♦ Slight Victorian feel with wall tiles and booths. Lively atmosphere is dis-
tinctly modern. Helpful and obliging service. Comprehensive seafood menu
from the on-view kitchen.

✗ Tate Cafe (7th Floor)   33 APV s
Tate Modern, Bankside, SE1 9TE, ✆ (020) 7401 5020, *Fax (020) 7401 5171*
≼ London skyline and River Thames – ✖️. 🆖 ᴀᴇ ⓪ 𝚅𝙸𝚂𝙰
closed 24-26 December – **Meals** (lunch only and dinner Friday-Saturday)
a la carte 19.75/26.50 ♀.
♦ Modernity to match the museum, with vast murals and huge windows
affording stunning views. Canteen-style menu at a sensible price with obliging service.

✗ Fish!   33 AQV s
Cathedral St, Borough Market, SE1 9AL, ✆ (020) 7407 3803, *borough@fishdin
er.couk, Fax (020) 7387 8636*
🏠 – ▤. 🆖 ᴀᴇ ⓪ 𝚅𝙸𝚂𝙰
closed 25 December and 1 January – **Meals** - Seafood - a la carte 24.45/
32.45 ♀.
♦ Under railway arches, an unusual structure made entirely of glass and
metal. Seafood menu where diners choose the fish as well as the accompany-
ing sauce.

Write to us...
If you have any comments on the contents of this Guide.
Your praise as well as your criticisms will receive careful
consideration and, with your assistance, we will be able to add
to our stock of information and, where necessary, amend
our judgments.
Thank you in advance!

SUTTON *Gtr London.*

Carshalton *Surrey – ✉ Surrey.*

XX La Veranda   6 EZ **c**
   18-19 Beynon Rd, SM5 3RL, ℰ (020) 8647 4370
   ▤, ⓜⓠ AE ① VISA
   closed Sunday and Bank Holidays – **Meals** - Italian - a la carte approx.
   23.00.
   ◆ The rather unassuming façade belies the friendly atmosphere. The regular
   clientele enjoy selecting their food from the extensive buffet. Traditional
   Italian cooking.

Sutton *Surrey – ✉ Surrey.*

   ⓘ₈, ⓘ₉ *Oak Sports Centre, Woodmansterne Rd, Carshalton* ℰ (020) 8643 8363.

🏛 Holiday Inn   6 DZ **a**
   Gibson Rd, SM1 2RF, ℰ (020) 8770 1311, *Fax (020) 8770 1539*
   ⅃₆, ⇌, ▨ – 🛗, ⇝ rm, ▤ TV ℰ ♿ P – 🔳 180. ⓜⓠ AE ① VISA JCB.
   ⅍
   Meals 15.00 and a la carte approx 21.00 – � 14.95 – **115 rm** 165.00,
   1 suite.
   ◆ Centrally located and modern. Offers comprehensive conference facilities.
   Spacious and well-equipped bedrooms. An ideal base for both corporate and
   leisure guests. Bright, modern, relaxed bar and restaurant.

🏛 Thatched House   6 DZ **e**
   135-141 Cheam Rd, SM1 2BN, ℰ (020) 8642 3131, *thatchedhouse@btconnect*
   .com, Fax (020) 8770 0684
   ⇌ – ⇝ rest, TV P – 🔳 50. ⓜⓠ ① VISA JCB. ⅍
   Meals *(closed Saturday-Sunday)* (bar lunch)/dinner 13.50 and a la carte 14.00/
   21.20 – **32 rm** ⊒ 85.00/100.00.
   ◆ Part thatched and gabled private hotel on busy main road just out of the
   town centre. Most comfortable and quietest rooms overlook the pretty
   gardens. Rustic-styled dining room.

   In this guide
   a symbol or a character,
   printed in **red** *or* **black**, *in light or bold type*
   does not have the same meaning.
   Pay particular attention to the explanatory pages.

TOWER HAMLETS *Gtr London.*

Blackwall *Gtr London – ✉ E14.*

🏛 Ibis   8 HV **c**
   1 Baffin Way, E14 9PE, ℰ (020) 7517 1100, *h2177@accor-hotels.com,*
   Fax (020) 7987 5916
   without rest. – 🛗, ⇝ rm, ▤ TV ℰ ♿. ⓜⓠ AE ① VISA JCB
   87 rm 71.95.
   ◆ Useful and sensibly priced accommodation, convenient for those visiting
   Canary Wharf. Bedrooms are all identically shaped, simply decorated and
   well-equipped.

Canary Wharf *Gtr London –* ✉ *E14.*

🏨 Four Seasons   3 GV **V**
Westferry Circus, E14 8RS, ✆ *(020) 7510 1999, Fax (020) 7510 1998*
≼, *ƒ₆*, ⇌s , 🔲 – |♿| ⇥ 🔲 TV 📞 ₺ ⟲ – ⚒ 200. 🆖 🆎 ⓪ *VISA* JCB. ⚡
Meals – (see *Quadrato* below) – ⌂ 20.00 – **128 rm** 352.50/411.25, 14 suites.
♦ Stylish hotel opened in 2000, with striking river and city views. Atrium lobby leading to modern bedrooms boasting every conceivable extra. Detailed service.

🏛 Circus Apartments   7 GV **a**
39 Westferry Circus, E14 8RW, ✆ *(020) 7719 7000, res@circusapartments.co.u k, Fax (020) 7719 7001*
without rest., *ƒ₆*, ⇌s , 🔲 – |♿| ⇥ 🔲 TV 📞 ⟲. 🆖 🆎 ⓪ *VISA* JCB. ⚡,
45 suites 293.75/346.60.
♦ Smart, contemporary, fully serviced appartment block close to Canary Wharf: rooms, comfortable and spacious, can be taken from one day to one year.

✗✗ Ubon by Nobu   7 GV **a**
34 Westferry Circus, E14 8RR, ✆ *(020) 7719 7800, ubon@noburestaurants.co m, Fax (020) 7719 7801*
≼ River Thames and city skyline – |♿| 🔲 P. 🆖 🆎 ⓪ *VISA* JCB
closed Christmas-New Year, Bank Holidays, Sunday and Saturday lunch –
Meals - Japanese - and a la carte approx. 75.00 **s**. ₤.
♦ Light, airy, open-plan restaurant, with floor to ceiling glass and great Thames views. Informal atmosphere. Large menu with wide selection of modern Japanese dishes.

✗✗ Quadrato (at Four Seasons H.)   3 GV **V**
Westferry Circus, E14 8RS, ✆ *(020) 7510 1999, Fax (020) 7510 1998*
⛱ – 🔲 ⟲. 🆖 🆎 ⓪ *VISA* JCB
Meals – Italian – 28.00/30.00 ₤.
♦ Striking, modern restaurant with terrace overlooking river. Sleek, stylish dining room with glass-fronted open-plan kitchen. Menu of northern Italian dishes; swift service.

East India Docks *Gtr London –* ✉ *E14.*

🏨 Travelodge   7 GV **S**
A 13 Coriander Ave, off East India Dock Rd, E14 2AA, off East India Dock Rd, ✆ *(08700) 850950, Fax (020) 7515 9178*
≼ – |♿|, ⇥ rm,) 🔲 rest, TV ₺ P. 🆖 🆎 ⓪ *VISA*. ⚡
Meals (grill rest.) – **232 rm** 79.95.
♦ Overlooking the Millennium Dome, a larger than average lodge-style hotel with uniform sized bedrooms. Acres of parking and an informal café-bar on the ground floor.

St Katherine's Dock *Gtr London –* ✉ *E1.*

✗✗ The Aquarium   34 ASV **a**
Ivory House, E1W 1AT, ✆ *(020) 7480 6116, info@theaquarium.co.uk, Fax (020) 7480 5973*
≼, ⛱ –🆖 🆎 ⓪ *VISA* JCB
closed 24-25 December, Monday dinner, Saturday lunch October-April, Sunday and Bank Holidays – **Meals** - Seafood - 20.50 a la carte 24.25/60.50 ₤.
♦ Seafood restaurant in a pleasant marina setting with views of the boats from some tables. Simple, smart modern décor. Menu of market-fresh, seafood dishes.

Spitalfields *Gtr London* – ✉ *E1.*

XX **Bengal Trader**   34 **AST X**
44 Artillery Lane, E1 7NA, ℘ (020) 7375 0072, *trader@bengalrestaurant.com,*
Fax (020) 7247 1002
🍽, **MO** 🅰🅴 **VISA**
Meals - Indian - a la carte 12.00/15.70.
♦ Contemporary Indian paintings feature in this stylish basement room beneath a ground floor bar. Menu provides ample choice of Indian dishes.

Whitechapel *Gtr London* – ✉ *E1.*

XX **Cafe Spice Namaste**   34 **ASU Z**
16 Prescot St, E1 8AZ, ℘ (020) 7488 9242, *info@cafespice.co.uk,*
Fax (020) 7481 0508
🍽, **MO** 🅰🅴 ⓪ **VISA** JCB
closed 1 week Christmas, Sunday, Saturday lunch and Bank Holidays – **Meals** -
Indian - 25.00 and a la carte 23.00/35.00 ♀.
♦ A riot of colour from the brightly painted walls to the flowing drapes. Sweet-natured service adds to the engaging feel. Fragrant and competitively priced Indian cooking.

Wapping *Gtr London* – ✉ *E1.*

X **Wapping Food**   20 **YZE n**
Wapping Wall, E1W 3ST, ℘ (020) 7680 2080, *wappingfood@wapping-wpt.com,*
Fax (020) 7680 2081
🏠 – 🅿, **MO** 🅰🅴 ⓪ **VISA**
closed 24 December-3 January and Sunday dinner – **Meals** a la carte 22.50/34.00.
♦ Something a little unusual; a combination of restaurant and gallery in a converted hydraulic power station. Enjoy the modern menu surrounded by turbines and TV screens.

WANDSWORTH *Gtr London.*

Battersea *Gtr London* – ✉ *SW8/SW11/SW18.*

🏨 **Express by Holiday Inn**   22 **OZH a**
Smugglers Way, SW18 1EG, ℘ (020) 8877 5950, *wandsworth@oreil-leisure.co.uk, Fax (020) 8877 0631*
without rest. – 🛗 ⫻ 🍽 📺 ✆ 🛏 🅿 – 🔥 35. **MO** 🅰🅴 ⓪ **VISA**. ✇
148 rm 92.00.
♦ Modern, purpose-built hotel on major roundabout, very much designed for the cost-conscious business guest or traveller. Adjacent steak house. Sizeable, well-kept bedrooms.

XX **Chada**   23 **QZH X**
208-210 Battersea Park Rd, SW11 4ND, ℘ (020) 7622 2209, *enquiry@chadathai.com, Fax (020) 7924 2178*
🍽, **MO** 🅰🅴 ⓪ **VISA** JCB
closed Sunday and Bank Holidays – **Meals** - Thai - (dinner only) a la carte 17.20/26.65 ♀.
♦ Weather notwithstanding, the Thai ornaments and charming staff in traditional silk costumes transport you to Bangkok. Carefully prepared and authentic dishes.

✂ **The Stepping Stone**   24 RZH **C**
123 Queenstown Rd, SW8 3RH, ℰ (020) 7622 0555, *thesteppingstone@aol.com, Fax (020) 7622 4230*
☰. **ⓜⓢ** **VISA**
closed 5 days Christmas, Saturday lunch, Sunday and Bank Holidays – **Meals** a la carte 18.00/27.00.
◆ Big bold colours and thoughtful service make this pleasant contemporary restaurant a local favourite. Eclectic, modern menu. Small bar to the rear.

✂ **Ransome's Dock**   23 QZG **C**
35-37 Parkgate Rd, SW11 4NP, ℰ (020) 7223 1611, *chef@ransomesdock.co.uk, Fax (020) 7924 2614*
☂ –**ⓜⓢ** **AE** **①** **VISA** **JCB**
closed Christmas, August Bank Holiday and Sunday dinner – **Meals** a la carte 18.75/35.75 ♀.
◆ Secreted in a warehouse development, with a dock-side terrace in summer. Vivid blue interior, crowded with pictures. Chef patron produces reliable brasserie-style cuisine.

Putney – ✉ SW15.

✗✗✗ **Putney Bridge**   22 MZH **U**
❀ Lower Richmond Rd, SW15 1LB, ℰ (020) 8780 1811, *Fax (020) 8780 1211*
≼ – ☰. **ⓜⓢ** **AE** **①** **VISA** **JCB**
closed 25-26 December, 1 January and Sunday dinner – **Meals** 22.00 (lunch) and a la carte 31.50/55.50 ♀.
◆ Winner of architectural awards, this striking glass and steel structure enjoys a charming riverside location. Exacting service; accomplished and detailed modern cooking.
Spec. Scallops with Jabugo ham and beurre noisette. Barbary duck with honey blossom and Szechuan pepper. Slow-roast lobster with orange and sweet spices.

✗✗ **Enoteca Turi**   22 MZH **n**
28 Putney High St, SW15 1SQ, ℰ (020) 8785 4449, *Fax (020) 8780 5409*
☰. **ⓜⓢ** **AE** **①** **VISA**
closed 25-26 December and Sunday – **Meals** - Italian - a la carte 21.75/31.75 ♀.
◆ A friendly neighbourhood Italian restaurant, overseen by the owner. Rustic cooking, with daily changing specials. Good selection of wine by the glass.

✂ **The Phoenix**   21 LZH **S**
Pentlow St, SW15 1LY, ℰ (020) 8780 3131, *phoenix@sonny's.co.uk, Fax (020) 8780 1114*
☂ – ☰. **ⓜⓢ** **AE** **①** **VISA**
closed Bank Holidays – **Meals** - Italian influences - 19.50 (lunch) and a la carte 21.00/34.75 ♀.
◆ Light and bright interior with French windows leading out on to a spacious terrace. Unfussy and considerate service. An eclectic element to the modern Mediterranean menu.

Southfields *Ctr London* – ✉ SW18.

✗✗ **Sarkhel's**   6 DX **e**
☙ 199 Replingham Rd, SW18 5LY, ℰ (020) 8870 1483, *veronica@sarkhels.co.uk, Fax (020) 8874 6603*
☰. **ⓜⓢ** **VISA**
closed 25-26 December – **Meals** - Indian - 10.00 (lunch) and a la carte 18.00/27.35 ♀.
◆ Recently expanded Indian restaurant with a large local following. Authentic, carefully prepared and well-priced dishes from many different Indian regions. Obliging service.

Tooting *Gtr London –* ⊠ *SW17.*

✗ Kastoori 6 EX V
188 Upper Tooting Rd, SW17 7EJ, ✆ (020) 8767 7027
▤. ⓂⓈ *VISA*
closed 25-26 December and lunch Monday and Tuesday – **Meals** - Indian Vegetarian - a la carte 12.75/24.50.
• Specialising in Indian vegetarian cooking with a subtle East African influence. Family-run for many years, a warm and welcoming establishment with helpful service.

✗ Oh Boy 6 EX C
843 Garratt Lane, SW17 0PG, ✆ (020) 8947 9760, *Fax (020) 8879 7867*
▤. ⓂⓈ AE Ⓞ *VISA* JCB
closed 25-26 December, 1 January and Monday – **Meals** - Thai - (dinner only) 22.00 and a la carte 12.25/18.35.
• Long-standing neighbourhood Thai restaurant. Extensive menu offers authentic and carefully prepared dishes, in simple but friendly surroundings.

Wandsworth *Gtr London –* ⊠ *SW12/SW17/SW18.*

✗✗ Chez Bruce (Poole) 6 EX e
⊛ 2 Bellevue Rd, SW17 7EG, ✆ (020) 8672 0114, *chezbruce2@aol.com,*
Fax (020) 8767 6648
✗⊱ ▤. ⓂⓈ AE Ⓞ *VISA*
closed 24-26 December and 1 January – **Meals** (booking essential) 23.50/ 30.00 ♀.
• An ever-popular restaurant, overlooking the Common. Simple yet considered modern British cooking. Convivial and informal, with enthusiastic service.
Spec. Red mullet with fennel, potato and olive salad. Grilled calf's kidney with balsamic vinegar. Strawberry and Champagne trifle.

✗✗ Ditto 6 EX n
55-57 East Hill, SW18 2QE, ✆ (020) 8877 0110, *christian-gilles@ditto1.fsnet.co. uk, Fax (020) 8875 0110*
ⓂⓈ *VISA*
closed 24-27 December, Sunday and Monday – **Meals** (bar lunch)/dinner 19.50 and a la carte 24.00/28.00 ♀.
• Relaxed bar on one side, informal restaurant on the other. Bright walls with modern pictures and a monthly changing modern menu. Personally run by the young owners.

✗ Bombay Bicycle Club 6 EX S
95 Nightingale Lane, SW12 8NX, ✆ (020) 8673 6217, *Fax (020) 8673 9100*
ⓂⓈ AE Ⓞ *VISA*
closed 25-26 December, Easter Monday and Sunday – **Meals** - Indian - (dinner only) a la carte 17.25/21.50 ♀.
• Nestling in a residential area and decorated with plants and murals. Relaxed atmosphere with an authentic, rustic appeal. Sound Indian cooking.

Write to us...
If you have any comments on the contents of this Guide.
Your praise as well as your criticisms will receive careful
consideration and, with your assistance, we will be able to add
to our stock of information and, where necessary, amend
our judgments.
Thank you in advance!

Bayswater and Maida Vale *Gtr London –* ✉ *NW6/W2/W9.*

Hilton London Paddington 28 ADU **a**
146 Praed St, W2 1EE, ☏ (020) 7850 0500, *paddington@hilton.com*, *Fax (020) 7850 0600*
♨ , ⇆ , ⚑ , ✻ rm, 🖃 TV ☎ ⓺ – 🛁 400. 🌕 ᴀᴇ ⓪ *VISA* ᴊᴄʙ. ✁
The Brasserie : Meals 20.00/33.00 ♀ – 立 18.50 – **335 rm** 229.10, 20 suites.
◆ Early Victorian railway hotel, sympathetically restored in contemporary style with Art Deco details. Co-ordinated bedrooms with high tech facilities continue the modern style. Contemporarily styled brasserie offering a modern menu.

Royal Lancaster 28 ADU **e**
Lancaster Terr, W2 2TY, ☏ (020) 7262 6737, *sales@royallancaster.com*, *Fax (020) 7724 3191*
≤ – ⚑ , ✻ rm, 🖃 TV ☎ ⓺ ᴘ – 🛁 1400. 🌕 ᴀᴇ ⓪ *VISA* ᴊᴄʙ. ✁
Meals – (see ***Nipa*** below) – 立 15.00 – **394 rm** 290.00/378.00, 22 suites.
◆ Imposing purpose-built hotel overlooking Hyde Park. Some of London's most extensive conference facilities. Well-equipped bedrooms are decorated in an Asian style. Park overlooks charming Italian Gardens. Pavement is a relaxed brasserie.

Hilton London Metropole 28 AET **C**
Edgware Rd, W2 1JU, ☏ (020) 7402 4141, *Fax (020) 7724 8866*
≤, ♨ , ⇆ , 🖵 – ⚑ , ✻ rm, 🖃 TV ☎ ᴘ – 🛁 2000. 🌕 ᴀᴇ ⓪ *VISA* ᴊᴄʙ. ✁
Meals a la carte 22.50/29.85 ♀ – 立 17.50 – **1033 rm** 175.00/198.50, 25 suites.
◆ One of London's most popular convention venues by virtue of both its size and transport links. Well-appointed and modern rooms have state-of-the-art facilities. Vibrant restaurant and bar.

The Hempel 28 ACU **a**
31-35 Craven Hill Gdns, W2 3EA, ☏ (020) 7298 9000, *hotel@the-hempel.co.uk*, *Fax (020) 7402 4666*
🤸 , 🚗 – ⚑ 🖃 TV ☎ ⓺ . 🌕 ᴀᴇ ⓪ *VISA* ᴊᴄʙ. ✁
closed 25-26 December –
I-Thai : Meals - Italian-Japanese-Thai - *(closed Sunday)* 60.00 and dinner a la carte – 立 21.00 – **40 rm** 346.60, 6 suites.
◆ A striking example of minimalist design. Individually appointed bedrooms are understated yet very comfortable. Relaxed ambience. Modern basement restaurant.

Marriott 10 NZB **C**
Plaza Parade, NW6 5RP, ☏ (020) 7543 6000, *marriottmaidavale@btinternet.com*, *Fax (020) 7543 2100*
♨ , ⇆ , 🖵 – ⚑ , ✻ rm, 🖃 TV ☎ ⓺ 🚗 – 🛁 200. 🌕 ᴀᴇ ⓪ *VISA* ᴊᴄʙ. ✁
Fratelli : Meals - Italian - *(closed Sunday)* (dinner only) a la carte 23.95/32.25 ♀ – 立 16.95 – **222 rm** 116.30, 16 suites.
◆ A capacious hotel, a short walk from Marble Arch and Oxford Street. Well-equipped with both business and leisure facilities including 12m pool. Suites have small kitchens. Informal restaurant and brasserie.

Thistle Hyde Park 28 ACU **V**
Bayswater Rd, 90-92 Lancaster Gate, W2 3NR, ☏ (020) 7262 2711, *Fax (020) 7262 2147*
⚑ ✻ 🖃 TV ᴘ – 🛁 25. 🌕 ᴀᴇ ⓪ *VISA* ᴊᴄʙ. ✁
Meals *(closed Sunday)* (bar lunch Saturday) 19.50 (lunch) and dinner a la carte 25.70/38.25 **s.** ♀ – 立 14.95 – **52 rm** 245.50/280.80, 2 suites.
◆ Behind the ornate pillared façade sits an attractively restored hotel. Appealing to the corporate and leisure traveller, the generally spacious rooms retain a period feel. Aperitifs in relaxed conservatory before formal dining.

🏨 **Colonnade Town House**   17 OZD e
2 Warrington Cres, W9 1ER, ☎ (020) 7286 1052, *colonnade@theetoncollectio
n.com, Fax (020) 7286 1057*
🌤 – |📶|, ⇆ rm, 🖪 📺 ☎, 📠 AE ① *VISA* JCB, ⌘
Enigma *(☎ (020) 7432 8455 :* Meals - Italian - *(closed Monday)* (light lunch)/
dinner 20.00/30.00 and a la carte 15.00/25.00 – ☲ 12.50 – **43 rm** 148.00/
270.00.
◆ Two Victorian townhouses with comfortable well-furnished communal
rooms decorated with fresh flowers. Stylish and comfortable bedrooms with
many extra touches. Enigma restaurant named after AlanTuring, the code-
breaker who was born here.

🏨 **Gresham Hyde Park**   28 ACU e
Lancaster Gate, W2 3NZ, ☎ (020) 7262 5090, *info@gresham-hydeparkhotel.co
m, Fax (020) 7723 1244*
£ъ – |📶|, ⇆ rm, 🖪 📺 ☎ – 🔏 25. 📠 AE ① *VISA*
Meals 30.00 (dinner) and a la carte 18.00/29.50 **s.** – ☲ 15.00 – **188 rm** 185.00.
◆ A smart hotel in the modern style in a quiet street just off Hyde Park.
Spacious brightly decorated rooms with every conceiveable facility including
robes, slippers etc. Contemporary style restaurant with serving a very concise
menu.

🏨 **Mornington**   28 ACU s
12 Lancaster Gate, W2 3LG, ☎ (020) 7262 7361, *london@mornington.co.uk,
Fax (020) 7706 1028*
without rest. – |📶| ⇆ 📺 ☎, 📠 AE ① *VISA* JCB
closed 24-27 December – **66 rm** ☲ 125.00/160.00.
◆ The classic portico facade belies the cool and modern Scandinavian influenced interior. Modern bedrooms are well-equipped and generally spacious.
Duplex rooms available.

🏨 **Commodore**   28 ACU r
50 Lancaster Gate, Hyde Park, W2 3NA, ☎ (020) 7402 5291, *reservations@com
modore-hotel.com, Fax (020) 7262 1088*
£ъ – |📶|, ⇆ rm, 📺 ☎, 📠 AE ① *VISA* JCB, ⌘
Meals (dinner only) 15.00/45.00 – **81 rm** 105.00/145.00, 3 suites.
◆ Three converted Georgian town houses in a leafy residential area. Bedrooms vary considerably in size and style. Largest rooms decorated with a
Victorian theme. Relaxed, casual bistro.

🏨 **Hilton London Hyde Park**   27 ABU c
129 Bayswater Rd, W2 4RJ, ☎ (020) 7221 2217, *reservations_hydepark@hilton
.com, Fax (020) 7229 0557*
|📶| ⇆, 🖪 rest, 📺 ☎ – 🔏 100. 📠 AE ① *VISA* JCB, ⌘
Meals (bar lunch)/dinner 21.95 and a la carte approx. 28.00 ♀ – ☲ 12.95 –
128 rm 145.70/157.45, 1 suite.
◆ Classical Victorian hotel on busy main road. Well-appointed bedrooms
enjoy up to date facilities. Rooms to front have Park views. Intimate dining
room or relaxed bar for meals.

🏨 **Delmere**   28 ADT v
130 Sussex Gdns, W2 1UB, ☎ (020) 7706 3344, *delmerehotel@compuserve.co
m, Fax (020) 7262 1863*
|📶|, ⇆ rm, 📺 ☎, 📠 AE ① *VISA* JCB, ⌘
Meals *(closed Sunday)* (dinner only) 19.00 – ☲ 6.00 – **36 rm** 86.00/107.00.
◆ Attractive stucco fronted and porticoed Victorian property. Now a friendly
private hotel. Compact bedrooms are both well-equipped and kept. Modest
prices. Bright, relaxed restaurant and adjacent bar.

🏠 **Miller's**   27 ABU **a**
111A Westbourne Grove, W2 4UW, ✆ (020) 7243 1024, *enquiries@millersuk.co m, Fax (020) 7243 1064*
without rest. – 📺 ✆. 📟 AE ① *VISA*. 🛇
8 rm 188.00/264.00.
♦ Victorian house brimming with antiques and knick-knacks. Charming sitting room provides the setting for a relaxed breakfast. Individual, theatrical rooms named after poets.

🏠 **Byron**   28 ACU **Z**
36-38 Queensborough Terr, W2 3SH, ✆ (020) 7243 0987, *byron@capricornhot els.co.uk, Fax (020) 7792 1957*
without rest. – 📶 🖥 📺, 📟 AE ① *VISA* JCB, 🛇
44 rm ⌓ 75.00/120.00, 1 suite.
♦ Centrally located and refurbished in the late 1990's - an ideal base for tourists. Bright and modern bedrooms are generally spacious and all have showers ensuite.

🍴🍴 **Nipa** (at Royal Lancaster H.)   28 ADU **e**
Lancaster Terr, W2 2TY, ✆ (020) 7262 6737, *Fax (020) 7724 3191*
🖥 📇 📟 AE ① *VISA* JCB
closed Saturday lunch, Sunday and Bank Holidays – **Meals** - Thai - 14.90/28.00 and a la carte 30.30/42.30 **s**.
♦ On the 1st floor and overlooking Hyde Park. Authentic and ornately decorated restaurant offers subtly spiced Thai cuisine. Keen to please staff in traditional silk costumes.

🍴🍴 **Al San Vincenzo**   29 AFU **a**
30 Connaught St, W2 2AF, ✆ (020) 7262 9623
📟 *VISA* JCB
closed Saturday lunch and Sunday – **Meals** - Italian - (booking essential) 34.50 ⓨ.
♦ A traditional Italian restaurant that continues to attract a loyal clientele. Rustic, authentic cooking and a wholly Italian wine list. Attentive service overseen by owner.

🍴🍴 **Jason's**   17 OZD **c**
Blomfield Rd, Little Venice, W9 2PA, ✆ (020) 7286 6752, *enquiries@jasons.co.u k, Fax (020) 7266 2656*
☂ –📟 AE ① *VISA*
closed Sunday dinner and Monday lunch – **Meals** - Seafood - 15.00 (lunch) and a la carte 23.45/35.00.
♦ Hidden behind a wall, one finds this charming spot beside Regent's Canal. Seafood can be enjoyed in the bright dining room or on the busy terrace beside the boats for hire.

🍴 **Green Olive**   17 OZD **a**
5 Warwick Pl, W9 2PX, ✆ (020) 7289 2469, *Fax (020) 7266 5522*
🖥. 📟 AE *VISA*
closed Christmas-New Year – **Meals** - Italian - (booking essential) 18.00/30.00 ⓨ.
♦ Attractive neighbourhood restaurant in a smart residential area. Modern Italian food served in the bright street level room or the more intimate basement.

※ **Assaggi** 27 AAU **C**

39 Chepstow Pl, (above Chepstow pub), W2 4TS, ✆ (020) 7792 5501, *nipi@assaggi1.demon.co.uk*

▤. 📶 ⓞ **VISA** JCB

closed 2 weeks Christmas, Sunday and Bank Holidays – **Meals** - Italian - a la carte 25.95/39.15.

✦ Polished wood flooring, tall windows and modern artwork provide the bright surroundings for this forever busy restaurant. Concise menu of robust Italian dishes.

※ **The Vale** 16 NZD **Z**

99 Chippenham Rd, W9 2AB, ✆ (020) 7266 0990, *thevale@hotmail.com*, Fax (020) 7286 7224

▤. 📶 ⓞ **VISA** JCB

closed 1 week Christmas, Easter, 25-31 August, Sunday dinner and lunch Monday and Saturday – **Meals** 12.00/15.00 and a la carte 19.00/25.00 ⓧ.

✦ Dine in either the light and spacious conservatory, or in the original bar of this converted pub. Modern British food with Mediterranean influences. Destination bar below.

※ **Ginger** 27 ABU **V**

115 Westbourne Grove, W2 4UP, ✆ (020) 7908 1990, *info@gingerrestaurant.co.uk*, Fax (020) 7908 1991

▤. 📶 AE **VISA** JCB

closed 25-26 December – **Meals** - Bangladeshi - a la carte 13.40/22.40.

✦ Bengali specialities served in contemporary styled dining room. True to its name, ginger is a key flavouring; dishes range from mild to spicy and are graded accordingly.

※ **L'Accento** 27 ABU **b**

16 Garway Rd, W2 4NH, ✆ (020) 7243 2201, *laccentorest@aol.com*, Fax (020) 7243 2201

📶 AE **VISA** JCB

closed 25-26 December and Sunday – **Meals** - Italian - a la carte 22.00/28.00.

✦ Rustic surroundings and provincial, well priced, Italian cooking. Menu specialises in tasty pasta, made on the premises, and shellfish. Rear conservatory for the summer.

※ **Formosa Dining Room** (at Prince Alfred) 17 OZD **n**

5A Formosa St, W9 1EE, ✆ (020) 7286 3287, *theprincealfred@thespiritgroup.com*, Fax (020) 7286 3383

▤. 📶 AE **VISA**

closed 25 December – **Meals** a la carte 24.50/37.00 ⓧ.

✦ Traditional pub appearance and a relaxed dining experience on offer behind the elegant main bar. Contemporary style of cooking.

🍴 **The Waterway** 17 OZD **p**

54 Formosa St, W9 2JU, ✆ (020) 7266 3557, Fax (020) 7266 3547

🌧 – ▤. 📶 AE **VISA**

closed 24-26 December – **Meals** 15.00 (lunch) and a la carte 23.00/34.50 ⓧ.

✦ Pub with a thoroughly modern, metropolitan ambience. Spacious bar and large decked terrace overlooking canal. Concise, well-balanced menu served in open plan dining room.

Belgravia *Ctr London –* ✉ *SW1.*

🏨🏨🏨🏨 **The Lanesborough** 37 AGX **a**
Hyde Park Corner, SW1X 7TA, ℘ (020) 7259 5599, *info@lanesborough.com*, *Fax (020) 7259 5606*
£ᵼ – |⚡|, ⇔ rm, ▤ 📺 ☎ ♿ 🅿 – 🛎 90. ⓜⓔ 🆎 ⑩ *VISA* ᴊᴄʙ. ⅋
The Conservatory : **Meals** 30.00/48.00 and a la carte 42.50/76.00 **s.** ♀ – ⌚ 24.50 – **86 rm** 334.80/528.75, 9 suites.
♦ Converted in the 1990s from 18C St George's Hospital. A grand and traditional atmosphere prevails. Butler service offered. Regency-era decorated, lavishly appointed rooms . Ornate, glass-roofed dining room with palm trees and fountains.

🏨🏨🏨🏨 **The Berkeley** 37 AGX **e**
Wilton Pl, SW1X 7RL, ℘ (020) 7235 6000, *info@the-berkeley.co.uk*, *Fax (020) 7235 4330*
£ᵼ, ⇔ₛ, 🔲 – |⚡| ⇔ rm, ▤ 📺 ☎ ⟷ – 🛎 220. ⓜⓔ 🆎 ⑩ *VISA* ᴊᴄʙ. ⅋
Boxwood Café *(℘ (020) 7235 1010) :* **Meals** a la carte 22.00/35.50 ♀ – (see also ***Pétrus*** below) – ⌚ 27.00 – **186 rm** 198.60/493.50, 28 suites.
♦ A gracious and discreet hotel. Relax in the gilded and panelled Lutyens lounge or enjoy a swim in the roof-top pool with its retracting roof. Opulent bedrooms. Split-level basement restaurant, divided by bar, with modern stylish décor; New York-style dining.

🏨🏨🏨 **The Halkin** 38 AHX **b**
5 Halkin St, SW1X 7DJ, ℘ (020) 7333 1000, *res@halkin.co.uk*, *Fax (020) 7333 1100*
|⚡| ⇔ rm ▤ 📺 ☎. ⓜⓔ 🆎 ⑩ *VISA* ᴊᴄʙ. ⅋
Meals – (see ***Nahm*** below) – ⌚ 22.00 – **37 rm** 364.25/464.10, 4 suites.
♦ One of London's first minimalist hotels. The cool, marbled reception and bar have an understated charm. Spacious rooms have every conceivable facility.

🏨🏨🏨 **Sheraton Belgravia** 37 AGX **u**
20 Chesham Pl, SW1X 8HQ, ℘ (020) 7235 6040, *central.london.reservations@sheraton.com, Fax (020) 7201 1926*
|⚡|, ⇔ rm, ▤ 📺 ☎ ♿ 🅿 – 🛎 25. ⓜⓔ 🆎 ⑩ *VISA* ᴊᴄʙ. ⅋
The Mulberry : **Meals** 22.00 (dinner) and a la carte 24.00/31.00 ♀ – ⌚ 17.50 – **82 rm** 329.00, 7 suites.
♦ Modern corporate hotel overlooking Chesham Place. Comfortable and well-equipped for the tourist and business traveller alike. A few minutes' walk from Harrods.

🏨🏨🏨 **The Lowndes** 37 AGX **h**
21 Lowndes St, SW1X 9ES, ℘ (020) 7823 1234, *contact@lowndeshotel.com*, *Fax (020) 7235 1154*
🌤 – |⚡|, ⇔ rm, ▤ 📺 ☎ 🅿 – 🛎 25. ⓜⓔ 🆎 ⑩ *VISA* ᴊᴄʙ. ⅋
Brasserie 21 : **Meals** 16.95 and a la carte 22.00/32.00 ♀ – ⌚ 17.50 – **77 rm** 305.50, 1 suite.
♦ Compact yet friendly modern corporate hotel within this exclusive residential area. Good levels of personal service offered. Close to the famous shops of Knightsbridge. Modern restaurant opens onto street terrace.

🏨 **Diplomat** 37 AGY **a**
2 Chesham St, SW1X 8DT, ℘ (020) 7235 1544, *diplomat.hotel@btinternet.co.uk, Fax (020) 7259 6153*
without rest. – |⚡| 📺. ⓜⓔ 🆎 ⑩ *VISA* ᴊᴄʙ. ⅋
26 rm ⌚ 95.00/170.00.
♦ Imposing Victorian corner house built in 1882 by Thomas Cubitt. Attractive glass-domed stairwell and sweeping staircase. Spacious and well-appointed bedrooms.

XXXX **Pétrus** (Wareing) (at The Berkeley H.) 37 AGX **e**
Wilton Pl, SW1X 7RL, ☎ (020) 7235 1200, *petrus@marcuswareing.com,
Fax (020) 7235 1266*

▣. ⓜⓞ ⒶⒺ VISA JCB

closed 2 weeks Christmas, Saturday lunch and Sunday – **Meals** 26.00/70.00 ⑨.
✦ Elegantly appointed restaurant named after one of the 40 Pétrus vintages
on the wine list. One table in the kitchen to watch the chefs at work. Ac-
complished modern cooking.
Spec. Lobster "Arnold Bennett". Braised hare, celeriac purée, Madeira sauce.
Peanut parfait, chocolate mousse and candied peanuts.

XX **Zafferano** 37 AGX **f**
15 Lowndes St, SW1X 9EY, ☎ (020) 7235 5800, *Fax (020) 7235 1971*

▣. ⓜⓞ ⒶⒺ ⓄVISA

closed 25 December and 1 January – **Meals** - Italian - 26.50/37.50 ⑨.
✦ Forever busy and relaxed. No frills, robust and gutsy Italian cooking, where
the quality of the produce shines through. Wholly Italian wine list has some
hidden treasures.
Spec. Green beans, cuttlefish salad and black olives. Flat linguini with lobster
and tomato. Tiramisu.

XX **Nahm** (at The Halkin H.) 38 AHX **b**
5 Halkin St, SW1X 7DJ, ☎ (020) 7333 1234, *Fax (020) 7333 1100*

▣. ⓜⓞ ⒶⒺ ⓄVISA JCB

closed lunch Saturday and Sunday – **Meals** - Thai - (booking essential) 26.00/
47.00 **s**. ⑨.
✦ Wood floored restaurant with uncovered tables and understated decor.
Menu offers the best of Thai cooking with some modern interpretation and
original use of ingredients.
Spec. Crab and pomelo with roasted coconut, peanuts and caramel dressing.
Salad of grilled duck with cashew nuts and Thai basil. Crispy fishcakes with
pork and salted eggs.

XX **Mango Tree** 38 AHX **a**
46 Grosvenor Pl, SW1X 7EQ, ☎ (020) 7823 1888, *mangotree@mangotree.org.
uk, Fax (020) 7838 9275*

▣. ⓜⓞ ⒶⒺ ⓄVISA JCB

closed 25-26 December and 1 January – **Meals** - Thai - 15.80/35.00
and a la carte 21.80/31.50 ⑧⑨ ⑨.
✦ Thai staff in regional dress in contemporarily styled dining room of refined
yet minimalist furnishings sums up the cuisine: authentic Thai dishes with
modern presentation.

XX **Noura Brasserie** 38 AHX **n**
16 Hobart Pl, SW1W 0HH, ☎ (020) 7235 9444, *Fax (020) 7235 9244*

▣. ⓜⓞ ⒶⒺ ⓄVISA

Meals - Lebanese - 14.50/31.00 and a la carte 23.00/30.00.
✦ Dine in either the bright bar or the comfortable, contemporary restaurant.
Authentic, modern Lebanese cooking specialises in char-grilled meats and
mezzes.

Write to us…
If you have any comments on the contents of this Guide.
Your praise as well as your criticisms will receive careful
consideration and, with your assistance, we will be able to add
to our stock of information and, where necessary, amend
our judgments.
Thank you in advance!

Hyde Park and Knightsbridge *Gtr London –* ⊠ *SW1/SW7.*

ⅠⅢⅢⅢ **Mandarin Oriental Hyde Park** 37 AGX **X**
66 Knightsbridge, SW1X 7LA, ℰ (020) 7235 2000, *molon-reservations@mohg. com, Fax (020) 7235 2001*
≤, Ⅰ₄, ☎ – |♯|, ✳ rm, 🖾 📺 ✆ 🕭 – 🏋 220. 🐵 🖭 ① *VISA* ᴊᴄʙ. ⅏
The Park : **Meals** 27.00 (lunch) and a la carte 26.00/43.00 – (see also ***Foliage*** below) – ⌸ 22.00 – **177 rm** 299.00/640.00, 23 suites.
◆ Built in 1889 this classic hotel, with striking façade, remains one of London's grandest. Many of the luxurious bedrooms enjoy Park views. Immaculate and detailed service.

ⅢⅢ **Knightsbridge Green** 37 AFX **Z**
159 Knightsbridge, SW1X 7PD, ℰ (020) 7584 6274, *reservations@thekghotel.c o.uk, Fax (020) 7225 1635*
without rest. – |♯| ✳ 🖾 📺 ✆. 🐵 🖭 ① *VISA*. ⅏ – ⌸ 10.50 – **16 rm** 110.00/145.00, 12 suites 170.00.
◆ Privately owned hotel, boasting peaceful sitting room with writing desk. Breakfast - sausage and bacon from Harrods! - served in the generously proportioned bedrooms.

ⅩⅩⅩ **Foliage** (at Mandarin Oriental Hyde Park H.) 37 AGX **X**
66 Knightsbridge, SW1X 7LA, ℰ (020) 7201 3723, *Fax (020) 7235 4552*
🖾. 🐵 🖭 ① *VISA* ᴊᴄʙ
Meals 27.00/42.50 ⓘ.
◆ Reached via a glass-enclosed walkway that houses the cellar. Hyde Park outside the window reflected in the foliage-themed décor. Gracious service, skilled modern cooking.
Spec. Duo of foie gras with caramelised endive Tarte Tatin. Ballottine of sole, roast tomato consommé and crab tortellini. Banana crème brûlée, caramel ice cream.

ⅩⅩⅩ **Isola** 37 AFX **h**
(basement) 145 Knightsbridge, SW1X 7PA, ℰ (020) 7838 1044, *Fax (020) 7838 1099*
🖾. 🐵 🖭 *VISA*
closed 24-26 December, 1 January and Sunday – **Meals** - Italian - 18.50/38.00 and dinner a la carte 29.50/39.50 ⓘ.
◆ In a contemporary basement, the main restaurant offers clean Italian cooking and prime ingredients. Large selection of wines by the glass.

ⅩⅩ **Zuma** 37 AFX **m**
5 Raphael St, SW7 1DL, ℰ (020) 7584 1010, *info@zumarestaurant.com, Fax (020) 7584 5005*
🖾. 🐵 🖭 ① *VISA*
closed 25-26 December – **Meals** - Japanese - a la carte 45.00/80.00 ⓘ.
◆ Strong modern feel with exposed pipes, modern lighting and granite flooring. A theatrical atmosphere around the Sushi bar and a varied and interesting modern Japanese menu.

ⅩⅩ **Mr Chow** 37 AFX **e**
151 Knightsbridge, SW1X 7PA, ℰ (020) 7589 7347, *mrchow@aol.com, Fax (020) 7584 5780*
🖾. 🐵 🖭 ① *VISA* ᴊᴄʙ
closed 24-26 December, 1 January and Easter Monday – **Meals** - Chinese - 18.00 (lunch) and a la carte 35.00/40.50 ⓘ.
◆ Cosmopolitan Chinese restaurant with branches in New York and L.A. Well established ambience. Walls covered with mirrors and modern art. House specialities worth opting for.

Mayfair *Ctr London –* ⊠ *W1.*

Dorchester 30 AHV **a**
Park Lane, W1A 2HJ, ℘ (020) 7629 8888, *reservations@dorchesterhotel.com,*
Fax (020) 7409 0114
Ι₆, ⇌s – |♦|, ⅍ rm, ▤ ▣ ☎ ᄾ ⇦ – ᇫ 550. ⚋ ᴁ ◑ *VISA* Jᴄв.
⅋

Meals – (see **The Oriental** and **Grill Room** below) – ⌷ 24.50 – **201 rm**
317.25/387.75, 49 suites 587.50/2,496.80.
♦ A sumptuously decorated, luxury hotel offering every possible facility.
Impressive marbled and pillared promenade. Rooms quintessentially English
in style. Faultless service.

Claridge's 30 AHU **c**
Brook St, W1A 2JQ, ℘ (020) 7629 8860, *info@claridges.co.uk,*
Fax (020) 7499 2210
Ι₆ – |♦|, ⅍ rm, ▤ ▣ ᄾ ᄾ – ᇫ 200. ⚋ ᴁ ◑ *VISA* Jᴄв. ⅋
Meals 29.50 and a la carte 33.50/60.00 ♀ – (see also **Gordon Ramsay at
Claridge's** below) – ⌷ 23.50 – **143 rm** 405.30/464.10, 60 suites.
♦ The epitome of English grandeur, celebrated for its Art Deco. Exceptionally
well-appointed and sumptuous bedrooms, all with butler service. Magnif-
icently restored foyer.

Grosvenor House 29 AGU **a**
Park Lane, W1K 7TN, ℘ (020) 7499 6363, *Fax (020) 7493 3341*
Ι₆, ⇌s, ▨ – |♦|, ⅍ rm, ▤ ▣ ᄾ ᄾ ⇦ – ᇫ 2000. ⚋ ᴁ ◑ *VISA* Jᴄв.
⅋
La Terrazza : **Meals** - Italian influences - *(closed Saturday lunch)* a la carte
24.00/38.00 ♀ – ⌷ 21.50 – **378 rm** 352.50, 74 suites.
♦ Over 70 years old and occupying an enviable position by the Park. Edwardian style décor. The Great Room, an ice rink in the 1920s, is Europe's
largest banqueting room. Bright, relaxing dining room with contemporary
feel.

Four Seasons 30 AHV **b**
Hamilton Pl, Park Lane, W1A 1AZ, ℘ (020) 7499 0888, *fsh.london@fourseason
s.com, Fax (020) 7493 1895*
Ι₆ – |♦|, ⅍ rm, ▤ ▣ ᄾ ᄾ ⇦ – ᇫ 500. ⚋ ᴁ ◑ *VISA* Jᴄв. ⅋
Lanes : **Meals** 36.00/33.50 and a la carte 35.50/59.50 **s.** ♀ – ⌷ 21.00 – **185 rm**
352.50/417.10, 35 suites.
♦ Set back from Park Lane so shielded from the traffic. Large, marbled lobby;
its lounge a popular spot for light meals. Spacious rooms, some with their
own conservatory. Restaurant's vivid blue and stained glass give modern, yet
relaxing, feel.

Le Meridien Piccadilly 31 AJV **a**
21 Piccadilly, W1J 0BH, ℘ (020) 7734 8000, *lmpiccres@lemeridien-hotels.com,*
Fax (020) 7437 3574
Ι₆, ⇌s, ▨, squash – |♦|, ⅍ rm, ▤ ▣ ᄾ ᄾ – ᇫ 250. ⚋ ᴁ ◑ *VISA* Jᴄв.
⅋
Meals – (see **Terrace** below) – ⌷ 22.50 – **248 rm** 170.30/217.30,
18 suites.
♦ Comfortable international hotel, in a central location. Boasts one of the
finest leisure clubs in London. Individually decorated bedrooms, with first
class facilities.

London Hilton
30 AHV e

22 Park Lane, W1K 4BE, ℰ (020) 7493 8000, *reservations@hilton.com*, *Fax (020) 7208 4146*

≼ London, 𝄐, ⇔ – |$|, ⇋ rm, ▤ TV 𝄐 ⟁ – 𝄐 1000. ⓜ AE ⓞ VISA JCB. ⊗

Trader Vics (ℰ *(020) 7208 4113*) **: Meals** *(closed lunch Saturday, Sunday and Bank Holidays)* 18.00 and a la carte 28.00/49.00 ℙ

Park Brasserie* : Meals** 22.50 (lunch) and a la carte 30.00/42.50 ℙ – (see also ***Windows below) – ⊑ 21.00 – **396 rm** 382.00, 65 suites.

♦ This 28 storey tower is one of the city's tallest hotels, providing impressive views from the upper floors. Club floor bedrooms are particularly comfortable. Exotic Trader Vics with bamboo and plants. A harpist adds to the relaxed feel of Park Brasserie.

Connaught
30 AHU e

16 Carlos Pl, W1K 2AL, ℰ (020) 7499 7070, *info@the-connaught.co.uk*, *Fax (020) 7495 3262*

𝄐 – |$| ▤ TV 𝄐 ⟁. ⓜ AE ⓞ VISA JCB. ⊗

Terrace* : Meals** a la carte 21.00/38.00 ℙ – (see also ***Menu and Grill below) – ⊑ 26.50 – **68 rm** 352.50/499.00, 23 suites.

♦ 19C quintessentially English hotel, with country house ambience. The grand mahogany staircase leads up to antique furnished bedrooms. Smart indoor terrace restaurant with green metal furniture. Attentive service. Menu ranging from one dish to a 3-course meal.

Brown's
30 AIV m

Albemarle St, W1S 4BP, ℰ (020) 7493 6020, *Fax (020) 7493 9381*

𝄐 – |$| ▤ TV 𝄐 – 𝄐 70. ⓜ AE ⓞ VISA. ⊗

Meals – (see ***1837*** below) – ⊑ 22.00 – **112 rm** 340.00/376.00, 6 suites.

♦ Opened in 1837, a classic English hotel, celebrated for its afternoon tea. Past guests include Alexander Graham Bell who made his successful telephone call from here.

Inter-Continental
30 AHV S

1 Hamilton Pl, Hyde Park Corner, W1J 7QY, ℰ (020) 7409 3131, *london@interc onti.com, Fax (020) 7493 3476*

≼, 𝄐, ⇔ – |$|, ⇋ rm, ▤ TV 𝄐 ⟁ ⟸ – 𝄐 1000. ⓜ AE ⓞ VISA JCB

Meals 26.00/30.00 and a la carte approx 38.00 :

***Le Souffle* : Meals** *(closed lunch Monday and Tuesday and Sunday dinner)* 29.50/40.00 and a la carte approx 46.00 ℙ – ⊑ 20.50 – **418 rm** 376.00/434.75, 40 suites.

♦ A large, purpose-built, international group hotel that dominates Hyde Park Corner. Spacious marbled lobby and lounge. Well-equipped bedrooms, many of which have Park views. Informal café style dining or more intimate Soufflé.

Park Lane
30 AHV X

Piccadilly, W1Y 8BX, ℰ (020) 7499 6321, *central.london.reservations@sherato n.com, Fax (020) 7499 1965*

𝄐 – |$|, ⇋ rm, ▤ TV 𝄐 ⟁ ⟸ – 𝄐 500. ⓜ AE ⓞ VISA JCB. ⊗

Citrus (ℰ *(020) 7290 7364*) **: Meals** 19.00/22.00 **s.** and a la carte ℙ – ⊑ 19.95 – **287 rm** 305.50, 20 suites.

♦ The history of the hotel is reflected in the elegant 'Palm Court' lounge and ballroom, both restored to their Art Deco origins. Bedrooms vary in shape and size. Summer pavement tables in restaurant opposite Hyde Park.

🏨 **London Marriott Park Lane**   29 AGU **b**
140 Park Lane, W1K 7AA, ℘ (020) 7493 7000, *mhrs.parklane@marriotthotels.com, Fax (020) 7493 8333*
🛏, 🖼 – |‡| ✛ 🔲 📺 ☎ ㊎ – 🏊 75. 🐵 🆎 ⓪ 🆅🆂🅰 🃏. ℀
140 Park Lane : Meals a la carte 23.00/38.00 ♀ – ☲ 18.95 – **148 rm** 323.10, 9 suites.
◆ Superbly located 'boutique' style hotel at intersection of Park Lane and Oxford Street. Attractive basement health club. Spacious, well-equipped rooms with luxurious elements. Attractive restaurant overlooking Marble Arch.

🏨 **Westbury**   30 AIU **a**
Bond St, W1S 2YF, ℘ (020) 7629 7755, *sales@westburymayfair.com, Fax (020) 7495 1163*
🛏 – |‡|, ✛ rm, 🔲 📺 ☎ ㊎ – 🏊 120. 🐵 🆎 ⓪ 🆅🆂🅰. ℀
Meals *(closed lunch Saturday and Sunday)* 19.50/21.50 and a la carte – ☲ 17.75 – **233 rm** 282.00/305.50, 21 suites.
◆ Surrounded by London's most fashionable shops; the renowned Polo bar and lounge provide soothing sanctuary. Some suites have their own terrace. Bright, fresh restaurant enhanced by modern art.

🏨 **The Metropolitan**   30 AHV **C**
Old Park Lane, W1Y 4LB, ℘ (020) 7447 1000, *res@metropolitan.co.uk, Fax (020) 7447 1100*
≼, 🛏 – |‡|, ✛ rm, 🔲 📺 ☎ 🚗. 🐵 🆎 ⓪ 🆅🆂🅰 🃏. ℀
Meals – (see *Nobu* below) – ☲ 20.00 – **147 rm** 305.50/569.80, 3 suites.
◆ Minimalist interior and a voguish reputation make this the favoured hotel of pop stars and celebrities. Innovative design and fashionably attired staff set it apart.

🏨 **Athenaeum**   30 AHV **g**
116 Piccadilly, W1J 7BS, ℘ (020) 7499 3464, *info@athenaeumhotel.com, Fax (020) 7493 1860*
🛏, ☲ – |‡|, ✛ rm, 🔲 📺 ☎ – 🏊 55. 🐵 🆎 ⓪ 🆅🆂🅰
Bulloch's at 116 : Meals *(closed lunch Saturday and Sunday)* 18.00 (lunch) and a la carte approx. 35.35 **s.** ♀ – ☲ 21.00 – **124 rm** 311.00/370.00, 33 suites.
◆ Built in 1925 as a luxury apartment block. Comfortable bedrooms with video and CD players. Individually designed suites are in an adjacent Edwardian townhouse. Conservatory roofed dining room renowned for its mosaics and malt whiskies.

🏨 **London Marriott Grosvenor Square**   30 AHU **S**
Duke St, Grosvenor Sq, W1K 6JP, ℘ (020) 7493 1232, *Fax (020) 7491 3201*
🛏 – |‡|, ✛ rm, 🔲 📺 ☎ ㊎ – 🏊 600. 🐵 🆎 ⓪ 🆅🆂🅰 🃏. ℀
Diplomat : Meals *(closed lunch Saturday and Monday-Tuesday dinner)* 15.95 and a la carte 22.25/37.85 ♀ – ☲ 15.95 – **209 rm** 270.00, 12 suites.
◆ A well-appointed international group hotel that benefits from an excellent location. Many of the bedrooms specifically equipped for the business traveller. Formal dining room with its own cocktail bar.

🏨 **Washington Mayfair**   30 AHV **d**
5-7 Curzon St, W1J 5HE, ℘ (020) 7499 7000, *sales@washington-mayfair.co.uk, Fax (020) 7495 6172*
🛏 – |‡|, ✛ rm, 🔲 📺 ☎ – 🏊 90. 🐵 🆎 ⓪ 🆅🆂🅰. ℀
Meals 17.95/33.85 **s.** and a la carte ♀ – ☲ 16.95 – **166 rm** 235.00, 5 suites.
◆ Successfully blends a classical style with modern amenities. Relaxing lounge with traditional English furniture and bedrooms with polished, burred oak. Piano bar annex to formal dining room.

🏛 Chesterfield
30 AHV **f**

35 Charles St, W1J 5EB, ✆ (020) 7491 2622, *bookch@chmail.com, Fax (020) 7491 4793*

📶, ⇌ rm, 🖥 📺 📞 – 🛁 110. 🆖 🆎 ⓞ 𝗩𝗜𝗦𝗔 🆓

Meals *(closed Saturday lunch)* 16.95/19.95 and a la carte 28.00/45.00 ⚊ – 🖵 16.50 – **106 rm** 264.30/346.60, 4 suites.

♦ An assuredly English feel to this Georgian house. Discreet lobby leads to a clubby bar and wood panelled library. Individually decorated bedrooms, with some antique pieces. Classically decorated restaurant.

🏛 Flemings
30 AIV **z**

Half Moon St, W1J 7BH, ✆ (020) 7499 2964, *sales@flemings-mayfair.co.uk, Fax (020) 7491 8866*

📶, ⇌ rm, 🖥 📺 📞 – 🛁 55. 🆖 🆎 ⓞ 𝗩𝗜𝗦𝗔 🆓 ⌘

Meals 25.00 ⚊ – 🖵 18.00 – **111 rm** 198.60/233.85, 10 suites.

♦ A Georgian town house where the oil paintings and English furniture add to the charm. Apartments located in adjoining house, once home to noted polymath Henry Wagner. Candlelit basement restaurant with oil paintings.

🏛 No.5 Maddox St
30 AIU **c**

5 Maddox St, W1S 2QD, ✆ (020) 7647 0200, *no5maddoxst@living-rooms.co.uk, Fax (020) 7647 0300*

without rest. – 🖥 📺 📞. 🆖 🆎 ⓞ 𝗩𝗜𝗦𝗔 🆓. ⌘ – 🖵 17.50, **12 suites** 287.80/705.00.

♦ No grand entrance or large foyer, just a discreet door bell and brass plaque. All rooms are stylish and contemporary suites, with kitchenettes and every conceivable mod con.

🏛 Hilton London Green Park
30 AIV **a**

Half Moon St, W1J 7BN, ✆ (020) 7629 7522, *Fax (020) 7491 8971*

📶 ⇌ 📺 – 🛁 130. 🆖 🆎 ⓞ 𝗩𝗜𝗦𝗔 🆓. ⌘

Meals 21.95/35.00 and a la carte 21.95/41.70 s. ⚊ – 🖵 17.50 – **161 rm** 198.50/210.30.

♦ A row of sympathetically adjoined townhouses, dating from the 1730s. Discreet marble lobby. Bedrooms share the same décor but vary in size and shape. Monet prints decorate light, airy dining room.

🏛 Hilton London Mews
30 AHV **u**

2 Stanhope Row, W1J 7BS, ✆ (020) 7493 7222, *Fax (020) 7629 9423*

📶 ⇌ 🖥 📺 – 🛁 50. 🆖 🆎 ⓞ 𝗩𝗜𝗦𝗔 🆓. ⌘

closed 24-28 December – **Meals** (dinner only) 20.00/35.00 and a la carte 21.95/34.95 s. ⚊ – 🖵 16.50 – **71 rm** 186.80/198.55.

♦ Tucked away in a discreet corner of Mayfair. This modern, group hotel manages to retain a cosy and intimate feel. Well-equipped bedrooms to meet corporate needs. Meals in cosy dining room or lounge.

XXXX Le Gavroche (Roux)
29 AGU **c**

❀❀

43 Upper Brook St, W1K 7QR, ✆ (020) 7408 0881, *bookings@le-gavroche.com, Fax (020) 7491 4387*

🖥. 🆖 🆎 ⓞ 𝗩𝗜𝗦𝗔 🆓

closed Christmas-New Year, Sunday, Saturday lunch and Bank Holidays – **Meals** - French - (booking essential) 42.00 (lunch) and a la carte 57.40/101.40.

♦ Long standing renowned restaurant with a clubby, formal atmosphere. Accomplished classical French cuisine, served by smartly attired and well-drilled staff.

Spec. Foie gras chaud et pastilla de canard à la cannelle. Râble de lapin et galette au parmesan. Le palet au chocolat amer et praline croustillant.

XXXX **The Oriental** (at Dorchester H.)   30 AHV **a**
Park Lane, W1A 2HJ, ✆ (020) 7317 6328, *Fax (020) 7317 6464*
▤. **MC AE ①** *VISA* JCB
closed Saturday lunch and Sunday – **Meals** - Chinese (Canton) - 17.00/48.00
and a la carte 27.00/67.50 **s.** ♀.
 ♦ London's grandest Chinese restaurant, decorated with sculptures, antique
silks and gilded mirrors. Asian themed private dining rooms. A variety of
menus available.

XXXX **Grill Room** (at Dorchester H.)   30 AHV **a**
Park Lane, W1A 2HJ, ✆ (020) 7317 6336, *Fax (020) 7317 6464*
▤. **MC AE ①** *VISA* JCB
Meals - English - 22.00/39.50 and a la carte 35.00/55.00 **s.** ♀.
 ♦ Ornate Spanish influenced, baroque decoration with gilded ceiling, tap-
estries and highly polished oak tables. Formal and immaculate service. Tradi-
tional English cooking.

XXXX **Menu and Grill** (at Connaught H.)   30 AHU **e**
❄ 16 Carlos Pl, W1K 2AL, ✆ (020) 7592 1222, *angelahartnett@the-connaught.co.
uk, Fax (020) 7592 1223*
✂ ▤. **MC AE ①** *VISA* JCB
Meals (booking essential) 25.00/60.00 ♀.
 ♦ Refined Italian influenced cooking can be enjoyed in the elegant panelled
'Menu'. The more intimate 'Grill' also offers a selection of traditional British
favourites.
Spec. Spaghetti with roast lobster, parsley and garlic. Caramelised duck
breast, balsamic onions and baby leeks. Lemon panna cotta with thyme
syrup.

XXXX **1837** (at Brown's H.)   30 AIV **m**
Albemarle St, W1S 4BP, ✆ (020) 7408 1837, *brownshotel@ukbusiness.com,
Fax (020) 7493 9381*
▤. **MC AE ①** *VISA*
closed Sunday – **Meals** a la carte 37.00/47.50 ♀.
 ♦ The name refers to the date the hotel opened. An elegant and comfort-
able wood panelled room that evokes a bygone age. By contrast, the kitchen
provides contemporary cooking.

XXXX **The Square** (Howard)   30 AIU **V**
❄❄ 6-10 Bruton St, W1J 6PU, ✆ (020) 7495 7100, *info@squarerestaurant.com,
Fax (020) 7495 7150*
▤. **MC AE ①** *VISA* JCB
*closed 25-26 December, 1 January and lunch Saturday, Sunday and Bank
Holidays* – **Meals** 30.00/55.00 ♀.
 ♦ Marble flooring and bold abstract canvasses add an air of modernity.
Extensive menus offer French influenced cooking of the highest order.
Prompt and efficient service.
Spec. Lasagne of crab with shellfish and basil cappuccino. Roast foie gras with
late picked Muscat grapes. Saddle of lamb with herb crust, shallot purée and
rosemary.

XXXX **Windows** (at London Hilton H.)   30 AHV **e**
22 Park Lane, W1Y 4BE, ✆ (020) 7208 4021, *wow@hilton.com,
Fax (020) 7208 4147*
❄ London – ▤. **MC AE ①** *VISA* JCB
closed Saturday lunch and dinner Sunday and Bank Holidays – **Meals** 39.50/
59.50 and dinner a la carte 47.50/62.00 ♀.
 ♦ Enjoys some of the city's best views. The lunchtime buffet provides a
popular alternative to the international menu. Formal service and a busy
adjoining piano bar.

Gordon Ramsay at Claridge's

30 AHU **C**

Brook St, W1A 2JQ, ℰ (020) 7499 0099, *reservations@gordonramsay.com*, *Fax (020) 7499 3099*

▤ . **MO** **AE** **VISA** **JCB**

Meals (booking essential) 25.00/60.00 ℚ.

◆ A thoroughly comfortable dining room with a charming and gracious atmosphere. Serves classically inspired food executed with a high degree of finesse.

Spec. Mosaïque of foie gras with smoked goose breast, baby spinach salad. Pigeon with caramelised parsnips and purée of dates. Baileys bread and butter pudding.

Mirabelle

30 AIV **X**

56 Curzon St, W1J 8PA, ℰ (020) 7499 4636, *sales@whitestarline.org.uk*, *Fax (020) 7499 5449*

⌂ – ▤ . **MO** **AE** **①** **VISA**

Meals 19.95 (lunch) and a la carte 31.95/53.50 ℚ.

◆ As celebrated now as it was in the 1950s. Stylish bar with screens and mirrors, leather banquettes and rows of windows. Modern interpretation of some classic dishes.

Spec. Ballottine of salmon Prunier. Tuna with aubergine caviar, sauce vierge. Bresse pigeon "en cocotte", confit of garlic.

The Greenhouse

30 AHV **m**

27a Hay's Mews, W1X 7RJ, ℰ (020) 7499 3331, *reservations@greenhouseresta urant.co.uk, Fax (020) 7499 5368*

▤ . **MO** **AE** **①** **VISA** **JCB**

closed January-February, Saturday lunch, Sunday and Bank Holidays – **Meals** 28.00 (lunch) and a la carte 45.00 ⚜ ℚ.

◆ A pleasant courtyard, off a quiet mews, leads to this well established restaurant. Original British cooking and inventive touches ensure an enjoyable dining experience.

Spec. Sweetcorn soup with roast langoustine, beans and liquorice. Cumin-roasted loin of lamb on smoked aubergine, samosa of braised shoulder. Iced caramel parfait, meringue and mango cream.

La Rascasse (at Café Grand Prix)

30 AIV **n**

50A Berkeley St, W1J 8HA, ℰ (020) 7629 0808, *reservations@cafegrandprix.co m, Fax (020) 7409 4708*

▤ . **MO** **AE** **VISA**

closed Saturday lunch, Sunday and Bank Holidays – **Meals** 15.00/20.00 and a la carte approx 33.00 ℚ.

◆ A basement restaurant with an interior of striking, stark elegance. Sit in sumptuous banquettes or armchairs at tables clad in crisp linen. Modern menus.

Benares

30 AIU **q**

12 Berkeley House, Berkeley Sq, W1X 5HG, ℰ (020) 7629 8886, *Fax (020) 7491 8883*

▤ . **MO** **AE** **VISA**

closed 24-30 December, lunch Saturday and Sunday and Bank Holidays – **Meals** - Indian - 12.95 (lunch) and a la carte 25.50/29.50 ℚ.

◆ Indian restaurant where pools of water scattered with petals and candles compensate for lack of natural light. Original Indian dishes; particularly good value at lunch.

XXX Embassy
30 AIU u

29 Old Burlington St, W1X 3AN, ℰ (020) 7851 0956, *embassy@embassylondon*
.com, Fax (020) 7734 3224

☂ – ▤. **M⑧** **AE** **VISA**

closed 25-26 December, Saturday lunch, Sunday and Monday – **Meals** 19.95
(lunch) and a la carte 29.40/46.40 ♀.

♦ Marble floors, ornate cornicing and a long bar create a characterful,
moody dining room. Tables are smartly laid and menus offer accomplished,
classic dishes.

XXX Sartoria
30 AIU b

20 Savile Row, W1X 1AE, ℰ (020) 7534 7000, *sartoriareservations@conran-rest*
aurants.co.uk, Fax (020) 7534 7070

▤. **M⑧** **AE** **①** **VISA**

closed Sunday lunch – **Meals** - Italian - 17.50/22.95 (lunch) and a la carte
29.90/44.50 ☜ ♀.

♦ In the street renowned for English tailoring, a coolly sophisticated restaurant to suit those looking for classic Italian cooking with modern touches.

XXX Brian Turner Mayfair (at Millennium Mayfair H.)
30 AHU x

44 Grosvenor Sq, W1K 2HP, ℰ (020) 7596 3444, *turner.mayfair@mill-cop.com,*
Fax (020) 7596 3443

☒. **M⑧** **AE** **VISA** **JCB**

closed 24-29 December, Saturday lunch and Sunday – **Meals** - English - 21.50
(lunch) and a la carte 28.25/40.75 ♀.

♦ Located within the Millennium Mayfair overlooking Grosvenor Square. Restaurant on several levels with sharp modern décor. Good English dishes with
modern twist.

XXX Tamarind
30 AHV h

20 Queen St, W1J 5PR, ℰ (020) 7629 3561, *tamarind.restaurant@virgin.net,*
Fax (020) 7499 5034

▤. **M⑧** **AE** **①** **VISA** **JCB**

closed 25-27 December and lunch Saturday and Bank Holidays – **Meals** -
Indian - 16.50 (lunch) and a la carte 25.75/42.50 ♀.

♦ Gold coloured pillars add to the opulence of this basement room. Windows
allow diners the chance to watch the kitchen prepare original and accomplished Indian dishes.

Spec. Khumb chaat (tandoor-grilled mushrooms). Peshawari champen (lamb
chops with Indian spices). Achari jhinga (prawns with pickling spices).

XXX Cecconi's
30 AIU d

5a Burlington Gdns, W1S 3EP, ℰ (020) 7434 1500, *info@cecconis.co.uk,*
Fax (020) 7494 2440

▤. **M⑧** **AE** **①** **VISA**

closed 25 December and Sunday lunch – **Meals** - Italian - a la carte 25.00/
48.50 ♀.

♦ A chic bar and a stylish, modern dining venue, invariably busy; the menus
call on the Italian classics with unusual touches.

XXX Terrace (at Le Meridien Piccadilly H.)
31 AJV a

21 Piccadilly, W1V 0BH, ℰ (020) 7851 3085, *Fax (020) 7851 3090*

☂ – ▤. **M⑧** **AE** **①** **VISA** **JCB**

Meals 16.00/40.00 and a la carte 24.00/38.00 **s.** ♀.

♦ On the second floor of the hotel, a bright and airy room. Large conservatory style glass ceiling and seating area by the balcony. Modern cooking with a
subtle French bias.

XXX **Berkeley Square Café**   30 AHU **W**
7 Davies St, W1K 3DD, ℰ (020) 7629 6993, *info@berkeleysquarecafe.com,*
Fax (020) 7491 9719
📶 –🅜🅞 🅰🅴 **VISA** 🄹🄲🄱
closed Christmas, 2 weeks August, Saturday, Sunday and Bank Holidays –
Meals 18.95/37.50 **s.** ⓨ.
♦ Despite its name, this is a fairly smart contemporary restaurant with pavement terrace and recordings of famous novels in the loos! Modern British food with original touches.

XXX **Scotts**   30 AHU **a**
20 Mount St, W1K 2HE, ℰ (020) 7629 5248, *bc@scottsrestaurant.co.uk,*
Fax (020) 7499 8246
🍽 🅜🅞 🅰🅴 🅞 **VISA** 🄹🄲🄱
closed 25 December, Good Friday, Saturday lunch and Bank Holidays – **Meals** - English - a la carte 31.00/50.75 ⓨ.
♦ Established in 1851 and a favoured haunt of Winston Churchill. Now a stylish and contemporary restaurant specialising in seafood. Pianist in the smart downstairs bar.

XXX **Kai**   30 AHV **n**
65 South Audley St, W1K 2QU, ℰ (020) 7493 8988, *kai@kaimayfair.com,*
Fax (020) 7493 1456
🍽 🅜🅞 🅰🅴 🅞 **VISA** 🄹🄲🄱
closed 25 December and 1 January – **Meals** - Chinese - 20.00/40.00 and a la carte 26.50/45.00 ⓨ.
♦ Marble flooring and mirrors add to the opulent feel of this smoothly run Chinese restaurant. Extensive menu offers dishes ranging from the luxury to the more familiar.

XX **Patterson's**   30 AIU **p**
4 Mill St, W1S 2AX, ℰ (020) 7499 1308, *enquiries@pattersonsrestaurant.com,*
Fax (020) 7491 2122
🍽 🅜🅞 🅰🅴 **VISA**
closed 25-26 December, 1 January, Saturday lunch, Sunday and Bank Holidays – **Meals** 16.00/30.00 ⓨ.
♦ Stylish modern interior in black and white. Elegant tables and attentive service. Modern British cooking with concise wine list and sensible prices.

XX **Deca**   30 AIU **X**
23 Conduit St, W1S 2XS, ℰ (020) 7493 7070, *Fax (020) 7493 7090*
🍽. 🅜🅞 🅰🅴 🅞 **VISA**
closed 10 days Christmas, 4 days Easter, Sunday and Bank Holiday Mondays –
Meals 12.50 (lunch) a la carte 30.00/46.00 ⓨ.
♦ Attractively styled and comfortable, personally-run restaurant. Menu offers an appealing mix of modern French and traditional English dishes.

XX **Teca**   30 AHU **f**
54 Brooks Mews, W1Y 2NY, ℰ (020) 7495 4774, *Fax (020) 7491 3545*
🍽. 🅜🅞 🅰🅴 🅞 **VISA**
closed 24 December-2 January, Sunday, Saturday lunch and Bank Holidays –
Meals - Italian - 19.50/36.00 ⓨ.
♦ A glass-enclosed cellar is one of the features of this modern, slick Italian restaurant. Set price menu, with the emphasis on fresh, seasonal produce.

XX **Alloro**   30 AIV r
19-20 Dover St, W1S 4LU, ℘ (020) 7495 4768, *Fax (020) 7629 5348*
▤. ⓜ⓪ AE ⓞ VISA
closed 25 December-2 January, Saturday lunch, Sunday and Bank Holidays –
Meals - Italian - 25.00/35.00 ₤.
♦ One of the new breed of stylish Italian restaurants, with contemporary art
and leather seating. A separate, bustling bar. Smoothly run, with modern
cooking.

XX **Hush**   30 AHU V
8 Lancashire Court, Brook St, W1S 1EY, ℘ (020) 7659 1500, *info@hush.co.uk,*
Fax (020) 7659 1501
🀫 – ▤ ▤. ⓜ⓪ AE ⓞ VISA JCB
hush down 🀫 *:* **Meals** a la carte 28.50/43.50 ₤
hush up : **Meals** *(closed Saturday lunch, Sunday and Bank Holidays)* (booking
essential) 26.50 (lunch) and a la carte 35.50/53.00 ₤.
♦ Tucked away down a side street: spacious, informal hush down brasserie
with a secluded courtyard terrace. Serves tasty modern classics. Join the
fashionable set in the busy bar or settle down on the banquettes at hush up.
Serves robust, satisfying dishes.

XX **Fakhreldine**   30 AIV e
85 Piccadilly, W1J 7NB, ℘ (020) 7493 3424, *info@fakhreldine.co.uk,*
Fax (020) 7495 1977
▤. ⓜ⓪ AE ⓞ VISA
closed 25 December and 1 January – **Meals** - Lebanese - a la carte 25.00/36.00 ₤.
♦ Long standing Lebanese restaurant with great view of Green Park. Large
selection of classic mezze dishes and more modern European styled menu of
original Lebanese dishes.

XX **Noble Rot**   30 AIU r
3-5 Mill St, W1S 2AU, ℘ (020) 7629 8877, *reception@noblerot.com,*
Fax (020) 7629 8878
▤. ⓜ⓪ AE ⓞ VISA
closed 25-26 December, 1 January, Saturday lunch, Sunday and Bank Holidays
– **Meals** 15.95/19.50 (lunch) and a la carte 30.00/41.45 ₤.
♦ A modern room with framed photographs, tiled flooring and venetian
blinds. Ambient lighting and music. Modern cooking with some French regional specialities.

XX **Nobu** (at The Metropolitan H.)   30 AHV C
❀
19 Old Park Lane, W1Y 4LB, ℘ (020) 7447 4747, *confirmations@noburestauran*
ts.com, Fax (020) 7447 4749
⪡ – ▤. ⓜ⓪ AE ⓞ VISA JCB
closed 25-26 December, 1 January and lunch Saturday-Sunday – **Meals** -
Japanese with South American influences - (booking essential) 50.00/70.00
and a la carte approx. 75.00 **s** ₤.
♦ Its celebrity clientele has made this one of the most glamorous spots. Staff
are fully conversant in the unique menu that adds South American influences
to Japanese cooking.
Spec. White fish tiradito. Black cod with miso. Peruvian style spicy rib-eye
steak.

XX **Taman Gang**   29 AGU e
140a Park Lane, W1K 7AA, ℘ (020) 7518 3160, *info@tamangang.com,*
Fax (020) 7518 3161
▤. ⓜ⓪ AE VISA JCB
closed 25-26 and 31 December, Sunday dinner and lunch Bank Holidays –
Meals - South East Asian - a la carte 35.00/75.00 ₤.
♦ Basement restaurant with largish bar and lounge area. Stylish but intimate
décor. Informal and intelligent service. Pan-Asian dishes presented in exciting
modern manner.

XX **Sumosan**   30 AIU e
26 Albemarle St, W1S 4HY, ☎ (020) 7495 5999, *info@sumosan.co.uk,
Fax (020) 7355 1247*
🍽 🚗 AE ① VISA
closed lunch Saturday, Sunday and Bank Holidays – **Meals** - Japanese - 25.00/
65.00 and a la carte 33.50/69.00 ☒.
◆ A very smart interior in which diners sit in comfy banquettes and armchairs. Sushi bar to the rear with some semi-private booths. Extensive menus
of Sushi and Sashimi.

XX **Chor Bizarre**   30 AIV s
16 Albemarle St, W1S 4HW, ☎ (020) 7629 9802, *chorbizarrelondon@oldworld
hospitality.com, Fax (020) 7493 7756*
🍽 🚗 AE ① VISA JCB
closed 25-26 and 31 December – **Meals** - Indian - 16.50 (lunch) and a la carte
24.50/33.50 **s**.
◆ Translates as 'thieves market' and the décor is equally vibrant; antiques,
curios, carvings and ornaments abound. Cooking and recipes chiefly from
north India and Kashmir.

XX **Yatra**   30 AIV b
34 Dover St, W1S 4NF, ☎ (020) 7493 0200, *yatra@lineone.net,
Fax (020) 7493 4228*
🍽 🚗 AE VISA
closed 25 December, Saturday lunch, Sunday dinner and Bank Holidays –
Meals - Indian - a la carte 22.75/27.50 ☒.
◆ Behind the large bar, a richly decorated room with a choice of high or low
level seating. Elaborate and ornate table setting. Indian cooking with an
innovative twist.

XX **Bentley's**   30 AJV e
11-15 Swallow St, W1B 4DG, ☎ (020) 7734 4756, *Fax (020) 7287 2972*
🍽 🚗 AE ① VISA JCB
closed 25-26 December and 1 January – **Meals** - Seafood - a la carte 32.65/
53.70 ☒.
◆ One of London's oldest restaurants. Ground floor oyster bar leads to the
upstairs dining room. Booth seating and walls adorned with oil paintings.
Specialises in seafood.

XX **Momo**   30 AIU n
25 Heddon St, W1B 4BH, ☎ (020) 7434 4040, *momoresto@aol.com,
Fax (020) 7287 0404*
🍴 – 🍽 🚗 AE ① VISA
closed 25-26 December, 1 January and Sunday lunch – **Meals** - Moroccan -
a la carte 23.00/35.50.
◆ Elaborate adornment of rugs, drapes and ornaments mixed with Arabic
music lend an authentic feel to this busy Moroccan restaurant. Helpful service. Popular basement bar.

X **Khew**   30 AHU r
43 South Molton St, W1K 5RS, ☎ (020) 7408 2236, *drew@khew.co.uk,
Fax (020) 7629 7507*
🍴 – ✦ 🍽 🚗 AE VISA
closed Sunday and Bank Holidays – **Meals** - South East Asian - 12.95
(lunch) and a la carte 19.50/29.75 ☒.
◆ Ground floor: a sushi counter; downstairs: a wonderfully curvaceous restaurant offering varied Asian menus exuding much originality amongst the
dim sum and tempura dishes.

✗ **The Cafe** (at Sotheby's)   30 AIU y
34-35 New Bond St, W1A 2AA, ✆ (020) 7293 5077, *Fax (020) 7293 5920*
✥, ⓝⓞ AE ⓞ *VISA*
closed 23 December-6 January, 15 August-1 September, Saturday, Sunday and
Bank Holidays – **Meals** (booking essential) (lunch only) a la carte 21.50/30.50 **s**.
Ⓩ.
   ◆ A velvet rope separates this simple room from the main lobby of this
famous auction house. Pleasant service from staff in aprons. Menu is short
but well-chosen and light.

✗ **Veeraswamy**   30 AIU t
Victory House, 99 Regent St, W1B 4RS, entrance on Swallow St,
✆ (020) 7734 1401, *info@realindianfood.com, Fax (020) 7439 8434*
▤, ⓝⓞ AE ⓞ *VISA* JCB
Meals - Indian - 14.75 (lunch) and a la carte 22.50/36.95 ⓥ Ⓩ.
   ◆ The country's oldest Indian restaurant boasts a new look with vivid col-
oured walls and glass screens. The menu also combines the familiar with
some modern twists.

✗ **Zinc Bar & Grill**   30 AIU f
21 Heddon St, W1R 7LF, ✆ (020) 7255 8899, *Fax (020) 7255 8888*
ⓝⓞ AE ⓞ *VISA*
closed Sunday – **Meals** 15.00 (lunch) and a la carte 18.75/35.95 ⓥ Ⓩ.
   ◆ The eponymous bar takes up half the room and is a popular after-work
meeting place. Parquet flooring and laminated tabletops. Offers a wide selection of modern cooking.

Regent's Park and Marylebone *Gtr London* – ✉ *NW1/NW8/W1.*

🏨 **Landmark London**   29 AFT a
222 Marylebone Rd, NW1 6JQ, ✆ (020) 7631 8000, *reservations@thelandmark.*
co.uk, Fax (020) 7631 8080
ⓕ, ⓢ, ◩ – ▯, ✥ rm, ▤ TV ☎ ✆ ⇔ – ⚿ 350. ⓝⓞ AE ⓞ *VISA*. ✗
Winter Garden : **Meals** 26.00 (lunch) and dinner a la carte 26.00/45.00 Ⓩ – 🖵
21.00 – **290 rm** 229.10/417.10, 9 suites.
   ◆ Imposing Victorian Gothic building with a vast glass enclosed atrium, overlooked by many of the modern, well-equipped bedrooms. Winter Garden
popular for afternoon tea.

🏨 **Langham Hilton**   30 AIT e
1c Portland Pl, Regent St, W1B 1JA, ✆ (020) 7636 1000, *langham@hilton.com,*
Fax (020) 7323 2340
ⓕ, ⓢ, ◩ – ▯, ✥ rm, ▤ TV ☎ ⚿ – ⚿ 250. ⓝⓞ AE ⓞ *VISA* JCB. ✗
Memories : **Meals** 19.00 (lunch) and a la carte 34.00/44.50 Ⓩ
Tsar's : **Meals** *(closed Saturday lunch and Sunday)* 17.00 (lunch)
and a la carte approx. 27.30 Ⓩ – 🖵 21.50 – **409 rm** 257.30, 20 suites.
   ◆ Opposite the BBC, with Colonial inspired décor. Polo themed bar and barrel
vaulted Palm Court. Concierge Club rooms offer superior comfort and butler
service. Memories is bright, elegant dining room. Russian influenced Tsar's:
hundreds of vodkas available.

🏨 **Churchill Inter-Continental**   29 AGT X
30 Portman Sq, W1A 4ZX, ✆ (020) 7486 5800, *churchill@interconti.com,*
Fax (020) 7486 1255
ⓕ, ⓢ, ✗ – ▯, ✥ rm, ▤ TV ☎ ✆ – ⚿ 300. ⓝⓞ AE ⓞ *VISA* JCB. ✗
Terrace on Portman Square : Meals a la carte 27.75/38.50 Ⓩ – 🖵 20.75 –
405 rm 399.50, 40 suites.
   ◆ Modern property overlooking attractive square. Elegant marbled lobby.
Cigar bar open until 2am for members. Well-appointed rooms have the
international traveller in mind. Restaurant provides popular Sunday brunch
entertainment.

🏨 **Charlotte Street**   31 AKT e
15 Charlotte St, W1T 1RJ, ℘ (020) 7806 2000, *charlotte@firmdale.com*,
Fax (020) 7806 2002
Ⅰ₅ – |≑| ▤ 📺 ✆ &. – 🔏 65. 🝏 🆎 *VISA*. ⅍
Meals – (see *Oscar* below) – ⌧ 18.00 – **44 rm** 229.10/364.20, 8 suites.
♦ Interior designed with a charming and understated English feel. Welcoming lobby laden with floral displays. Individually decorated rooms with CDs and mobile phones.

🏨 **Sanderson**   31 AJT c
50 Berners St, W1P 3NG, ℘ (020) 7300 1400, *sanderson@ianschragerhotels.com*, *Fax (020) 7300 1401*
🛁, Ⅰ₅ – |≑|, ⅍⇚ rm, ▤ 📺 ✆. 🝏 🆎 ① *VISA*. ⅍
Spoon : **Meals** a la carte 38.00/58.00 ♀ – ⌧ 20.00 – **150 rm** 370.00/393.60.
♦ Designed by Philipe Starck: the height of contemporary design. Bar is the place to see and be seen. Bedrooms with minimalistic white décor have DVDs and striking bathrooms. Stylish Spoon allows diners to construct own dishes.

🏨 **The Leonard**   29 AGU n
15 Seymour St, W1H 7JW, ℘ (020) 7935 2010, *theleonard@dial.pipex.com*,
Fax (020) 7935 6700
Ⅰ₅ – |≑| ⅍⇚ ▤ 📺 ✆. 🝏 🆎 ① *VISA* JCB. ⅍
Meals (room service only) – ⌧ 18.50 – **21 rm** 200.00/258.50, **20 suites** 329.00/646.00.
♦ Around the corner from Selfridges, an attractive Georgian townhouse: antiques and oil paintings abound. Informal, stylish café bar offers light snacks. Well-appointed rooms.

🏨 **Radisson SAS Portman**   29 AGT a
22 Portman Sq, W1H 7BG, ℘ (020) 7208 6000, *sales.london@radissonsas.com*, *Fax (020) 7208 6001*
Ⅰ₅, ⇆S, ⅍ – |≑|, ⅍⇚ rm, ▤ 📺 ✆ – 🔏 650. 🝏 🆎 ① *VISA* JCB. ⅍
Talavera : **Meals** (buffet lunch)/dinner a la carte 37.50/55.00 **s.** – ⌧ 19.50 – **265 rm** 229.10/235.00, 7 suites.
♦ This modern, corporate hotel offers check-in for both British Midland and SAS airlines. Rooms in attached towers decorated in Scandinavian, Chinese and Italian styles. Restaurant renowned for its elaborate buffet lunch.

🏨 **Montcalm**   29 AGU d
Great Cumberland Pl, W1H 7TW, ℘ (020) 7402 4288, *montcalm@montcalm.co.uk*, *Fax (020) 7724 9180*
|≑|, ⅍⇚ rm, ▤ 📺 ✆ – 🔏 80. 🝏 🆎 ① *VISA* JCB. ⅍
Meals – (see *The Crescent* below) – ⌧ 17.95 – **110 rm** 270.25/293.75, 10 suites.
♦ Named after the 18C French general, the Marquis de Montcalm. In a charming crescent a short walk from Hyde Park. Spacious bedrooms with a subtle oriental feel.

🏨 **Ramada Plaza**   17 PZC v
18 Lodge Rd, NW8 7JT, ℘ (020) 7722 7722, *sales.plazalondon@ramadajarvis.co.uk, Fax (020) 7483 2408*
|≑|, ⅍⇚ rm, ▤ 📺 ✆ ℙ – 🔏 150. 🝏 🆎 ① *VISA* JCB. ⅍
Minsky's : **Meals** 19.50/20.95 and a la carte 18.50/35.00 ♀ – ⌧ 15.50 – **376 rm** 199.00, 1 suite.
♦ Modern hotel offers extensive conference facilities. Some of the functional bedrooms either overlook Regent's Park or Lord's cricket ground. Minsky's is designed on a New York deli theme. Kashinoki has Oriental ambience.

Berners 31 AJT r

10 Berners St, W1A 3BE, ☎ (020) 7666 2000, *berners@berners.co.uk, Fax (020) 7666 2001*

|♦|, ⇆ rm, ▤ rest, TV ☏ ♿ – 🪑 160. MC AE ① VISA JCB. ✈

Meals *(closed Saturday lunch)* (carving lunch) 17.95/19.95 and a la carte 26.95/40.15 – ☕ 15.95 – **213 rm** 190.00/260.00, 3 suites.

♦ Series of five converted Georgian houses. Impressive lobby with ornately carved plasterwork ceiling. The floor of club rooms have their own lounge and compact gym. Art Deco themed restaurant.

Jurys Clifton Ford 30 AHT a

47 Welbeck St, W1M 8DN, ☎ (020) 7486 6600, *clifton@jurysdoyle.com, Fax (020) 7486 7492*

Ⅎ₆, ≘s, ▢ – |♦|, ⇆ rm, ▤ TV ☏ ♿ – 🪑 230. MC AE ① VISA. ✈

Meals a la carte approx. 22.95 – ☕ 16.00 – **253 rm** 225.00, 2 suites.

♦ A fairly quiet spot, despite being a short stroll away from the Oxford Street shops. Modern, corporate hotel benefits from an extensive leisure club. Spacious modern rooms. Subtly Irish influence to menu.

Holiday Inn Regent's Park 18 RZD j

Carburton St, W1W 5EE, ☎ (0870) 4009111, *reservations-londonregentspark@ichotelsgroup.com, Fax (020) 7387 2806*

|♦|, ⇆ rm, TV ☏ – 🪑 350. MC AE ① VISA JCB. ✈

Junction : **Meals** *(closed Saturday lunch)* 15.50 and a la carte 16.35/25.45 **s.** – ☕ 14.95 – **333 rm** 179.00.

♦ Modern corporate hotel and a forever busy conference destination. 1st floor lounges are particularly spacious. Bright bedrooms have a certain Scandinavian feel. International menus.

London Marriott Marble Arch 29 AFT j

134 George St, W1H 5DN, ☎ (0870) 400 7255, *salesadmin.marblearch@marriott.co.uk, Fax (020) 7402 0666*

Ⅎ₆, ≘s, ▢ – |♦|, ⇆ rm, ▤ TV ☏ ♿ P – 🪑 150. MC AE ① VISA JCB. ✈

Mediterrano : **Meals** *(closed lunch Saturday and Sunday)* a la carte 19.85/29.85 ♀ – ☕ 16.45 – **240 rm** 198.50/233.80.

♦ Centrally located and modern. Offers comprehensive conference facilities. Leisure centre underground. An ideal base for both corporate and leisure guests. Mediterranean-influenced cooking.

Berkshire 30 AHU n

350 Oxford St, W1N 0BY, ☎ (020) 7629 7474, *resberk@radisson.com, Fax (020) 7629 8156*

|♦|, ⇆ rm, ▤ TV ☏ – 🪑 40. MC AE ① VISA JCB. ✈

Ascots : **Meals** (dinner only) 27.50 and a la carte 30.00/36.00 – ☕ 15.00 – **145 rm** 290.20/370.10, 2 suites.

♦ Above the shops of Oxford St. Reception areas have a pleasant traditional charm. Comfortably appointed bedrooms have plenty of thoughtful touches. Personable staff. Stylish, relaxed dining room.

Durrants 29 AGT e

26-32 George St, W1H 5BJ, ☎ (020) 7935 8131, *enquiries@durrantshotel.co.uk, Fax (020) 7487 3510*

|♦|, ▤ rest, TV ☏ – 🪑 55. MC AE VISA. ✈

Meals 17.50 (lunch) and a la carte 26.75/36.75 – ☕ 13.50 – **88 rm** 92.50/165.00, 4 suites.

♦ First opened in 1790 and family owned since 1921. Traditionally English feel with the charm of a bygone era. Cosy wood panelled bar. Attractive rooms vary somewhat in size. Semi-private booths in quintessentially British dining room.

🏨 **Dorset Square**   17 QZD S

39-40 Dorset Sq, NW1 6QN, ℘ (020) 7723 7874, *reservations@dorsetsquare.c o.uk, Fax (020) 7724 3328*

🚗 – |♦| ▤ TV 📞. ⑩ AE VISA ✗

***The Potting Shed* : Meals** *(closed Saturday lunch and Sunday dinner)* (booking essential) (live music Tuesday and Saturday dinner) 19.50 and a la carte 23.50/29.00 ♀ – ☐ 15.75 – **37 rm** 147.00/211.50.

♦ Converted Regency townhouses in a charming square and the site of the original Lord's cricket ground. A relaxed country house in the city. Individually decorated rooms. The Potting Shed features live entertainment.

🏨 **Sherlock Holmes**   29 AGT C

108 Baker St, W1U 6LJ, ℘ (020) 7486 6161, *info@sherlockholmeshotel.com, Fax (020) 7958 5211*

♪₅, 🏋 – ✗ ▤ TV 📞. 🏋 45. ⑩ AE ① VISA JCB

Meals 16.50 (lunch) and a la carte 28.00/42.00 ♀ – ☐ 12.75 – **116 rm** 252.60.
♦ A stylish building with a relaxed contemporary feel. Comfortable guests' lounge with Holmes pictures on the walls. Bedrooms welcoming and smart, some with wood floors. Brasserie style dining.

🏨 **10 Manchester Street**   29 AGT b

10 Manchester St, W1U 4DG, ℘ (020) 7486 6669, *stay@10manchesterstreet.fs net.co.uk, Fax (020) 7224 0348*

without rest. – |♦| TV. ⑩ AE VISA JCB. ✗ – ☐ 5.00 – **37 rm** 120.00/150.00, 9 suites.
♦ Redbrick hotel built in 1919; speciality shops and Wallace Collection are on the doorstep. Thoughtful extras such as mineral water, chocolates complement comfortable rooms.

🏠 **Hart House**   29 AGT d

51 Gloucester Pl, W1U 8JF, ℘ (020) 7935 2288, *reservations@harthouse.co.uk, Fax (020) 7935 8516*

without rest. – ✗ TV. ⑩ AE ① VISA JCB. ✗
15 rm ☐ 70.00/105.00.
♦ Once home to French nobility escaping the 1789 Revolution. Now an attractive Georgian, mid-terraced private hotel. Warm and welcoming service. Well kept bedrooms.

🏠 **St George**   29 AGT h

49 Gloucester Pl, W1U 8JE, ℘ (020) 7486 8586, *reservations@stgeorge-hotel. net, Fax (020) 7486 6567*

without rest. – ✗ TV 📞. ⑩ AE ① VISA. ✗
19 rm ☐ 95.00/135.00.
♦ Terraced house on a busy street, usefully located within walking distance of many attractions. Offers a warm welcome and comfortable bedrooms which are spotlessly maintained.

XXX **Orrery**   18 RZD a
✿
55 Marylebone High St, W1M 3AE, ℘ (020) 7616 8000, *Fax (020) 7616 8080*

|♦| ⑩ AE ① VISA JCB

closed 1-3 January and August Bank Holiday – **Meals** (booking essential) 23.50 (lunch) and a la carte 31.50/50.50 ♀.

♦ Contemporary elegance: a smoothly run 1st floor restaurant in converted 19C stables, with a Conran shop below. Accomplished modern British cooking.
Spec. Ballottine of chicken, foie gras and celeriac, Muscat grapes. Whole roasted Barbury duck. Chocolate fondant, milk ice cream.

XXX Locanda Locatelli ☸   29 AGU   r

8 Seymour St, W1H 7JZ, ℰ (020) 7935 9088, *info@locandalocatelli.com*, *Fax (020) 7935 1149*

📖. **⬤ᴊ** AE VISA

closed Christmas, Easter, Sunday and Bank Holidays – **Meals** - Italian - a la carte 34.50/52.50 ♀.

♦ Very stylishly appointed restaurant with banquettes and cherry wood or glass dividers which contribute to an intimate and relaxing ambience. Accomplished Italian cooking.

Spec. Roast rabbit wrapped in ham with polenta. Linguini with chilli and crab. Nettle risotto.

XX The Crescent (at Montcalm H.)   29 AGU   d

Great Cumberland Pl, W1H 7TW, ℰ (020) 7402 4288, *reservations@montcalm. co.uk, Fax (020) 7724 9180*

📖. **⬤ᴊ** AE **①** VISA JCB

closed lunch Saturday, Sunday and Bank Holidays – **Meals** 25.00 ♀.

♦ Discreetly appointed room favoured by local residents. Best tables overlook a pretty square. Frequently changing fixed price modern menu includes half bottle of house wine.

XX Six13   30 AHT   n

19 Wigmore St, W1H 9UA, ℰ (020) 7629 6133, *info@six13.com*, *Fax (020) 7629 6135*

📖. **⬤ᴊ** AE **①** VISA

closed 25 December, Friday, Saturday and Sunday – **Meals** - Kosher - 24.50 (lunch) and a la carte 31.75/37.75 ♀.

♦ Stylish and immaculate with banquette seating. Strictly kosher menu supervised by the Shama offering interesting cooking with a modern slant.

XX Oscar (at Charlotte Street H.)   31 AKT   e

15 Charlotte St, W1T 1RJ, ℰ (020) 7907 4005, *charlotte@firmdale.com*, *Fax (020) 7806 2002*

📖. **⬤ᴊ** AE VISA

closed Sunday lunch – **Meals** (booking essential) a la carte 32.50/47.50 ♀.

♦ Adjacent to hotel lobby and dominated by a large, vivid mural of contemporary London life. Sophisticated dishes served by attentive staff: oysters, wasabi and soya dressing.

XX The Providores   30 AHT   S

109 Marylebone High St, W1U 4RX, ℰ (020) 7935 6175, *anyone@theprovidore s.co.uk, Fax (020) 7935 6877*

↞⇥. **⬤ᴊ** AE VISA JCB

closed 25 December, 1 January and Bank Holidays – **Meals** a la carte 18.50/33.50 ♀.

♦ Swish, stylish restaurant on first floor; unusual dishes with New World base and fusion of Asian, Mediterranean influences. Tapas and light meals in downstairs Tapa Room.

XX La Porte des Indes   29 AGU   S

32 Bryanston St, W1H 7EG, ℰ (020) 7224 0055, *pilondon@aol.com*, *Fax (020) 7224 1144*

📖. **⬤ᴊ** AE **①** VISA JCB

closed 25-26 December, 1 January and Saturday lunch – **Meals** - Indian - 33.00/35.00 and a la carte 30.50/46.50 ♀.

♦ Don't be fooled by the discreet entrance: inside there is a spectacularly unrestrained display of palm trees, murals and waterfalls. French influenced Indian cuisine.

XX **Rosmarino** 11 PZB **r**
1 Blenheim Terr, NW8 0EH, ✆ (020) 7328 5014, *Fax (020) 7625 2639*
🏠 – ▤. ⓜⓢ Ⓐ Ⓔ Ⓞ 𝘝𝘐𝘚𝘈
closed 25-27 December and 1-3 January – **Meals** - Italian - 19.50/35.00 ♀.
♦ Modern, understated and relaxed. Friendly and approachable service of robust and rustic Italian dishes. Set priced menu is carefully balanced.

XX **Ozer** 30 AIT **Z**
4-5 Langham Pl, Regent St, W1B 3DG, ✆ (020) 7323 0505, *info@sofra.co.uk,*
Fax (020) 7323 0111
▤. ⓜⓢ Ⓐ Ⓔ Ⓞ 𝘝𝘐𝘚𝘈
Meals - Turkish - 11.00 (lunch) and a la carte 14.75/21.80 ♀.
♦ Behind the busy and vibrantly decorated bar you'll find a smart modern restaurant. Lively atmosphere and efficient service of modern, light and aromatic Turkish cooking.

XX **Rasa Samudra** 31 AKT **r**
5 Charlotte St, W1T 1RE, ✆ (020) 7637 0222, *Fax (020) 7637 0224*
✖. ⓜⓢ Ⓐ Ⓔ Ⓞ 𝘝𝘐𝘚𝘈
closed 24-30 December, 1 January and Sunday lunch – **Meals** - Indian Seafood and Vegetarian - 22.50/30.00 and a la carte 13.25/24.40.
♦ Comfortably appointed, richly decorated and modern Indian restaurant. Authentic Keralan (south Indian) cooking with seafood and vegetarian specialities.

XX **Levant** 30 AHT **C**
Jason Court, 76 Wigmore St, W1H 9DQ, ✆ (020) 7224 1111,
Fax (020) 7486 1216
▤. ⓜⓢ Ⓐ Ⓔ Ⓞ 𝘝𝘐𝘚𝘈 ⒿⒸⒷ
Meals - Lebanese - 8.50/39.50 and a la carte ♀.
♦ The somewhat unpromising entrance leads down to a vibrantly decorated basement. Modern Lebanese cooking featuring subtly spiced dishes.

XX **Latium** 31 AJT **n**
21 Berners St, Fitzrovia, W1T 3LP, ✆ (020) 7323 9123, *info@latiumrestaurant.c om, Fax (020) 7323 3205*
▤. ⓜⓢ Ⓐ Ⓔ 𝘝𝘐𝘚𝘈
closed Sunday – **Meals** - Italian - 18.00/23.50 ♀.
♦ Latium, the Latin for Lazio, reflects the patron's interest in football. The minimalist décor is enlivened by the colourful artwork Italian country cooking; daily specials.

XX **Caldesi** 30 AHT **e**
15-17 Marylebone Lane, W1U 2NE, ✆ (020) 7935 9226, *Fax (020) 7935 9228*
▤. ⓜⓢ Ⓐ Ⓔ Ⓞ 𝘝𝘐𝘚𝘈 ⒿⒸⒷ
closed Saturday lunch, Sunday and Bank Holidays – **Meals** - Italian - a la carte 30.40/43.50.
♦ A traditional Italian restaurant that continues to attract a loyal clientele. Robust and authentic dishes with Tuscan specialities. Attentive service by established team.

XX **Bertorelli** 31 AJT **V**
19-23 Charlotte St, W1T 1RL, ✆ (020) 7636 4174, *bertorellisc@groupechezger ard.co.uk, Fax (020) 7467 8902*
▤. ⓜⓢ Ⓐ Ⓔ Ⓞ 𝘝𝘐𝘚𝘈 ⒿⒸⒷ
closed 25-26 December, Saturday lunch, Sunday and Bank Holidays – **Meals** - Italian - 18.50 and a la carte 30.00/35.00 ♀.
♦ Above the informal and busy bar/café. Bright and airy room with vibrant décor and informal atmosphere. Extensive menu combines traditional and new wave Italian dishes.

XX **Blandford Street** 30 AHT **V**
5-7 Blandford St, W1U 3DB, ✆ (020) 7486 9696, *info@blandford-street.co.uk, Fax (020) 7486 5067*
▤. **MO AE O** **VISA**
closed 25 December-4 January, Easter Saturday, Saturday lunch, Sunday and Bank Holidays – **Meals** 15.00 (lunch) and a la carte 21.50/31.50 ♒ ♉.
♦ Understated interior with plain walls hung with modern pictures and subtle spot-lighting. Contemporary menu with a notably European character.

XX **L'Aventure** 11 PZB **b**
3 Blenheim Terr, NW8 0EH, ✆ (020) 7624 6232, *Fax (020) 7625 5548*
⛱ –**MO AE** **VISA**
closed first 2 weeks January, Easter, Sunday, Saturday lunch and Bank Holidays – **Meals** - French - 18.50/32.50.
♦ Behind the pretty tree lined entrance you'll find a charming neighbourhood restaurant. Relaxed atmosphere and service by personable owner. Authentic French cuisine.

X **Villandry** 30 AIT **S**
170 Great Portland St, W1W 5QB, ✆ (020) 7631 3131, *Fax (020) 7631 3030*
✗⛱ ▤. **MO AE O** **VISA**
closed 25 December, 1 January and Sunday – **Meals** a la carte 19.00/35.45 ♉.
♦ The senses are heightened by passing through the well-stocked deli to the dining room behind. Bare walls, wooden tables and a menu offering simple, tasty dishes.

X **Union Café** 30 AHT **d**
96 Marylebone Lane, W1U 2QA, ✆ (020) 7486 4860, *unioncafe@brinkleys.com, Fax (020) 7486 4860*
MO AE **VISA**
closed Sunday – **Meals** a la carte 25.50/29.00 ♉.
♦ No standing on ceremony at this bright, relaxed restaurant. The open kitchen at one end produces modern Mediterranean cuisine. Ideal for visitors to the Wallace Collection.

X **Caffè Caldesi** 30 AHT **S**
1st Floor, 118 Marylebone Lane, W1U 2QF, ✆ (020) 7935 1144, *people@caldesi .com, Fax (020) 7935 8832*
▤. **MO AE O** **VISA** **JCB**
closed Sunday and Bank Holidays – **Meals** - Italian - a la carte 20.00/30.50 ♉.
♦ Converted pub with a simple modern interior in which to enjoy tasty, uncomplicated Italian dishes. Downstairs is a lively bar with a deli counter serving pizzas and pastas.

X **Chada Chada** 30 AHU **b**
16-17 Picton Pl, W1M 5DE, ✆ (020) 7935 8212, *enquiry@chadathai.com, Fax (020) 7924 2178*
▤. **MO AE O** **VISA** **JCB**
closed Sunday and Bank Holidays – **Meals** - Thai - a la carte 17.20/26.65 ♉.
♦ Authentic and fragrant Thai cooking; the good value menu offers some interesting departures from the norm. Service is eager to please in the compact and cosy rooms.

X **No.6 George St** 30 AHT **a**
6 George St, W1U 3QX, ✆ (020) 7935 1910, *Fax (020) 7935 6036*
✗⛱ ▤. **MO** **VISA**
closed 2 weeks August, 2 weeks Christmas, Saturday and Sunday – **Meals** (lunch only) a la carte 25.40/32.95.
♦ To the front is a charming delicatessen offering fresh produce and behind is a simple, well-kept dining room. Daily changing menu with good use of fresh ingredients.

✗ **La Contenta** 30 AHT **f**
90-92 Wigmore St, W1H 9DR, ☎ (020) 7486 1912, *Fax (020) 7486 1913*
▤ ◍ AE ◑ *VISA*
closed dinner 24 December-26 December and 1 January – **Meals** a la carte
17.00/26.50.
♦ Light and airy open dining room with simple columned décor and some
banquette seating. Menu of modern dishes.

St James's *Gtr London* – ✉ *W1/SW1*.

🏨 **Ritz** 30 AIV **c**
150 Piccadilly, W1J 9BR, ☎ (020) 7493 8181, *enquire@theritzlondon.com*,
Fax (020) 7493 2687
f∂ – |✿|, ↩ rm, ▤ TV ☎ – 🔏 50. ◍ AE ◑ *VISA* JCB. ✵
Meals – (see **The Restaurant** below) – ☷ 26.00 – **116 rm** 352.50/428.80,
17 suites.
♦ Opened 1906, a fine example of Louis XVI architecture and decoration.
Elegant Palm Court famed for afternoon tea. Many of the lavishly appointed
rooms overlook the park.

🏨 **Sofitel St James London** 31 AKV **a**
6 Waterloo Pl, SW1Y 4AN, ☎ (020) 7747 2200, *h3144@accor-hotels.com*,
Fax (020) 7747 2210
f∂ – |✿|, ↩ rm, ▤ TV ☎ ᵹ – 🔏 180. ◍ AE ◑ *VISA* JCB, ✵
Meals – (see **Brasserie Roux** below) – ☷ 19.50 – **179 rm** 323.12/423.00,
7 suites.
♦ Grade II listed building in smart Pall Mall location. Classically English interiors
include floral Rose Lounge and club-style St. James bar. Comfortable, well-
fitted bedrooms.

🏨 **Dukes** 30 AIV **f**
35 St James's Pl, SW1A 1NY, ☎ (020) 7491 4840, *bookings@dukeshotel.com*,
Fax (020) 7493 1264
🅂, *f∂* – |✿|, ↩ rest, ▤ TV ☎ – 🔏 50. ◍ AE ◑ *VISA*. ✵
Meals *(closed Saturday lunch)* (residents only) 19.50 (lunch) and a la carte
29.50/43.50 ♈ – ☷ 16.00 – **82 rm** 229.00/305.50, 7 suites.
♦ Privately owned, discreet and quiet hotel. Traditional bar, famous for its
martini's and Cognac collection. Well-kept spacious rooms in a country house
style.

🏨 **Hilton London Trafalgar** 31 AKV **b**
2 Spring Gdns, SW1A 2TS, ☎ (020) 7870 2900, *lontshirm@hilton.com*,
Fax (020) 7870 2911
|✿|, ↩ rm, ▤ TV ☎ ᵹ – 🔏 50. ◍ AE ◑ *VISA* JCB. ✵
Jago : **Meals** *(closed Saturday lunch and Sunday)* a la carte 27.00/45.00 ♈ – ☷
18.50 – **127 rm** 233.80, 2 suites.
♦ Enjoys a commanding position on the square of which the deluxe rooms,
some split-level, have views. Bedrooms are in pastel shades with leather
armchairs or stools; mod cons. Low-lit restaurant with open-plan kitchen.

🏨 **Stafford** 30 AIV **u**
16-18 St James's Pl, SW1A 1NJ, ☎ (020) 7493 0111, *info@thestaffordhotel.co.
uk*, *Fax (020) 7493 7121*
🅂 – |✿| ▤ TV ☎ – 🔏 40. ◍ AE ◑ *VISA*
Meals *(closed Saturday lunch)* 32.50 (lunch) and dinner a la carte 42.00/
70.00 **s.** ♈ – ☷ 16.50 – **75 rm** 264.30/376.00, 6 suites.
♦ A genteel atmosphere prevails in this elegant and discreet country house
in the city. Do not miss the famed American bar. Well-appointed rooms
created from 18C stables. Refined, elegant, intimate dining room.

🏨 Cavendish
30 AIV **V**

81 Jermyn St, SW1Y 6JF, ☎ (020) 7930 2111, *cavendish.reservations@devere-hotels.com, Fax (020) 7839 2125*

📶, ⇆ rm, 🖥 📺 ☎ 🚗 – 🛗 100. 🅰🅴 🅰🅴 ⓞ 𝗩𝗜𝗦𝗔 JCB. ✗

Meals *(closed lunch Saturday and Sunday)* a la carte 29.00/44.00 ⚥ – 🍽 16.95 – **227 rm** 276.10/311.30, 3 suites.

◆ Modern hotel opposite Fortnum & Mason. Contemporary, minimalist style of rooms with moody prints of London; too five floors offer far-reaching views over and beyond the city. Classic styled restaurant overlooks Jermyn Street.

🏨 22 Jermyn Street
31 AKV **e**

22 Jermyn St, SW1Y 6HL, ☎ (020) 7734 2353, *office@22jermyn.com, Fax (020) 7734 0750*

📶 🖥 📺 ☎. 🅰🅴 🅰🅴 ⓞ 𝗩𝗜𝗦𝗔 JCB. ✗

Meals (room service only) – 🍽 12.65 – **5 rm** 246.75, **13 suites** 346.60/393.60.

◆ Discreet entrance amid famous shirt-makers' shops leads to this exclusive boutique hotel. Stylishly decorated bedrooms more than compensate for the lack of lounge space.

🍴🍴🍴🍴🍴 The Restaurant (at Ritz H.)
30 AIV **c**

150 Piccadilly, W1V 9DG, ☎ (020) 7493 8181, *Fax (020) 7493 2687*

🏡 – 🖥. 🅰🅴 🅰🅴 ⓞ 𝗩𝗜𝗦𝗔 JCB

Meals (dancing Friday and Saturday evenings) 37.00/43.00 and a la carte 46.50/103.00 **s.** ⚥.

◆ The height of opulence: magnificent Louis XVI décor with trompe l'oeil and ornate gilding. Delightful terrace over Green Park. Refined service, classic and modern menu.

🍴🍴🍴 L'Oranger
30 AIV **d**

❀ 5 St James's St, SW1A 1EF, ☎ (020) 7839 3774, *Fax (020) 7839 4330*

🖥. 🅰🅴 🅰🅴 ⓞ 𝗩𝗜𝗦𝗔

closed 24 December-2 January, Saturday lunch, Sunday and Bank Holidays – **Meals** 26.00/45.00 ⚥.

◆ Behind the period façade lies a stylish, understated and comfortable restaurant. The refined and precise dishes are enjoyed by the regular clientele. Booking recommended.

Spec. Terrine of foie gras and artichoke. Roast fillet of John Dory with langoustine. Chocolate fondant, vanilla and nougatine ice cream.

🍴🍴 Osia
31 AKV **n**

11 Haymarket, SW1Y 4BP, ☎ (020) 7976 1313, *Fax (020) 7976 1919*

🖥. 🅰🅴 🅰🅴 𝗩𝗜𝗦𝗔

closed 25 December, 1 January, Saturday lunch and Sunday – **Meals** 23.00 (lunch) and a la carte 27.50/34.50 ⚥.

◆ Converted bank with high ornate ceilings; dining hall separated by wine display case from long bar in leather boothed lounge. Interesting menus of Asian and Australian dishes.

🍴🍴 Quaglino's
30 AIV **j**

16 Bury St, SW1Y 6AL, ☎ (020) 7930 6767, *Fax (020) 7839 2866*

🖥. 🅰🅴 🅰🅴 ⓞ 𝗩𝗜𝗦𝗔

Meals (booking essential) 18.50 (lunch) and a la carte 23.25/37.50 🍽 ⚥.

◆ Descend the sweeping staircase into the capacious room where a busy and buzzy atmosphere prevails. Watch the chefs prepare everything from osso bucco to fish and chips.

%%% **Mint Leaf** 31 AKV k

Suffolk Pl, SW1Y 4HX, ☏ (020) 7930 9020, *reservations@mintleafrestaurant.com, Fax (020) 7930 6205*

▤. ⓂⓈ ⒶⒺ Ⓞ VISA

closed 25-26 December, 1 January and lunch Saturday and Sunday – **Meals** - Indian - 15.00 (lunch) and a la carte 23.00/35.00 ☺ ♀.

◆ Basement restaurant in theatreland. Cavernous dining room incorporating busy, trendy bar with unique cocktail list and loud music. Helpful service. Contemporary Indian dishes.

%%% **Criterion Grill Marco Pierre White** 31 AKU c

224 Piccadilly, W1J 9HP, ☏ (020) 7930 0488, *sales@whitestarline.org.uk, Fax (020) 7930 8380*

▤. ⓂⓈ ⒶⒺ Ⓞ VISA JCB

closed Sunday – **Meals** 17.95 (lunch) and a la carte 23.00/43.50 ☺ ♀.

◆ A stunning modern brasserie behind the revolving doors. Ornate gilding, columns and mirrors aplenty. Bustling, characterful atmosphere, Pre and post-theatre menus.

%%% **Brasserie Roux** 31 AKV a

🕭 8 Pall Mall, SW1Y 5NG, ☏ (020) 7968 2900, *h3144-fb4@accor-hotels.com, Fax (020) 7747 2242*

▤. ⓂⓈ ⒶⒺ Ⓞ VISA JCB

Meals - French - a la carte 18.50/33.50 ☺ ♀.

◆ Informal, smart, classic brasserie style with large windows making the most of the location. Large menu of French classics with many daily specials; comprehensive wine list.

%%% **Le Caprice** 30 AIV h

Arlington House, Arlington St, SW1A 1RT, ☏ (020) 7629 2239, *Fax (020) 7493 9040*

▤. ⓂⓈ ⒶⒺ Ⓞ VISA JCB

closed 25-26 December, 1 January and August Bank Holiday – **Meals** (Sunday brunch) a la carte 26.75/61.25 ♀.

◆ Still attracting a fashionable clientele and as busy as ever. Dine at the bar or in the smoothly run restaurant. Food combines timeless classics with modern dishes.

%%% **The Avenue** 30 AIV y

7-9 St James's St, SW1A 1EE, ☏ (020) 7321 2111, *avenue@egami.co.uk, Fax (020) 7321 2500*

▤. ⓂⓈ ⒶⒺ Ⓞ VISA JCB

closed 25-26 December and 1 January – **Meals** 17.95/19.95 and a la carte 19.95/29.75 ☺ ♀.

◆ The attractive and stylish bar is a local favourite. Behind is a striking, modern and busy restaurant. Appealing and contemporary food. Pre-theatre menu available.

%%% **Matsuri** 30 AIV w

15 Bury St, SW1Y 6AL, ☏ (020) 7839 1101, *dine@matsuri-restaurant.com, Fax (020) 7930 7010*

▤. ⓂⓈ ⒶⒺ Ⓞ VISA JCB

closed 25 December and Bank Holidays – **Meals** - Japanese (Teppan-Yaki, Sushi) - a la carte 24.00/45.50 ♀.

◆ Specialising in theatrical and precise teppan-yaki cooking. Separate restaurant offers sushi delicacies. Charming service by traditionally dressed staff.

✗ **Al Duca**   31 AJV **r**

4-5 Duke of York St, SW1Y 6LA, ℰ (020) 7839 3090, *info@alduca-restaurants.c o.uk, Fax (020) 7839 4050*

▤. **MO AE O VISA JCB**

closed 25-26 December, 1 January and Sunday – **Meals** - Italian - 20.50/24.00 ▨ ♈.

◆ Relaxed, modern, stylish restaurant. Friendly and approachable service of robust and rustic Italian dishes. Set priced menu is good value.

Soho *Gtr London* – ✉ *W1/WC2.*

Hampshire   31 AKU **s**

Leicester Sq, WC2H 7LH, ℰ (020) 7839 9399, *reshamp@radisson.com, Fax (020) 7930 8122*

🏠, *l₆* – |♦|, ✕ rm, ▤ **TV** ✆ – ⛎ 100. **MO AE O VISA JCB**. ✼

The Apex *:* **Meals** 27.50 and a la carte 30.00/36.00 – ☲ 16.00 – **119 rm** 386.50/507.60, 5 suites.

◆ The bright lights of the city are literally outside and many rooms overlook the bustling Square. Inside, it is tranquil and comfortable, with well-appointed bedrooms.

Hazlitt's   31 AKU **u**

6 Frith St, W1D 3JA, ℰ (020) 7434 1771, *reservations@hazlitts.co.uk, Fax (020) 7439 1524*

without rest. – **TV** ✆. **MO AE O VISA JCB**

22 rm 205.60/240.80, 1 suite.

◆ A row of three adjoining early 18c town houses and former home of the eponymous essayist. Individual and charming bedrooms, many with antique furniture and Victorian baths.

✕✕✕✕ **L'Escargot**   31 AKU **b**

48 Greek St, W1D 5EF, ℰ (020) 7437 2679, *sales@whitestarline.org.uk, Fax (020) 7437 0790*

▤. **MO AE O VISA JCB**

▨

Ground Floor *:* **Meals** *(closed 25-26 December, 1 January, Sunday and lunch Saturday)* 17.95 (lunch) and a la carte approx. 26.95 ♈

Picasso Room *:* **Meals** *(closed 2 weeks Christmas-New Year, August, Sunday, Monday and Saturday lunch)* 25.50/42.00.

◆ Ground Floor is chic, vibrant brasserie with early-evening buzz of theatre-goers. Finely judged modern dishes. Intimate and more formal upstairs Picasso Room famed for its limited edition art.

Spec. Ravioli of langoustine, fennel bouillon. Squab pigeon "en vessie" with ravioli of wild mushroom, thyme jus. Millefeuille of Muscat grapes and liquorice.

✕✕✕ **Quo Vadis**   31 AKU **v**

26-29 Dean St, W1D 3LL, ℰ (020) 7437 9585, *sales@whitestarline.org.uk, Fax (020) 7734 7593*

▤. **MO AE O VISA**

closed 25-26 December, 1 January, Sunday and Saturday lunch – **Meals** - Italian - 19.95 (lunch) and a la carte 28.00/38.00 ▨ ♈.

◆ Stained glass windows and a neon sign hint at the smooth modernity of the interior. Modern artwork abounds. Contemporary cooking and a serious wine list.

XXX **Red Fort** 31 AKU **X**
77 Dean St, W1D 3SH, ℘ (020) 7437 2525, *info@redfort.co.uk,*
Fax (020) 7434 0721
▤. 🅼🅾 🆎 🅾 **VISA**
closed 23-29 December and Sunday – **Meals** - Indian - 12.00 (lunch)
and a la carte 23.45/31.50 🕭 ⅌.
♦ Smart, stylish restaurant with modern water feature and glass ceiling to
rear. Seasonally changing menus of authentic dishes handed down over
generations.

XX **Richard Corrigan at Lindsay House** 31 AKU **f**
❀ 21 Romilly St, W1D 5AF, ℘ (020) 7439 0450, *richardcorrigan@lindsayhouse.co.*
uk, Fax (020) 7437 7349
▤. 🅼🅾 🆎 🅾 **VISA**
closed 1 week Christmas, 2 weeks summer, Sunday and Saturday lunch –
Meals 23.00/48.00 🕭 ⅌.
♦ One rings the doorbell before being welcomed into this handsome 18C
town house, retaining many original features. Skilled and individual cooking
with a subtle Irish hint.
Spec. Organic hen's egg, leeks and lobster. Scallops with pork belly and
spiced carrots. Granny Smith apple parfait with chocolate and mint.

XX **Café Lazeez** 31 AKU **d**
21 Dean St, W1V 5AH, ℘ (020) 7434 9393, *soho@cafelazeez.com,*
Fax (020) 7434 0022
▤. 🅼🅾 🆎 🅾 **VISA**
closed 25-26 December, 1 January, Sunday and Bank Holidays – **Meals** - North
Indian - a la carte 16.55/23.15 🕭 ⅌.
♦ In the same building as Soho Theatre; the bar hums before shows, restau-
rant is popular for pre- and post-theatre meals of modern Indian fare.
Refined décor; private booths.

XX **The Sugar Club** 30 AIU **h**
21 Warwick St, W1R 5RB, ℘ (020) 7437 7776, *reservations@thesugarclub.co.u*
k, Fax (020) 7437 7778
⇥ ▤. 🅼🅾 🆎 🅾 **VISA** **JCB**
closed lunch Saturday-Monday and restricted opening Christmas-New Year –
Meals 19.50 (lunch) and a la carte 25.90/42.40 ⅌.
♦ Light interior with a glass-fronted bar and additional basement seating.
Asian and Oriental influenced cuisine with good use of diverse ingredients
and combinations.

XX **Mezzo** 31 AKU **g**
Lower Ground Floor, 100 Wardour St, W1F 0TN, ℘ (020) 7314 4000, *info@conr*
an-restaurants.co.uk, Fax (020) 7314 4040
▤. 🅼🅾 🆎 🅾 **VISA**
closed Sunday and lunch Monday, Tuesday and Saturday – **Meals** 16.50
(lunch) and a la carte 23.50/38.50 🕭 ⅌.
♦ Through the vast bar and down the sweeping staircase to this enormous
and sonorous basement. Well-drilled service. Windows into the kitchen which
produces modern cooking.

X **Bertorelli** 31 AKU **t**
11-13 Frith St, W1D 4RB, ℘ (020) 7494 3491, *bertorelli-soho@groupechezger*
ard.co.uk, Fax (020) 7439 9431
🍸 – ▤. 🅼🅾 🆎 🅾 **VISA**
closed 25-26 December, Saturday lunch, Sunday and Bank Holidays – **Meals** -
Italian - 18.50 and a la carte 30.00/35.00 ⅌.
♦ A haven of tranquilllity from the bustling street below. Discreet and professionally run first floor restaurant with Italian menu. Popular ground floor
café.

✗ **La Trouvaille** 30 AIU **g**
12A Newburgh St, W1F 7RR, ☏ (020) 7287 8488, *Fax (020) 7434 4170*
🍽 –⓪⓪ AE ⓪ VISA
closed Sunday and Bank Holidays – **Meals** - French - 19.75 (lunch) and a la carte 23.00/32.45 🍷 ⚱.
◆ Atmospheric restaurant located just off Carnaby Street. Hearty, robust French cooking with a rustic character. French wine list with the emphasis on southern regions.

✗ **Alastair Little** 31 AKU **y**
49 Frith St, W1D 5SG, ☏ (020) 7734 5183, *Fax (020) 7734 5206*
▤. ⓪⓪ AE ⓪ VISA
closed 25-26 December, 1 January, Sunday, Saturday lunch and Bank Holidays – **Meals** (booking essential) 29.00/35.00.
◆ The eponymous owner was at the vanguard of Soho's culinary renaissance. Tasty, daily changing British based cuisine; the compact room is rustic and simple.

✗ **Vasco and Piero's Pavilion** 31 AJU **b**
15 Poland St, W1F 8QE, ☏ (020) 7437 8774, *vascosfood@hotmail.com*, *Fax (020) 7437 0467*
▤. ⓪⓪ AE ⓪ VISA JCB
closed Sunday, Saturday lunch and Bank Holidays – **Meals** - Italian - (lunch booking essential) 23.50 and lunch a la carte 27.00/31.00.
◆ A long standing, family run Italian restaurant with a loyal local following. Pleasant service under the owners' guidance. Warm décor and traditional cooking.

✗ **itsu** 31 AKU **m**
103 Wardour St, W1V 3TD, ☏ (020) 7479 4790, *glenn.edwards@itsu.co.uk*, *Fax (020) 7479 4795*
🍽✗ ▤. ⓪⓪ AE VISA
closed 25 December and 1 January – **Meals** - Japanese - (bookings not accepted) a la carte 15.00/20.00.
◆ Japanese dishes of Sushi, Sashimi, handrolls and miso soup turn on a conveyor belt in a pleasingly hypnotic fashion. Hot bowls of chicken and coconut soup also appear.

✗ **Aurora** 31 AJU **e**
49 Lexington St, W1F 9AJ, ☏ (020) 7494 0514, *Fax (020) 7494 4357*
🍽 VISA
closed 24 December-5 January, Sunday and Bank Holidays – **Meals** (booking essential) a la carte 19.40/24.45 🍷.
◆ An informal, no-nonsense, bohemian style bistro with a small, but pretty, walled garden terrace. Short but balanced menu; simple fresh food. Pleasant, languid atmosphere.

✗ **Soho Spice** 31 AKU **w**
🍴 124-126 Wardour St, W1F 0TY, ☏ (020) 7434 0808, *info@sohospice.co.uk*, *Fax (020) 7434 0799*
🍽✗ ▤. ⓪⓪ AE ⓪ VISA
closed 25-26 December – **Meals** - Indian - (bookings not accepted) a la carte 15.40/20.40 🍷.
◆ Busy, buzzy, café-style Indian restaurant with basement cocktail bar. Vivid colours on the wall matched by the staff uniforms. Indian food with a contemporary twist.

✕ **Fung Shing**　　　　　　　　　　　　　　　　**31** AKU　**j**
15 Lisle St, WC2H 7BE, ℘ (020) 7437 1539, *Fax (020) 7734 0284*
🖿 ⓪❻ ⒶⒺ ⓪ *VISA*
closed 24-26 December and lunch Bank Holidays – **Meals** - Chinese (Canton) -
17.00/30.00 and a la carte 14.10/23.10 ℡.
　◆ A long-standing Chinese restaurant on the edge of Chinatown. Chatty and
pleasant service. A mix of authentic, rustic dishes and the more adventurous
chef's specials.

Strand and Covent Garden *Gtr London* – ✉ *WC2*.

🏛 **Savoy**　　　　　　　　　　　　　　　　　　**31** ALU　**a**
Strand,　　WC2R　　0EU,　　℘ (020) 7836 4343,　　*info@the-savoy.co.uk,*
Fax (020) 7240 6040
f₆, ⓵⓹, 🖾 – ⦷, ✝ rm, 🖿 📺 ☏ ☞ – 🛎 500. ⓪❻ ⒶⒺ ⓪ *VISA*. ✀
River : **Meals** (dancing Friday and Saturday dinner) 33.50/52.50 and a la carte
℡ – (see also *The Savoy Grill* below) – ☐ 24.50 – **236 rm** 340.75/434.75,
27 suites.
　◆ Famous the world over, since 1889, as the epitome of English elegance
and style. Celebrated for its Art Deco features and luxurious bedrooms.
Immaculate service from classical menus at River.

🏛 **Swissôtel London, The Howard**　　　　　　　**32** AMU　**e**
Temple Pl, WC2R 2PR, ℘ (020) 7836 3555, *reservations.london@swissotel.co*
m, Fax (020) 7379 4547
≼, 🏠 – ⦷, ✝ rm, 🖿 📺 ☏ ☞ – 🛎 150. ⓪❻ ⒶⒺ ⓪ *VISA* ⒿⒸⒷ. ✀
Meals – (see *Jaan* below) ℡ – ☐ 23.00 – **148 rm** 346.60, 41 suites.
　◆ Cool elegance is the order of the order of the day at this handsomely
appointed hotel. Many of the comfortable rooms enjoy balcony views of the
Thames. Attentive service.

🏛 **One Aldwych**　　　　　　　　　　　　　　　　**32** AMU　**r**
1 Aldwych, WC2B 4RH, ℘ (020) 7300 1000, *reservations@onealdwych.com,*
Fax (020) 7300 1001
f₆, ⓵⓹, 🖾 – ⦷, ✝ rm, 🖿 📺 ☏ ⅙ ℗ – 🛎 50. ⓪❻ ⒶⒺ ⓪ *VISA* ⒿⒸⒷ. ✀
Indigo : **Meals** a la carte 25.55/36.40 ℡ – (see also *Axis* below) – ☐ 19.25 –
96 rm 346.00/446.50, 9 suites.
　◆ Decorative Edwardian building, former home to the Morning Post news-
paper. Now a stylish and contemporary address with modern artwork, a
screening room and hi-tech bedrooms. All-day restaurant looks down on
fashionable bar.

🏛 **St Martins Lane**　　　　　　　　　　　　　　**31** ALU　**e**
45 St Martin's Lane, WC2N 4HX, ℘ (020) 7300 5500, *sml@ianschragerhotels.co*
m, Fax (020) 7300 5501
🏠, *f₆* – ⦷, ✝ rm, 🖿 📺 ☏ ☞ – 🛎 40. ⓪❻ ⒶⒺ ⓪ *VISA*. ✀
Asia de Cuba : **Meals** - Asian - 25.00 and a la carte 50.00/71.00 – ☐ 20.00 –
200 rm 311.30/334.80, 4 suites.
　◆ The unmistakable hand of Philippe Starck evident at this most contemporary of hotels. Unique and stylish, from the starkly modern lobby to the
state-of-the-art rooms. 350 varieties of rum at fashionable Asia de Cuba.

🏛 **Thistle Charing Cross**　　　　　　　　　　　**31** ALY　**a**
Strand,　　WC2N　　5HX,　　℘ (020) 7839 7282,　　*charingcross@thistle.co.uk,*
Fax (020) 7839 3933
⦷, ✝ rm, 🖿 📺 ☏ ⅙ – 🛎 150. ⓪❻ ⒶⒺ ⓪ *VISA* ⒿⒸⒷ. ✀
The Strand Terrace : **Meals** 15.95/17.95 and a la carte 26.40/31.35 – ☐
16.95 – **239 rm** 293.75/329.00.
　◆ Classic Victorian hotel built above the station. In keeping with its origins,
rooms in the Buckingham wing are traditionally styled whilst others have
contemporary décor. Watch the world go by from restaurant's pleasant
vantage point.

XXXX ✿ **The Savoy Grill** (at Savoy H.)   31 ALU **a**
Strand, WC2R 0EU, ✆ (020) 7592 1600, *savoygrill@marcuswareing.com,*
Fax (020) 7592 1601

🍴, 🆎 **AE** **VISA** **JCB**

Meals 25.00/55.00 ♈.

✦ Redesigned in 2003 to conserve its best traditions, the Grill buzzes at
midday and in the evening. Formal service; menu of modern European dishes
and the Savoy classics.

Spec. King prawn tortellini with lime and chervil. Braised pork belly with
Jerusalem artichoke and braised red onions. Sherry trifle.

XXX **Ivy**   31 AKU **p**
1 West St, WC2H 9NQ, ✆ (020) 7836 4751, *Fax (020) 7240 9333*

🍴, 🆎 **AE** **①** **VISA** **JCB**

closed dinner 24-26 and 31 December, 1 January and August Bank Holiday –
Meals a la carte 23.50/51.50 ♈.

✦ Wood panelling and stained glass combine with an unpretentious menu to
create a veritable institution. A favourite of 'celebrities', so securing a table
can be challenging.

XXX **Axis**   31 AMU **r**
1 Aldwych, WC2B 4RH, ✆ (020) 7300 0300, *sales@onealdwych.co.uk,*
Fax (020) 7300 0301

🍴, 🆎 **AE** **①** **VISA** **JCB**

closed Saturday lunch and Sunday – **Meals** (live jazz at dinner Tuesday and
Wednesday) 19.75 (lunch) and a la carte 23.15/39.95 🍷 ♈.

✦ Lower-level room overlooked by gallery bar. Muted tones, black leather
chairs and vast futuristic mural appeal to the fashion cognoscenti. Globally-
influenced menu.

XXX **Jaan** (at Swissôtel London, The Howard)   37 EX **e**
Temple Pl, WC2R 2PR, ✆ (020) 7300 1700, *jaan.london@swissotel.com,*
Fax (020) 7240 7816

� – 🍴, 🆎 **AE** **①** **VISA** **JCB**

closed lunch Saturday and Sunday – **Meals** 19.50/22.00 and a la carte 25.00/
35.00 ♈.

✦ Bright room on the ground floor of the hotel with large windows overlooking an attractive terrace. Original cooking - modern French with Cambo-
dian flavours and ingredients.

XX **J.Sheekey**   31 ALU **v**
28-32 St Martin's Court, WC2N 4AL, ✆ (020) 7240 2565, *Fax (020) 7240 8114*

🍴, 🆎 **AE** **①** **VISA** **JCB**

closed dinner 24-26 December, 1 January and August Bank Holidays – **Meals** -
Seafood - (booking essential) a la carte 23.50/57.50 🍷 ♈.

✦ Festooned with photographs of actors and linked to the theatrical world
since opening in 1890. Wood panels and alcove tables add famed intimacy.
Traditional British cooking.

XX **Rules**   31 ALU **n**
35 Maiden Lane, WC2E 7LB, ✆ (020) 7836 5314, *info@rules.co.uk,*
Fax (020) 7497 1081

✦✕ 🍴, 🆎 **AE** **①** **VISA** **JCB**

closed 4 days Christmas and 1 January – **Meals** - English - (booking essential)
a la carte 27.40/36.40 🍷 ♈.

✦ London's oldest restaurant boasts a fine collection of antique cartoons,
drawings and paintings. Tradition continues in the menu, specialising in game
from its own estate.

XX **Adam Street**   31 ALU **C**
9 Adam St, WC2N 6AA, ☏ (020) 7379 8000, *info@adamstreet.co.uk, Fax (020) 7379 1444*
▤. **MO AE VISA**
closed Christmas-New Year, Saturday, Sunday and Bank Holidays – **Meals** (lunch only) 17.95 and a la carte 19.50/35.00 ♈.
♦ Set in the striking vaults of a private members club just off the Strand. Sumptuous suede banquettes and elegantly laid tables. Well executed classic and modern English food.

XX **The Admiralty**   32 AMU **a**
Somerset House, The Strand, WC2R 1LA, ☏ (020) 7845 4646, *Fax (020) 7845 4658*
✦⚡. **MO AE ① VISA JCB**
closed 24-26 December and dinner Sunday and Bank Holidays – **Meals** 25.00/33.00 ♈.
♦ Interconnecting rooms with bold colours and informal service contrast with its setting within the restored Georgian splendour of Somerset House. 'Cuisine de terroir'.

XX **Bank**   32 AMU **S**
1 Kingsway, Aldwych, WC2B 6XF, ☏ (020) 7379 9797, *aldres@bankrestaurants. com, Fax (020) 7379 5070*
▤. **MO AE ① VISA**
closed 25-26 December and 1 January – **Meals** 15.00 (lunch) and a la carte 22.75/35.95 ✿ ♈.
♦ Ceiling decoration of hanging glass shards creates a high level of interest in this bustling converted bank. Open-plan kitchen provides an extensive array of modern dishes.

XX **Le Deuxième**   31 ALU **b**
65a Long Acre, WC2E 9JH, ☏ (020) 7379 0033, *Fax (020) 7379 0066*
▤. **MO AE VISA**
closed 24-25 December – **Meals** 14.50 (lunch) and a la carte 22.00/28.50 ✿ ♈.
♦ Caters well for theatregoers: opens early, closes late. Buzzy eatery, quietly decorated in white with subtle lighting. Varied International menu: Japanese to Mediterranean.

XX **Maggiore's**   31 ALU **Z**
33 King St, WC2 8JD, ☏ (020) 7379 9696, *enquiries@maggiores.uk.com, Fax (020) 7379 6767*
▤. **MO AE ① VISA JCB**
closed 24-26 December and 1 January – **Meals** - Bistro - 17.50 (lunch) and dinner a la carte 24.20/40.80 ✿ ♈.
♦ Narrow glass-roofed dining room with distinctive lighting and greenery creating a woodland atmosphere. Quick service and good value wide-ranging pre-theatre menu.

X **Le Café du Jardin**   31 ALU **f**
28 Wellington St, WC2E 7BD, ☏ (020) 7836 8769, *Fax (020) 7836 4123*
▤. **MO AE VISA**
closed 24-25 December – **Meals** 14.50 (lunch) and a la carte 21.50/26.50 ♈.
♦ Divided into two floors with the downstairs slightly more comfortable. Light and contemporary interior with European-influenced cooking. Ideally placed for the Opera House.

※ **Livebait** 32 AMU u

21 Wellington St, WC2E 7DN, ✆ (020) 7836 7161, *lb-coventgdn@groupechezg erard.co.uk, Fax (020) 7836 7141*

⓴⓾ AE ⓞ VISA

closed 25-26 December, 1 January, Sunday and Bank Holidays – **Meals** - Seafood - 15.95 (lunch) and a la carte 30.00/40.00 ♀.

♦ Busy front bar and back restaurant both decorated with black and white tiles. Energetic service and a menu offering fresh seafood in relaxed surroundings.

Victoria *Gtr London –* ⊠ *SW1.*

🛈 *Victoria Station Forecourt.*

🏨 **Royal Horseguards** 31 ALV a

2 Whitehall Court, SW1A 2EJ, ✆ (0870) 333 9122, *royalhorseguards@thistle.co .uk, Fax (0870) 333 9222*

🛋, *Is* – |♯|, ⅍ rm, 🗏 TV ✆ – 🕍 200. ⓶⓾ AE ⓞ VISA. ⅍

One Twenty One Two : Meals *(closed lunch Saturday, Sunday and Bank Holidays)* 19.50/25.50 and dinner a la carte 27.75/38.90 – ⌲ 17.50 – **276 rm** 333.70/385.40, 4 suites.

♦ Imposing Grade I listed property in Whitehall overlooking the Thames and close to London Eye. Impressive meeting rooms. Some of the well-appointed bedrooms have river views. Stylish restaurant, sub-divided into intimate rooms.

🏨 **Crowne Plaza London St James** 39 AJX e

45 Buckingham Gate, SW1E 6AF, ✆ (020) 7834 6655, *sales@cplonsj.co.uk, Fax (020) 7630 7587*

Is, ⅀s – |♯|, ⅍ rm, 🗏 TV ✆ ⅙ – 🕍 180. ⓶⓾ AE ⓞ VISA. ⅍

Méditerranée : Meals 15.00 (lunch) and a la carte 21.45/47.00 ♀ – (see also **Quilon** and **Bank** below) – ⌲ 15.20 – **323 rm** 293.70, 19 suites.

♦ Built in 1897 as serviced accommodation for visiting aristocrats. Behind the impressive Edwardian façade lies an equally elegant interior. Quietest rooms overlook courtyard. Bright and informal café style restaurant.

🏨 **51 Buckingham Gate** 39 AJX s

51 Buckingham Gate, SW1E 6AF, ✆ (020) 7769 7766, *info@51-buckinghamgat e.co.uk, Fax (020) 7828 5909*

Is, ⅀s – |♯| 🗏 TV ✆. ⓶⓾ AE ⓞ VISA

Meals – (see **Quilon** and **Bank** below) – ⌲ 17.50 – **82 suites** 370.00/940.00.

♦ Canopied entrance leads to luxurious suites: every detail considered, every mod con provided. Colour schemes echoed in plants and paintings. Butler and nanny service.

🏨 **The Goring** 38 AIX a

15 Beeston Pl, Grosvenor Gdns, SW1W 0JW, ✆ (020) 7396 9000, *reception@go ringhotel.co.uk, Fax (020) 7834 4393*

🛋 – |♯| 🗏 TV ✆ – 🕍 50. ⓶⓾ AE ⓞ VISA. ⅍

Meals *(closed Saturday lunch)* 25.00/38.00 ♀ – ⌲ 16.50 – **68 rm** 232.60/ 293.70, 6 suites.

♦ Opened in 1910 as a quintessentially English hotel. The fourth generation of Goring is now at the helm. Many of the attractive rooms overlook a peaceful garden. Elegantly appointed restaurant provides memorable dining experience.

🏨 **41** 38 AIX n

41 Buckingham Palace Rd, SW1W 0PS, ✆ (020) 7300 0041, *book41@rchmail.co m, Fax (020) 7300 0141*

without rest. – |♯| 🗏 TV ✆. ⓶⓾ AE ⓞ VISA JCB

17 rm 258.50/371.30, 1 suite.

♦ Take the lift to the 5th floor- London's first all-inclusive hotel. Relaxed and exclusive club-like lounge where meals and most drinks complimentary. State-of-the-art rooms.

🏨 **The Rubens at The Palace** 38 AIX n
39 Buckingham Palace Rd, SW1W 0PS, ℰ (020) 7834 6600, *bookrb@rchmail.co m*, Fax (020) 7828 5401
🛗 ✎ 🖥 📺 ℰ – 🛎 90. 🆗 🅰🅴 ① *VISA* 🃏
Meals *(closed lunch Saturday and Sunday)* (carvery) 16.95 ♀:
***The Library* : Meals** (dinner only) a la carte 26.50/35.00 ♀ – ⌷ 15.00 – **170 rm** 235.00/264.30, 2 suites.
♦ Traditional hotel with an air of understated elegance. Tastefully furnished rooms: the Royal Wing, themed after British Kings and Queens, features TVs in the bathrooms. Intimate, richly decorated Library restaurant has sumptuous armchairs.

🏨 **Dolphin Square** 39 AJZ a
Dolphin Sq, Chichester St, SW1V 3LX, ℰ (020) 7834 3800, *reservations@dolphi nsquarehotel.co.uk*, Fax (020) 7798 8735
🛌, ⊜s, 🔲, 🎯, 🍽, squash – 🛗 ✎, 🖥 rest, 📺 ℰ 🚗 – 🛎 85. 🆗 🅰🅴 ①
VISA 🃏. 🕱
The Brasserie* : Meals** 14.50 and a la carte – (see also ***Allium below) – ⌷ 13.50 – **30 rm** 205.00/229.00, **118 suites** 229.00/529.00.
♦ Built in 1935 and shared with residential apartments. Art Deco influence remains in the Clipper bar overlooking the leisure club. Spacious suites with contemporary styling. Brasserie overlooks the swimming pool.

🏨 **Jolly St Ermin's** 39 AKX a
Caxton St, SW1H 0QW, ℰ (020) 7222 7888, *reservations@jollyhotels.co.uk*, Fax (020) 7222 6914
🛗, ✎ rm, 📺 ℰ – 🛎 150. 🆗 🅰🅴 ① *VISA*. 🕱
***Cloisters Brasserie* : Meals** 22.50 ♀ – ⌷ 11.95 – **282 rm** 205.00/229.00, 8 suites.
♦ Ornate plasterwork to both the lobby and the balconied former ballroom are particularly striking features. Club rooms have both air conditioning and a private lounge. Grand brasserie with ornate ceiling.

🏨 **Thistle Victoria** 38 AIY e
101 Buckingham Palace Rd, SW1W 0SJ, ℰ (020) 7834 9494, *victoria@thistle.co. uk*, Fax (020) 7630 1978
🛗, ✎ rm, 📺 ℰ – 🛎 200. 🆗 🅰🅴 ① *VISA* 🃏. 🕱
Meals 18.00 ♀ – ⌷ 13.50 – **361 rm** 245.50, 3 suites.
♦ Former Victorian railway hotel with ornate front entrance and grand reception. Harvard bar particularly noteworthy. Well-appointed rooms are generally spacious.

🏨 **Thistle Westminster** 38 AIX z
49 Buckingham Palace Rd, SW1W 0QT, ℰ (0207) 834 1821, *westminster@thistl e.co.uk*, Fax (0207) 931 7542
🛗, ✎ rm, 🖥 📺 ℰ – 🛎 150. 🆗 🅰🅴 ① *VISA* 🃏. 🕱
Meals 20.00 and a la carte 18.50/23.50 – ⌷ 13.95 – **134 rm** 242.05/337.20.
♦ Proximity to station and Palaces make this a popular destination for corporate and leisure guests. Comfortable and well-equipped bedrooms benefit from mini-bars and safes. Shelves with cook books for sale in restaurant.

🏨 **City Inn** 31 ALY a
30 John Isup St, SW1P 4DD, ℰ (020) 7932 4602, *westminster@cityinn.com*, Fax (020) 7233 7575
Ⓜ, 🛌 – 🛗 ✎ 🖥 📺 ℰ ♿ – 🛎 100. 🆗 🅰🅴 ① *VISA* 🃏. 🕱
***City Cafe* : Meals** 17.50 and a la carte 17.50/30.00 ♀ – ⌷ 19.00 – **444 rm** 185.00, 16 suites.
♦ Modern hotel five minutes' walk from Westminster Abbey and Tate Britain. Well-appointed rooms with high-tech equipment and some with pleasant views of London. Brasserie serving modern style food next to a glass covered terrace with artwork feature.

Tophams Belgravia
38 AHY e

28 Ebury St, SW1W 0LU, ℘ (020) 7730 8147, *tophams_belgravia@compuserve.com*, Fax (020) 7823 5966

[symbols] 30. 📷 AE ① VISA JCB. ✸

closed 24 December-2 January – **Meals** *(closed Saturday and Sunday)* (dinner only) a la carte 17.45/23.45 **s.** – **36 rm** ⊆ 115.00/170.00.

♦ Family owned and run since 1937, this hotel has a certain traditional charm. Cosy lounges, roaring fires and antique furniture aplenty. Individually decorated bedrooms. Homely basement dining room.

Winchester
38 AIY s

17 Belgrave Rd, SW1V 1RB, ℘ (020) 7828 2972, *winchesterhotel17@hotmail.com*, Fax (020) 7828 5191

without rest. – 📷. ✸

closed 24-26 December – **18 rm** ⊆ 85.00/100.00.

♦ Behind the portico entrance one finds a friendly, well-kept private hotel. The generally spacious rooms are pleasantly appointed. Comprehensive English breakfast offered.

Express by Holiday Inn
39 AJZ c

106-110 Belgrave Rd, SW1V 2BJ, ℘ (020) 7630 8888, *info@hiexpressvictoria.co.uk*, Fax (020) 7828 0441

without rest. – [symbols] 📷 ✆ &. 📷 AE ① VISA JCB. ✸

52 rm 105.00.

♦ Converted Georgian terraced houses a short walk from station. Despite property's age, all rooms are stylish and modern with good range of facilities including TV movies.

Allium (at Dolphin Square H.)
39 AJZ a

Dolphin Sq, Chichester St, SW1V 3LX, ℘ (020) 7798 6888, *info@allium.co.uk*, Fax (020) 7798 5685

▤. 📷 AE ① VISA

closed Saturday lunch, Sunday dinner and Monday – **Meals** 22.50/32.50 and a la carte 30.00/34.20 ⊆.

♦ A calm atmosphere prevails in this richly decorated room. Raised tables to rear with sumptuous banquettes for more privacy. Interesting and assured modern British cooking.

The Cinnamon Club
39 AKX c

Great Smith St, SW1P 3BU, ℘ (020) 7222 2555, *info@cinnamonclub.com*, Fax (020) 7222 1333

▤ P. 📷 AE ① VISA

closed 24-31 December, Saturday lunch and Sunday – **Meals** - Indian - 19.00/22.00 (lunch) and a la carte 30.93/57.38 **s.** 🍴 ⊆.

♦ Housed in former Westminster Library: exterior has ornate detail, interior is stylish and modern. Walls are lined with books. New Wave Indian cooking with plenty of choice.

Quilon (at Crowne Plaza London St James H.)
39 AJX e

45 Buckingham Gate, SW1 6AF, ℘ (020) 7821 1899, Fax (020) 7828 5802

▤. 📷 AE ① VISA

closed 1 week Christmas, Sunday, Saturday lunch and Bank Holidays – **Meals** - Indian - 15.95 (lunch) and dinner a la carte 17.50/28.95 🍴 ⊆.

♦ A selection of Eastern pictures adorn the walls in this smart, modern and busy restaurant. Specialising in progressive south coastal Indian cooking.

XXX **L'Incontro**   37 AGZ **U**

87 Pimlico Rd, SW1W 8PH, ✆ (020) 7730 6327, *cristiano@lincontro-restaurant. com, Fax (020) 7730 5062*

▤ ⃞ **AE ⃝ VISA JCB**

closed Easter, 25-26 December and lunch Saturday and Sunday – **Meals** - Italian - 19.50 (lunch) and a la carte 28.50/47.50.

◆ Cool, understated and comfortable with attentive service. Simple, unfussy, traditional Italian cooking; set lunch good value. Private dining downstairs for 30 people.

XXX **Santini**   38 AHY **V**

29 Ebury St, SW1W 0NZ, ✆ (020) 7730 4094, *Fax (020) 7730 0544*

▤ ⃞ **AE ⃝ VISA JCB**

closed 25-26 December, lunch Saturday, Sunday and Bank Holidays – **Meals** - Italian - 26.00 (lunch) and a la carte 29.00/51.00 ♀.

◆ Discreet, refined and elegant modern Italian restaurant. Assured and professional service. Extensive selection of modern dishes and a more affordable set lunch menu.

XXX **Shepherd's**   39 AKY **Z**

Marsham Court, Marsham St, SW1P 4LA, ✆ (020) 7834 9552, *admin@langansr estaurants.co.uk, Fax (020) 7233 6047*

▤ ⃞ **AE ⃝ VISA JCB**

closed Saturday, Sunday and Bank Holidays – **Meals** - English - (booking essential) 28.00.

◆ A truly English restaurant where game and traditional puddings are a highlight. Popular with those from Westminster - the booths offer a degree of privacy.

XX **Roussillon**   38 AHZ **C**

✿ 16 St Barnabas St, SW1W 8PE, ✆ (020) 7730 5550, *alexis@roussillon.co.uk, Fax (020) 7824 8617*

▤ ⃞ **AE VISA JCB**

closed Sunday and lunch Monday and Tuesday – **Meals** - French - 21.00/ 45.00 ♀.

◆ Tucked away in an smart residential area. Cooking clearly focuses on the quality of the ingredients. Seasonal menu with inventive elementsand a French base.

Spec. Late summer fruit and vegetables truffle broth. Venison with poached pear, celeriac and truffles. Spicy soufflé, gingerbread "soldiers" and maple syrup.

XX **The Ebury (Dining Room)**   38 AHZ **Z**

1st Floor, 11 Pimlico Rd, SW1W 8NA, ✆ (020) 7730 6784, *info@theebury.co.uk, Fax (020) 7730 6149*

▤ ⃞ **AE VISA**

closed 24-26 December – **Meals** (lunch by arrangement Monday-Friday) 29.50 ♀.

◆ Mount the spiral stair to the formal restaurant with tall windows overlooking the street. Open-plan kitchen provides set gastronomic style menu using first-class ingredients.

XX **Il Convivio**   38 AHY **a**

143 Ebury St, SW1W 9QN, ✆ (020) 7730 4099, *comments@etruscagroup.co.u k, Fax (020) 7730 4103* – ⸙ – ▤ ⃞ **AE ⃝ VISA**

closed 25 December, 1 January and Sunday – **Meals** - Italian - 19.50/32.50 and a la carte 20.25/30.50 ♀.

◆ A retractable roof provides alfresco dining to part of this comfortable and modern restaurant. Contemporary and traditional Italian menu, with home-made pasta specialities.

XX **Simply Nico**　　　　　　　　　　　　　　　　　　39 AJY **a**
48a Rochester Row, SW1P 1JU, ℘ (020) 7630 8061, *westminster@simplynico.c
o.uk, Fax (020) 7828 8541* – **⬤☻** **AE** **①** **VISA**
*closed Easter, 24-26 and 31 December, 1 January, Saturday lunch, Sunday and
Bank Holidays* – **Meals** (booking essential) a la carte 24.00/30.20 ₤.
  ◆ Relaxed and discreet restaurant with a certain bistro atmosphere. Lunch is
especially busy. Short, Anglo-French menu. One of a small chain.

XX **Bank**　　　　　　　　　　　　　　　　　　　　39 AJX **e**
45 Buckingham Gate, SW1E 6BS, ℘ (020) 7379 9797, *westres@bankrestaurant
s.com, Fax (020) 7379 5070* – 🛋 – 🗐. **⬤☻** **AE** **①** **VISA** **JCB**
closed 25-26 December, 1 January, Saturday lunch, Sunday and Bank Holidays
– **Meals** 15.00 (lunch) and a la carte 25.15/40.95 🖂 ₤.
  ◆ The understated entrance belies the vibrant contemporary interior. One of
Europe's longest bars has a lively atmosphere. Conservatory restaurant, modern European cooking.

XX **Boisdale**　　　　　　　　　　　　　　　　　　38 AHY **C**
15 Eccleston St, SW1W 9LX, ℘ (020) 7730 6922, *katarina@boisdale.co.uk,
Fax (020) 7730 0548* – 🛋 – 🗐. **⬤☻** **AE** **①** **VISA** **JCB**
closed Saturday lunch, Sunday and Bank Holidays – **Meals** - Scottish - (live jazz
at dinner) 14.00/17.45 and a la carte 27.50/49.00 ₤.
  ◆ Popular haunt of politicians; dark green, lacquer red panelled interior. Run
by a Scot of Clanranald, hence modern British dishes with Scottish flavour:
Crofter's pie.

XX **Tate Britain**　　　　　　　　　　　　　　　　　39 ALZ **C**
Tate Gallery, Millbank, SW1P 4RG, ℘ (020) 7887 8825, *tate.restaurant@tate.org
.uk, Fax (020) 7887 8902* – 🗐. **⬤☻** **AE** **①** **VISA**
Meals (booking essential) (lunch only) 21.50 and a la carte 24.75/31.75 ₤.
  ◆ Continue your appreciation of art when lunching in this basement room
decorated with original Rex Whistler murals. Forever busy, it offers modern
British fare.

XX **Memories of China**　　　　　　　　　　　　　　39 AHY **U**
65-69 Ebury St, SW1W 0NZ, ℘ (020) 7730 7734, *Fax (020) 7730 2992*
🗐. **⬤☻** **AE** **①** **VISA** – *closed 25 December* – **Meals** a la carte 20.50/45.15 ₤.
  ◆ An air of tranquillity pervades this traditionally furnished room. Lattice
screens add extra privacy. Extensive Chinese menu: bold flavours with a clean,
fresh style.

X **The Ebury (Brasserie)**　　　　　　　　　　　　38 AHZ **Z**
Ground Floor, 11 Pimlico Rd, SW1W 8NA, ℘ (020) 7730 6784, *info@theebury.c
o.uk, Fax (020) 7730 6149* – 🗐. **⬤☻** **AE** **VISA**
closed 24-26 December – **Meals** a la carte 20.00/40.00 ₤.
  ◆ Victorian corner pub restaurant with walnut bar, tables and seafood bar.
Friendly service. Wide-ranging menu from snacks to full meals.

X **Olivo**　　　　　　　　　　　　　　　　　　　39 AHY **Z**
21 Eccleston St, SW1W 9LX, ℘ (020) 7730 2505, *maurosanna@oliveto.fsnet.co
.uk, Fax (020) 7823 5377* – 🗐. **⬤☻** **AE** **VISA** **JCB**
closed lunch Saturday and Sunday and Bank Holidays – **Meals** - Italian - 18.00
(lunch) and dinner a la carte 23.25/27.50.
  ◆ Rustic, informal Italian restaurant. Relaxed atmosphere provided by the
friendly staff. Simple, non-fussy cuisine with emphasis on best available fresh
produce.

X **La Poule au Pot**　　　　　　　　　　　　　　　38 AHY **a**
231 Ebury St, SW1W 8UT, ℘ (020) 7730 7763, *Fax (020) 7259 9651*
🛋 – 🗐. **⬤☻** **AE** **①** **VISA** **JCB**
Meals - French - 16.00 (lunch) and a la carte 25.50/39.50.
  ◆ The subdued lighting and friendly informality make this one of London's
more romantic restaurants. Classic French menu with extensive plats du jour.

Note: when making an international call, do not dial the first «0» of the city codes (except for calls to Italy).

Indicatifs Téléphoniques Internationaux

Important : pour les communications internationales, le zéro (0) initial de l'indicatif interurbain n'est pas à composer (excepté pour les appels vers l'Italie).

from \ to	A	B	CH	CZ	D	DK	E	FIN	F	GB	GR
A Austria		0032	0041	00420	0049	0045	0034	00358	0033	0044	0030
B Belgium	0043		0041	00420	0049	0045	0034	00358	0033	0044	0030
CH Switzerland	0043	0032		00420	0049	0045	0034	00358	0033	0044	0030
CZ Czech Republic	0043	0032	0041		0049	0045	0034	00358	0033	0044	0030
D Germany	0043	0032	0041	00420		0045	0034	00358	0033	0044	0030
DK Denmark	0043	0032	0041	00420	0049		0034	00358	0033	0044	0030
E Spain	0043	0032	0041	00420	0049	0045		00358	0033	0044	0030
FIN Finland	0043	0032	0041	00420	0049	0045	0034		0033	0044	0030
F France	0043	0032	0041	00420	0049	0045	0034	00358		0044	0030
GB United Kingdom	0043	0032	0041	00420	0049	0045	0034	00358	0033		0030
GR Greece	0043	0032	0041	00420	0049	0045	0034	00358	0033	0044	
H Hungary	0043	0032	0041	00420	0049	0045	0034	00358	0033	0044	0030
I Italy	0043	0032	0041	00420	0049	0045	0034	00358	0033	0044	0030
IRL Ireland	0043	0032	0041	00420	0049	0045	0034	00358	0033	0044	0030
J Japan	00143	00132	00141	001420	00149	00145	00134	001358	00133	00144	00130
L Luxembourg	0043	0032	0041	00420	0049	0045	0034	00358	0033	0044	0030
N Norway	0043	0032	0041	00420	0049	0045	0034	00358	0033	0044	0030
NL Netherlands	0043	0032	0041	00420	0049	0045	0034	00358	0033	0044	0030
PL Poland	0043	0032	0041	00420	0049	0045	0034	00358	0033	0044	0030
P Portugal	0043	0032	0041	00420	0049	0045	0034	00358	0033	0044	0030
RUS Russia	81043	81032	810420	6420	81049	81045	*	810358	81033	81044	*
S Sweden	0043	0032	0041	00420	0049	0045	0034	00358	0033	0044	0030
USA	01143	01132	01141	001420	01149	01145	01134	1358	01133	01144	01130

*Direct dialling not possible   *Pas de sélection automatique

Indicativi Telefonici Internationali

Importante: per le comunicazioni internazionali, non bisogna comporre lo zero (0) iniziale dell'indicativo interurbano (escluse le chiamate per l'Italia)

H	I	IRL	J	L	N	NL	PL	P	RUS	S	USA	
0036	0039	00353	0081	00352	0047	0031	0048	00351	007	0046	001	**A Austria**
0036	0039	00353	0081	00352	0047	0031	0048	00351	007	0046	001	**B Belgium**
0036	0039	00353	0081	00352	0047	0031	0048	00351	007	0046	001	**CH Switzerland**
0036	0039	00353	0081	00352	0047	0031	0048	00351	007	0046	001	**CZ Czech Republic**
0036	0039	00353	0081	00352	0047	0031	0048	00351	007	0046	001	**D Germany**
0036	0039	00353	0081	00352	0047	0031	0048	00351	007	0046	001	**DK Denmark**
0036	0039	00353	0081	00352	0047	0031	0048	00351	007	0046	001	**E Spain**
0036	0039	00353	0081	00352	0047	0031	0048	00351	007	0046	001	**FIN Finland**
0036	0039	00353	0081	00352	0047	0031	0048	00351	007	0046	001	**F France**
0036	0039	00353	0081	00352	0047	0031	0048	00351	007	0046	001	**GB United Kingdom**
0036	0039	00353	0081	00352	0047	0031	0048	00351	007	0046	001	**GR Greece**
	0039	00353	0081	00352	0047	0031	0048	00351	007	0046	001	**H Hungary**
0036		00353	0081	00352	0047	0031	0048	00351	*	0046	001	**I Italy**
0036	0039		0081	00352	0047	0031	0048	00351	007	0046	001	**IRL Ireland**
00136	00139	001353		001352	00147	00131	00148	001351	*	00146	0011	**J Japan**
0036	0039	00353	0081		0047	0031	0048	00351	007	0046	001	**L Luxembourg**
0036	0039	00353	0081	00352		0031	0048	00351	007	0046	001	**N Norway**
0036	0039	00353	0081	00352	0047		0048	00351	007	0046	001	**NL Netherlands**
0036	0039	00353	0081	00352	0047	0031		00351	007	0046	001	**PL Poland**
0036	0039	00353	0081	00352	0047	0031	0048		007	0046	001	**P Portugal**
81036	*	*	*	*	*	81031	81048	*		*	*	**RUS Russia**
0036	0039	00353	0081	00352	0047	0031	0048	00351	007		001	**S Sweden**
01136	01139	011353	01181	011352	01147	01131	01148	011351	*	011146		**USA**

*Selezione automatica impossibile   *Automatische Vorwahl nicht möglich

GREAT BRITAIN: Based on Ordnance Survey of Great Britain with the permission of the Controller of Her Majesty's Stationery Office.© Crown Copyright 39923X.

Manufacture française des pneumatiques Michelin

Société en commandite par actions au capital de 304 000 000 EUR.
Place des Carmes-Déchaux – 63 Clermont-Ferrand (France)
R.C.S. Clermont-Fd B 855 200 507

© Michelin et Cie, Propriétaires-Éditeurs, 2004

Dépôt légal Janvier 2004– ISBN 2-06-710247-8

Printed in France 12-03

Photocompositeur : A.P.S., Tours
Imprimeur, brocheur : Imprimerie CLERC, St-Amand-Montrond

Illustrations Cécile Imbert/MICHELIN : pages 4, 6 à 12, 20, 22 à 28, 32, 34 à 40
Narratif Systèmes/Geneclo : pages 5, 21, 33
Rodolphe Corbel pages 18, 30, 46, 219

In the same series ●

Dans la même collection ●

Altri titoli della collezione ●

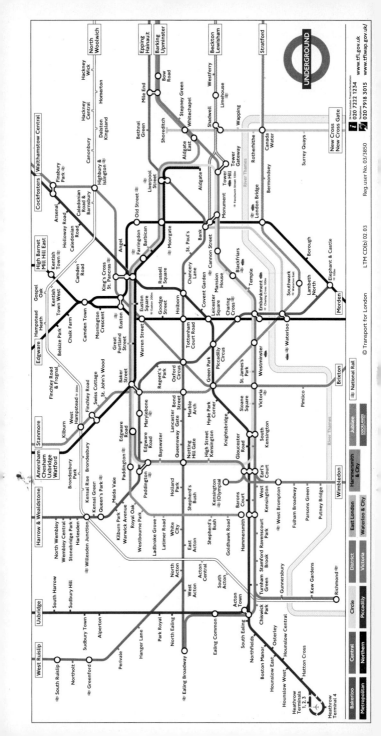